JUN 1 2 2015

W9-CAJ-323
3 9043 09792275 6

⊗

A PLUME BOOK

ROMANCE IS MY DAY JOB

PATIENCE BLOOM has been a romance editor at Harlequin for sixteen years. After living in Connecticut, New Mexico, and Paris, she now lives in New York City.

Praise for *Romance Is My Day Job*

"What makes *Romance Is My Day Job* unique and charming is the author's arc: a quirky combination of professional, survivor, romance genre fan, and Desperately Seeking Single. . . . And since she shows us her best and her worst while becoming a heroine worthy of her real hero, we like her, and find her pretty brave."

—Bobbi Dumas, NPR.org

"The beautiful irony of the title says it all—erudite romance editor by day, lonely girl by night. Bloom (editor, Harlequin) offers the American, real, and highly relatable version of Helen Fielding's Bridget Jones . . . that's bound to be consumed in great gulps. Highly recommended for romantics of all stripes."

—*Library Journal* (starred review)

"In the end, it's not romance but something more elusive that Bloom finds: intimacy. Romance may wane as the quotidian details of cohabitation intrude on hearts and flowers, but that's when true love begins."

—*Kirkus Reviews*

"Bloom's lively memoir is sure to captivate those engrossed in the worlds of romance fictional and real." —*Booklist*

"Ultimately, Patience's heroism lies in her extraordinary optimism about the male sex despite the abundance of evidence she encounters to the contrary." —Bookreporter.com

"An absolute delight. Funny, charming, and totally honest. I was transported. Patience Bloom will make you believe in the power of a great happily-ever-after!"

—Susan Mallery, *New York Times* bestselling author of *Three Little Words*

"This book is fantastic! Patience Bloom has written a real-life fairy tale. *Romance Is My Day Job* is for romance readers and memoir readers alike."

—Tracey Garvis Graves, *New York Times* bestselling author of *On the Island* and *Covet*

"I love everything about this book. Prepare to have your heart stolen and your faith renewed."

—Marie Ferrarella, *USA Today* bestselling author of *A Small Fortune*

"Beautifully written, laugh-out-loud funny, and poignant."

—Mary Burton, *USA Today* bestselling author of *The Seventh Victim*

DALY CITY PUBLIC LIBRARY
DALY CITY, CALIFORNIA

DISCARDED

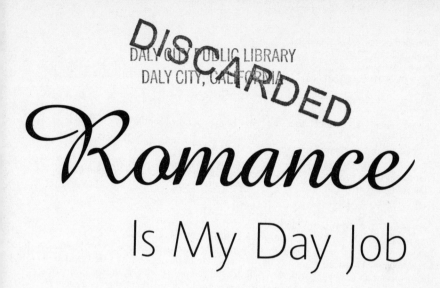

Romance

Is My Day Job

—◆▬◆▬◆—

A MEMOIR OF

FINDING LOVE AT LAST

Patience Bloom

A PLUME BOOK

W

PLUME
Published by the Penguin Group
Penguin Group (USA) LLC
375 Hudson Street
New York, New York 10014

USA | Canada | UK | Ireland | Australia | New Zealand | India | South Africa | China
penguin.com
A Penguin Random House Company

First published in the United States of America by Dutton, a member of Penguin Group
(USA) LLC, 2014
First Plume Printing 2015

Copyright © 2014 by Patience Bloom
Photographs © 2014 by Sam Bloom, Patrick Smith, and Chris Cozzone
Penguin supports copyright. Copyright fuels creativity, encourages diverse voices, promotes
free speech, and creates a vibrant culture. Thank you for buying an authorized edition of
this book and for complying with copyright laws by not reproducing, scanning, or distrib-
uting any part of it in any form without permission. You are supporting writers and allowing
Penguin to continue to publish books for every reader.

P REGISTERED TRADEMARK—MARCA REGISTRADA

THE LIBRARY OF CONGRESS HAS CATALOGED THE DUTTON EDITION AS FOLLOWS:

Bloom, Patience.
Romance is my day job : a memoir of finding love at last / Patience Bloom.
pages cm
ISBN 978-0-525-95438-5 (hc.)
ISBN 978-0-14-218139-3 (pbk.)
1. Bloom, Patience.   2. Editors—United States—Biography.
3. Book editors—United States—Biography.   4. Harlequin Enterprises.
5. Love stories—Publishing—United States.   I. Title.
PN149.9.B56A3 2014
070.5092—dc23
[B]
2013024050

Printed in the United States of America
10 9 8 7 6 5 4 3 2 1

Set in ITC Berkeley Old Style
Original hardcover design by Alissa Amell

While the author has made every effort to provide accurate telephone numbers, Internet
addresses, and other contact information at the time of publication, neither the publisher
nor the author assumes any responsibility for errors or for changes that occur after publication. Further, publisher does not have any control over and does not assume any responsibility for author or third-party Web sites or their content.

*Penguin is committed to publishing works of quality and integrity. In that spirit, we are proud to offer
this book to our readers; however, the story, the experiences, and the words are the author's alone.*

For Cookie

Contents

Prelude to a Romance xi

PART I

CHAPTER ONE

High School Dances Don't End Like Romance Novels

(Except Maybe If There's a Pregnancy) 3

CHAPTER TWO

Tragic Heroes Are Romantic on the Page

but Sad in Real Life 23

CHAPTER THREE

When in Crisis, Go Party in Paris! 45

CHAPTER FOUR

Harrison Ford Isn't Coming to Cleveland 63

CHAPTER FIVE

If He Says He Doesn't Reciprocate Your Feelings,

Believe Him and Run 81

PART II

CHAPTER SIX

Romance on Paper Can Help a Girl Through a Long
Dry Spell, and It's Not as Messy as the Real Thing   111

CHAPTER SEVEN

A Hero for All Seasons   131

CHAPTER EIGHT

Never Discount the Power of a Birthday Wish   147

CHAPTER NINE

The Voice from Five Thousand Miles and
Twenty-Six Years Away   163

CHAPTER TEN

Is This My Romance or One of Those Strange
Friendships That Goes Nowhere?   181

PART III

CHAPTER ELEVEN

The Airport Scene   207

CHAPTER TWELVE

Eat, Pray, Move in on the First Date   231

CHAPTER THIRTEEN

Where There's a Ring   247

CHAPTER FOURTEEN

Wedding Planning and Taking the High Road   263

CHAPTER FIFTEEN

Happily Wedded Ever After
(but Someone Will Puke)   285

Acknowledgments   303

Prelude to a Romance

I know there's a reason why I'm here, all pouty and sullen on this Amtrak train speeding back to New York City. There has to be. It's one of the first beautiful days of spring in 2009, but I'm not appreciating it the way I should. My situation is causing me some confusion. If the irony of my lame love life and my profession as a romance editor is a cosmic accident, then life is truly absurd. This is why I need a chocolate doughnut before boarding.

The boyfriend I call Superman is sitting next to me, looking extremely gorgeous. He's that elusive alpha male I've always dreamed of dating, the hero who fills up the pages of many romance novels—and he was mine for five months. Now we're not speaking. The weekend at his country home was a disaster. I can't wait to be home.

I have no idea what I'm doing anymore. At forty, I should have this part of my life figured out. And I of all people really should know better, right? I've been a romance editor at Harlequin for more than ten years. As a supposed expert in the field, the mechanics of love are familiar to me. I've read the dating books (combined with a dizzying number of romances) and given real-life romance my full attention for over twenty-five years. Though I never deluded myself that my hero would be James Bond or Heathcliff (who was a head case, by the way), you'd think I'd have come close. I have this vast knowledge of romance in print, a gigantic dating pool in Manhattan, and I'm no Quasimodo. But it's been a long time, and I haven't met anyone close to Mr. Darcy. Maybe it's time to take a break.

But never a break from reading love stories. The novelty of editing romance is still there: I read romance through terrible times and it gives me a boost. Every day, I work with friendly, smart people at my job. I get to deal with writers who love writing about love. They make me love love, even when I hate it. These books even compel me to hope that everyone finds her own happily-ever-after—not just me. And it's not because authors send me chocolate on Valentine's Day, always ask about my personal life, supply me with manuscripts to feed my book-reading obsession, and are interesting people. Who doesn't want to escape for a little while? Really, it's sick that I get paid to do this.

Imagine the agony I endure on a day-to-day basis: A surly FBI agent—let's call him Jake Hunter—has to find the latest serial killer menacing a small community. Even though he has been through hell—maybe his wife died in a car crash or his partner was killed by a drug cartel—he has this crazy attraction to the town's knitting-store owner with a name like, say, Cassie McBride, who happens to be a virgin. Knitting Girl has no clue a stalker—most likely an ex-boyfriend or jealous friend from high school—wants her dead because she's so unforgettable. And why is an FBI agent in her knitting store? He's definitely sexy, and it's been a while since Cassie's no-good boyfriend dumped her.

Yes. This is what I want to read most of the time. My average day is a good one. In the morning, the sun hits my neck, and I'm drinking my coffee and plunging into a tale of characters overcoming obstacles, having amazing simultaneous-orgasm sex, and then realizing they're destined for each other. It's a far cry from this sad, depressing Amtrak ride.

I gave dating my best shot. I did everything I was supposed to do: made myself available but not too much, dated like I shopped, online-dated on numerous sites, went out, was cheerful, didn't talk about my ex(es) or whine. I took extra care with hair, clothes, and makeup. I was ready for any opportunity. But then years—decades—went by and here I am, still. I've read so much, tried so hard, and I figure I'm happy even without real romance in my life. I'm okay if it's just me. The final verdict is: My life is nothing like these books, not even a little bit.

Or, maybe my real-life romance is just around the corner. . . .

PART I

A lady's imagination is very rapid; it jumps from admiration to love, from love to matrimony, in a moment.

—Jane Austen, *Pride and Prejudice*

CHAPTER ONE

—◆◀◆▶◆—

High School Dances Don't End Like

Romance Novels

(Except Maybe If There's a Pregnancy)

1984

It's dance night. February 25, 1984, at the Taft School in bucolic Watertown, Connecticut. My little boarding school is a haven, nestled in rolling hills, with green trees, manicured grounds, and charming buildings. When you drive up to the main building, you might think "old" and "elitist." Inside, though, you become part of an energized stream of high school students, legendary teachers, and history in the making. CEOs' and politicians' children go here.

I am Patience Smith, a sophomore and the daughter of two historians. As a scholarship student, I'm used to living on a budget (sort of). Being not-rich at Taft doesn't affect me as much as it should. We all live in tiny rooms, eat the same food, sit through a two-hour study hall, and attend the same classes. So I wear velour instead of a Fair Isle sweater. My choice of a mullet doesn't quite mesh with the sea of bobs. I may not have a BMW waiting for me on my sixteenth birthday or all the preppy clothes, but I still spend Daddy's money, mostly on low-rent items like yogurt peanuts I charge to his account.

Lately, though, I've been starving myself to fit into my dress for the dance. This is no hardship since I'm nervous and not up to my usual vanilla shake with fries after every meal. It's time for the big winter formal, and my date is Harlequin-hero gorgeous, someone I want as my boyfriend. Dating my formal date would put me into the stratosphere known as "popular," not that I'm a social climber. It's just a thought.

I check myself out in the mirror in my dorm room. I look amazing. My dress is deep blue and lacy, skintight over my hourglass shape. You can see that I have a body. Maybe I don't need oversize pants and baggy shirts cinched with a Madonna belt. This is a dress worthy of the Academy Awards. It will shock everyone that I am, in fact, a glamorous movie star.

All I need to do is convey my amazingness to Kent. My long red hair is curled, and my sparkling blue eye shadow has been deftly applied along with mascara and thick black eyeliner. Shiny frosted pink lipstick, of course, because that's the thing. Not coral as in a romance novel, but simple, shimmering pink. The face is perfect.

My dorm, Mac House, is buzzing with dance anticipation. Freshman and sophomore girls stand around, admiring one another's hair and the explosion of taffeta. I wait and wait, shifting in my heels on the shaggy purple rug on the first floor. Then in walks my dream.

Kent saunters through the entrance of the dorm. "You look nice," he says when I greet him.

The compliment makes me glow. Even though I'm anxious, I note how dashing Kent looks in a white tuxedo. I've never seen one before. Maybe it's a New Canaan/Greenwich/Darien, Connecticut, thing. In some ways, I feel out of place, like I came from a different club. My parents—who divorced each other, then remarried other academics— are professional bookworms and not exactly silver-spoon material. Although thanks to them, I got to live in Paris for a few years, which lends sophistication to my profile. I am bilingual, but mostly just grown-ups think that's cool. So many of my classmates have known one another since birth. Our different backgrounds and financial portfolios don't alienate me, except when I think of what I might have missed: lawn parties, Talbots, croquet, and Izod shirts. But then there's my roommate, Nici, who knows about lawn parties and has a few more pennies to rub together than I do. She and I are two gig-gling fools, attached at the hip.

Nici is this pretty, pleasingly plump girl with light brown hair, fair coloring, and a smile that lights up a room, very younger Lady Di and girl next door, with part of a screw loose (in a fun way). Her big heart attracts a range of friends, though she obsesses about boys to such an extent that a listener's eyes might glaze over—which makes her the perfect friend for me since I am also boy-crazy. She is "an incurable romantic." I'm not sure where she heard that phrase, but that's how she describes herself, as if it's a good thing. I start to wonder what would happen if she did catch the boy she wants. In the meantime, I marvel at her careful orchestration of romantic scenes—stealing a boy's sneaker and running to the pond, hoping he'll chase her, which he does because he wants his sneaker back. This kind of plan tends to backfire and she winds up in our room sobbing her brains out.

You can't fault a girl for trying . . . really, really hard. This is only a small part of what makes her lovable, why I spend most of my time with her.

This whole Kent predicament is Nici's fault, by the way. She convinced me that asking Kent to the dance was a good idea, just like she got me hooked on romance novels last year. I am already obsessed with Duran Duran to the point where I might need medication. Did I need more imaginary romance in my life? Probably not.

Last spring, when Nici first handed me a Harlequin romance novel, I pretended not to be interested. Of course, I devoured the book, on the morning of my Latin exam—and still got an A. Who wouldn't adore the story of a plain Jane who meets a hunky millionaire who treats her like crap before declaring a soft "I love you" at the end? Plus, it's a little dirty—enough for me anyway.

I just wish I could translate the romance novel into real life. Love is so effortless between the pages of these juicy clinch covers.

Secretly, I'm dying to have a real boyfriend. Everyone around me claims to be having sex, and I've never kissed anyone. It's a little embarrassing, so much so that I start to make up boyfriends from my past—even to Nici. You'd think living with my peers would produce scads of romantic possibilities, but for a shy girl like me, the opportunities are the same. I get mind-numbing crushes that go nowhere.

On the other hand, I like how it feels to have a crush on someone, that giddy feeling where you can't wait to see him. The step from crush to dating goes way too fast here at school. Where is the hand-holding that looks like so much fun, the long conversations about your painful childhoods? The kissing that you see in movies? My classmates talk about *other* things that they've done, like actual intercourse in gym locker rooms, the cemetery, one another's rooms, graphic details about acts involving body parts.

Romance is supposed to be close to what happens on *The Love Boat,* my all-time favorite show. *The Love Boat* could even be deemed educational since it teaches about meeting new people and how easily love can flourish over a three-day period. You share that flicker of attraction from across the room. The man asks you to dance, then you go out on the Lido Deck to make out. I'm not sure what happens after this, though there are a lot of bathrobes and trips to see Doc. It would be too cruel if romance had more to do with that crazy stuff in *Our Bodies, Ourselves.*

My dorm-mates describe what they do with boys. It's terrifying to me. One girl was almost raped by a boy out on the soccer field after dark. When he got too rough, she kicked him in that special place. I'd die if that happened to me. Another girl talked about a blow job, which, only months ago, I thought had something to do with a hair dryer. I'm still not sure what's supposed to happen there.

In romance novels and *The Love Boat,* these kinds of icky details are nonexistent. All sexual contact produces severe ecstasy (and is consensual), but it's mostly about the emotion, the romantic conflict. The heroine—let's call her Faun, since this is the eighties and that's the kind of name she'd have—has no idea what's about to happen to her. She's not really looking for love. Her insouciance is adorable. She's just like Bambi, getting her sea legs. She can barely pour her own Cheerios, much less show anyone her slinky lingerie (the underwear and bra always match—no granny panties here).

Inevitably, she comes face-to-face with her future deflowering man-stallion hero, a.k.a. the Boss. Let's call him Devlin, because it sounds like *devil* and he's one demon in the sack—and impossibly well endowed. I'm still not sure how the size of his endowment is advantageous, but in these books, he's never not hung like a horse. Devlin sees Faun and his pants feel tighter. If you unzipped Devlin's fly, it would spring free, leveling skyscrapers; it is just that powerful. Poor Devlin, though. He's kind of a dick (note to self: Dickish behavior means true love). Secretly, long ago, in his darkest past, Devlin was kicked around by love, maybe even beaten by his drunken father who slept with Devlin's ex-fiancée the night before his wedding. Faun misunderstands his meanness, avoids him—though can't stop blushing with (sexual) awareness. He keeps showing up, barking at her and being all dark and sullen (attractive). At one point, Faun sees his underbelly (and his perfect, perfect abs). Clothes fly off. Maybe it hurts at first, but Faun soon adores sex with this man. It's the most natural thing, and they're like rabbits all night long. They spend the night cuddling, a first for Devlin. In the morning, he's pissed for no reason and leaves, and she thinks he hates her. Separation ensues, at the end of which she runs to the bathroom to puke up her breakfast. Pregnancy. Marriage. She thinks it's just for the baby, that he's too damaged to love her, but actually, he does love her and they are happy for always.

You can see how easy it is to get hooked.

I read about all kinds of destined couples—an earl who falls for the less comely girl, a cranky millionaire who butts heads and body parts with his dead wife's sister, the secretary who marries the wrong groom . . . the list goes on. The romances encourage me to dream. I'll meet my husband someday—maybe on a windswept beach in Malibu—and he will be John Taylor, bass guitarist of Duran Duran. JT is my idea of the perfect man with his hairless, preadult chest and the red, shiny suit he wears in the "Rio" video. He's eight years older than I am, but he looks younger. I'm fifteen, he's twenty-three: We could totally date! I love him so much that I look up the word *prawns* since that's one of his favorite foods (according to *Tiger Beat*).

No, it's time to find a real boyfriend, and having a date to the dance seems like the logical first step. Being shy and bookish is just not fun anymore. Do I want to spend another year watching all my friends go out and date? Nici and I are on the same page.

At the beginning of the year, we went through the roster of new students, making notes on who's hooked up with whom and their secret nicknames. Nici is in love with Promising Actor and with Senior Who Doesn't Know She Exists. She's written reams of poetry about them, drawn countless roses with her married initials scrawled inside. I noticed Kent immediately because he is so tall and has that "life is effortless" look about him, which I love. I'm not sure what color his eyes are since his floppy blond hair covers them. The instant he walks into a room, my stomach goes cold.

My reaction and our connection is a lot like a Harlequin romance, I insist to Nici, and explain my findings: Kent seems casual, as if he doesn't care about me, just like Devlin's attitude toward Faun when she comes to work as his secretary. It's almost a hostile relationship. With Kent, I almost feel as if he secretly loves me but pretends not to know who I am. How could he *not* know who I am? It's a small school. The final piece of evidence is that I'm falling deeply in love, absolutely freaking out inside because he's so beautiful. It must be fate that we wind up together. Nici agrees with me, and she's the expert.

"Maybe you should ask him to the formal," Nici suggested just last month between drags of a cigarette. We were sitting in the "butt room," our dorm's smoking lounge, where we conduct our top-level discussions. It's a tiny, dark room, like a filthy jail, littered with cigarette butts, the perfect place for us to deal with our new problem. My good friend Diane was also with us. She is an intellectually curious, blue-eyed blonde who is direct like Rizzo from *Grease* and dreams of a man-sandwich with Sting and Billy Idol. Her motto is usually, "Go for it!" Between these two, I knew I was in trouble with the whole Kent idea, because they would encourage me.

The Sadie Hawkins winter formal was fast approaching and I intended to find myself a date—and not just a platonic guy friend, but a real *date* date. The problem was that I had to do the asking.

"Okay, I'll ask Kent." I took a giant gulp of my Tab soda, then a drag.

"No, really, I dare you." Nici blew out a long stream of smoke.

"Sure, I'll do it."

"*Do it!*" Diane said loudly, urging me on.

This is how a bad idea was born.

Our main worry was the competition from the rash of new sophomore girls, known as "mid chicks." *Mid* was the Taft term for *sophomore*, and adding *chick* must have been organic since, truly, they were babes, the fresh new faces to our old sack of potatoes. They sashayed into the dorm, squealing over concerts attended, vacations had, parties thrown. They overshadowed us with their miniskirts and long, tan legs. The mid chicks made it all seem easy, like they just woke up from a fabulous nap. The boys noticed them immediately. They were exciting and bombshell gorgeous. And, worst of all, mostly nice. We had to hate them on sight since they were stealing our chance to star in a romance novel come to life. These girls were in my universe for a reason, to make me fight harder for the cute boy. So I had a little competition. I could still snag the hero of my dreams.

Faun always pulls courage out of thin air—if the stakes are high enough. She needs someone to drive her to visit her mentally unstable brother in jail (who then tries to kill her). Faun doesn't really drive or operate any kind of machinery, unless it's a typewriter. At first, she insists on walking the twelve miles to the penitentiary even though she might miss visiting hours (logic sometimes goes astray). Then she sees Devlin in his sleek Jaguar and asks him for a ride, her chin defiantly stuck out. She almost dares him to say no.

I am so like Faun. I want this. It was my destiny to ask Kent to the dance, my bold attempt to be less of a wallflower. Kent and I will experience lasting happiness through thick and thin. Then we'll get married.

Isn't that how the story goes?

I agonized for weeks over asking Kent, how to get to know him since we'd never spoken before. Not even hello. He had no obvious reputation, and I couldn't investigate him without arousing suspicion. Our friends were leagues apart. Telling Nici and Diane about my crush was bad enough, and now I wanted to ask this stranger to a dance? That was eye-twitchingly insane. It would take serious work to bridge the gap between Kent and me, especially since I wanted to marry him in the future.

Like any infatuated girl, I spent a lot of time watching him, though he appeared unaware of this. I did my usual timed hallway run-ins, post-dinner lagging in his general area, and showing up at the snack bar after study hall and lurking around his friends. Nothing quite worked, which didn't stop me. The imagined romantic conflict between us filled many pages of my diary, my ultimate confidant. Kent took Spanish, I took Latin and French. He liked the Dead, I liked Duran Duran, Culture Club, and Wham! He lived in the boys' dorm, I was in the girls' (obviously). We were both quiet. Only a miracle would bring us together.

But miracles happen in the perfect love story, and I devised a plan of attack. I didn't have time for a gradual getting-to-know-you montage, so I dove in, ready for all outcomes.

On weeknights, we had a lecture of some kind in the main auditorium, given by the headmaster, teacher, or some educational luminary. Wearing coats and ties, skirts and dresses, the entire school attended. It was twenty minutes of reflection or cultural enrichment, and many of us fidgeted, dozed off, or flirted with whoever sat next to us. One time, during the assembly, Nici made herself pass out by pressing on her jugular vein for too long, just to see what would happen.

The appointed evening arrived, and during the night's lecture, I squirmed in my seat and mustered my courage to do the deed. Between the lecture and dinner was my window of opportunity.

At the end, I rushed out of the auditorium and waited for his section to let out. I was going to do this crazy thing, so unlike me, as if an alien had taken over my body. But this was how love stories began—with inspiration (Kent) and one person taking that leap of faith. Sweet Faun goes out in front of the school and belts out an amazing song. Or perhaps Devlin is in the hospital—poor guy fell down five flights of stairs trying to catch Faun's kidnapper. He's been unconscious for days. Only Faun can defy modern medicine by kissing him out of his coma. And then Devlin whips out a diamond ring.

If I made a fool of myself, I'd be mortified, but not for long. I could hide in our dorm's smoking lounge until my humiliation dissipated. My imaginary boyfriend "Jason" could emerge on this special occasion. If Kent rejected me, I'd tell a whopper—"Oh, I forgot, Jason might drive all the way from Cape Cod for the dance." There was the option of chickening out, too, but once I decided to ask, I had to follow through.

Here came Kent—Devlin—sauntering out the door with his signature shuffle, hair in his face. I couldn't fathom how he saw two feet in front of him, but I was ready to lead him in life, shape his future.

I pounced. Hard. "Hi. Can I ask you something?"

He had a blank look on his face, no doubt because my identity was a complete mystery to him. Was this a joke?

"Would you go to the dance with me?" I blurted out with students milling around me, no doubt oblivious because they would never expect me to do something so daring.

He seemed to consider my request for a second or two. "Sure," Devlin said, shrugging, maybe even amused.

Oh God. Really? "Great."

This was so easy and the beginning of my better social life. Next stop, a romantic picnic in the north field with us holding hands and smiling at each other. I'd bring a basket of fried chicken, potato salad, and pie—typical romance-novel picnic fare. No idea where I'd get those items from, but who cares?

Kent hesitated. "So, what's your name?"

The embarrassing question didn't matter. It was one of those cute anecdotes you tell your grandchildren.

Over the following week, I spent hours thinking of how to act, what would be the perfect dress, whether he would want to go out with me. I couldn't sleep. Nici and I had many, many emergency strategizing sessions in the dorm's smoking lounge.

"What are you going to wear?"

"I don't know. A dress."

"Make sure it's not too baggy."

"What if he says something to me?"

"You just talk. It's called conversation."

"But what do I say?"

"I dunno, that you grew up in France?"

That would impress him. But Kent and I rarely talked during those weeks leading up to the dance. We said hello at the snack bar yet had no other contact. Could you have great love just by staring? We needed to interact on another level, like talk or share interests. Though, in romance novels, you don't need a lot of talk or shared interests. Well, okay, that wasn't true, since Devlin displays astounding knowledge of, say, gargoyles on European cathedrals, usually in just one scene as he and Faun are walking down the Seine, thereby proving to her that he is an intellectual as well as the owner of a giant appendage in his pants (not that I want to see this firsthand). Maybe Devlin secretly has a PhD in archaeology as well as an MBA, but Faun doesn't know this until some benevolent fairy godmother tells her the truth about him, that he's full of depth—not just chiseled features. Really, Devlin is beyond mysterious. Which made me think Kent could be perfect for me, since I knew nothing about him.

Deep down, I started to dread the dance and had the feeling it would be a failure. How could Kent become my boyfriend out of nowhere? I had overthought the whole thing. My future love with Kent could be all in my head.

———

Well, the moment has arrived. There's no turning back now. I am on this date with Kent. As we go toward the school cafeteria I feel like Cinderella, with a few jitters and some doubts. Maybe, though, he'll kiss me at the end of the night even if it seems wrong. Walking next to him, this giant blond boy, I can't imagine us as a real couple. This is what happens when I try to turn the Joy of Staring into a viable relationship.

We move into the cafeteria, where the dance is taking place, with its special lighting, streamers, and posters galore. Outside the cafeteria, a line of couples in their taffeta and tuxes wait to get their photographs taken. For some reason, Kent and I glide by the photographers, perhaps because the line is too long, the punch is too irresistible, or they're playing "Rock Lobster." As such, there will be no evidence that we ever went to the dance together.

I'm sure Kent and I should talk about something, but we don't. People sort of leave us alone, walking around us as if we're a museum exhibit. On *The Love Boat,* conversation is effortless. Julie McCoy, your cruise director, would know how to seduce a sixteen-year-old boy, no problem. I'm disappointed we're not this easy-breezy couple. The awkwardness is more than I can bear, and it's due in part to our not knowing much about each other—plus my idea of flirtation is to show up. Dances are not about fun at all, mostly just freaking out over nothing and a depressing walk back to the dorm at the end of the night.

So it's a little obvious to me this is a wrong turn in my love story, but not fatal. Maybe we won't be an ecstatic couple. At least I know this. He won't kiss me under a full moon or father my child accidentally on the topmost soccer field. As the music gets going, with decked-out couples dancing away, there are no fireworks between me and Kent. This I can admit to myself, though it gives me an empty feeling—like, who do I have a crush on now? I do feel some relief, too, because I expended a lot of energy thinking about Kent. We are not made for each other, and I can always go back to obsessing about John Taylor, who is perfect (and the tabloids say he's a virgin!).

I start to rally and notice how the cafeteria has been transformed into the dance of our dreams with the cheesy decorations, the refreshments, and the sea of couples on the dance floor. There are other occasions when my peers dress up, but the gowns and tuxes take my breath away. My classmates clean up good. It's preparation for their lives ahead, with professional functions, weddings, parties, and fundraisers. These students are the hope of the future. Tonight, they look the part.

Kent and I dance a little. Most eighties music brings out the beast in me on the dance floor. For instance, that laugh at the beginning of "Hungry Like the Wolf" jump-starts me to the point where I have to find Nici and then thrash in front of the nearest speaker. This time, I hold back on any wild moves since Kent is a mellow side-to-side dancer. As other people jump and twirl around us, Kent and I smile at each other now and then, not quite participating in the real festivities. I start to feel uncomfortable, like I should have left him alone so that he could have a better time with his own friends. I don't hate him at all for being such a sedate date. He's a really nice guy, just not my partner on my real-life *Love Boat*.

Within the hour, I am alone.

I know this happens a lot at dances. The year before, I ditched someone, ran to hide in a stairwell, and I know I hurt him. This is karma paying me back for spurning such a tender heart. Kent is not my Devlin. He's an affable Deadhead with great hair—and he has vanished. I'm not sure how or when, maybe when he went off with a group of friends. I totally expected this and don't even try to find him. How could I have ever mistaken him for Devlin?

And yet I'm sad. Paranoid, too, that he devised some secret plan to escape my clutches. If that's even true, I won't let it get me down. Maybe I could just blend in and pretend everything is okay. No one will see my disappointment. What's so special about *this* dance anyway?

It's like any other, with four different years of classes mingling and moving on the dance floor. As I scan the room, I see Nici is happily losing her sanity—and her heart—dancing with Prescott, a tall new sophomore boy with a drawl. A skilled seducer with a fleet of adoring girls, Prescott easily indulges Nici—another female—on most levels, laps up the attention, and pays her those crucial compliments (you look pretty; aw, you're so nice; wow, you're intense; I'm sure he likes you, he'd be stupid not to; screw him, you deserve better). Judging from her glow, he might become a serious addition to her stable of crushes—which means hours of deliberation and romantic scene planning in the butt room for us.

Along with the movement of colors and shimmering fabric, I watch how some couples hold each other in public, while others dance in large unisex groups. Real romances start on this very dance floor. Then the couples move out to the patio off the cafeteria. They sit out on the stone wall and talk and kiss until curfew. Or they go out to the cemetery next door. . . .

With every dance, there's a new expectation that this one will change my life—someone will appear and declare himself, will want me, that little red-haired girl who sits in the bleachers. But not this dance. Certainly not with Kent.

I do my best to dance in heels and appear sinewy in my tight blue dress, but I wind up on the sidelines, nursing that too-sweet punch. Maybe in an hour, I can make a quiet escape, count this night as a total failure. But at least I tried. I always try.

Tears threaten, but I force them back.

It's almost a losing battle when, suddenly, the unthinkable happens.

"You wanna dance?"

I turn around and see Sam, the popular senior with a reputation for funny and crazy behavior. Dumbfounded, I stare up into his animated face, his big green eyes full of mischief. He once threw a boy's whole bed out the window. He often pulls crazy stunts like running full speed at the wall to test the strength of a helmet. Without hesitation, Sam damages school property, lovingly torments his teachers, and sets up residence in the infirmary with his many injuries. Maybe he should have gotten kicked out, but he always just teeters on the edge. He is untouchable, and no one hates him—except maybe his football coach, but only when Sam turned warm-up exercises into a Chippendales show.

To me, Sam is that boy who basically runs the school. And now he's looking at me with this smile on his face.

I nod automatically. Who wouldn't dance with him?

His hand grabs mine and whisks me onto the floor, guiding us to some pop song, possibly "In a Big Country," but the song doesn't register in my head. I'm too stunned. How does Sam even know to pick me? He has no clue I exist and now here he is, grinning down at me, his hand on my waist. He doesn't sense what I'm going through, does he? We're just having fun, and my mood changes in an instant.

Sam is one of those experimental dancers, as in he jumps high in the air like David Lee Roth, then comes down in a split. I laugh, just marveling at how insane he must be. He laughs with me. There's warmth behind his eyes, and I wonder what he's like when he's serious. I feel as if he can see through me, but I go with it, taking in the fact that this is the boy who launched wet balls of toilet paper out the window at visitors. The scary imp you don't want to double-cross because he will come back at you ten times harder.

One wouldn't call him a ladies' man, though he is fiendishly cute. The class clown doesn't usually attract a flock of females, not until later. At the same time, it's hard not to go dreamy-eyed over his fearlessness, how he hurls himself at bigger men in football. Just recently, for good luck, our stern headmaster asked Sam to rub his bald head in order break their football team's losing streak—in front of the entire school. This is the power of Sam.

I'm thrilled he's paying attention to me. Delirious but preparing myself for the bucket of blood falling from the ceiling like in the movie *Carrie*. The night has mostly been a disaster . . . except for now.

Sam twirls me on the dance floor, encouraging me to break free of myself. I like how he feels in my arms. He's a little sweaty, but that endears him to me even more. Could he be nervous or is it just that he sweats a lot when he moves? He's holding me as if I were a delicate creature—and then leads me into a fast-and-furious square dance from hell. The more I look at his face, the more I like it. I didn't notice before just how gorgeous he is with his sparkling eyes, that wide smile. I'm a little breathless.

Though I can't move too much in my tight dress, I do my best. Most of all, I have fun and take in this special moment. A real dance with a school legend.

Any guy who rescues a newly dateless girl at a dance has to be the nicest person ever. He's that hero who swoops in after a miserable night. I had no idea anything like this could happen to me, that I could be the target of such a person. It dawns on me now how sexy he is, how he might be that romance-novel hero. The key element is the unexpected.

When the music ends, I make as if to leave, but Sam has other plans and takes my hand. Faun would never argue over such a bold gesture, and I won't either. He brings me along to chat with his friends, the big stars of the senior class. One of them is the vice president's nephew. Vice president of the United States, the one who became president later. They are extremely nice to me, as if I've been hanging with them for years.

"Let's take a picture," Sam says insistently, shepherding me to the photographer and pulling me into the frame with him. While he's not affectionate with me, he's attentive in a way that brightens my night. I know that he has another date at the dance and is just being a nice guy. It doesn't even occur to me to be jealous of the girl he's with. How could I when this night was deemed a downer? He could have seen my suffering on the dance floor and wanted to make me feel better. Mission accomplished.

I'm so dazed over Sam's request that my jaw drops just as the bulb flashes. This is the official picture, the one I should have taken with Kent. For a few minutes, I feel cherished, like someone's princess, like I had a real date experience.

All too soon, the lights come on. Sam folds back into his super-pack and Kent finds me at the end to say good night. I prepare myself for the inevitable kiss-off and because I can smell rejection from far away, I explain to Kent that no-no-no, I don't have unreal fantasies of our dating since that would upset my boyfriend, Jason from Cape Cod. All is well. I am secretly grateful Kent said yes to me in the first place. I return to my room, let go of the night, and keep one precious memory of the popular boy sweeping me off my feet.

We all move on from this dance. Kent continues being cute and friendly—but out of my social sphere, and never again masquerading as Devlin. Despite the lack of romance with Kent, I'm grateful that he inspired me to be audacious, really go after what I want. Everyone should ask out their Kent. He might say yes, and if he says no, you'll get over it.

Nici and I keep dreaming about the perfect guy, reading our romance novels. My soul mate is someone else—possibly John Taylor, who finally learns of my existence for about thirty seconds when a classmate of mine meets him at a party years later. "I like her name," he says, though this entire story could be a vicious lie. I write a fifty-page term paper on Duran Duran for sophomore English class, which brings me no closer to attracting a boyfriend at Taft. The paper does cement my legend as Taft's number one Duran Duran fan. I thoroughly investigate the band's roots in funk, its goal to create danceable, happy music, its meteoric rise due to those sultry MTV videos, and then I do a thorough analysis of Simon Le Bon's lyrics and how they compare to T. S. Eliot's poetry (not that I've read any Eliot or know who he is).

My winter formal savior, Sam, and I don't interact after our dance, except for a few smiles in the hall. He has his own troubles. Not only does he fall short in his quest to break a world record by eating the most ravioli squares in an hour, but in a failed mooning attempt, he puts his butt through a glass window and needs thirty-seven stitches in his ass. He has to stand for the rest of his classes that semester.

He is way too cool for me, the unattainable hero I don't even try to dream about.

Maybe somewhere, someone is out there for me.

CHAPTER TWO

——◆◂◆▸◆——

Tragic Heroes Are Romantic on the Page but Sad in Real Life

Summer 1987

It's a mistake for me to read *The Thorn Birds,* years after everyone else went crazy over the televised miniseries and book. It's not even about birds. It's about forbidden, holy love. The thorn bird is a metaphor for people who impale themselves on one burst of awesomeness, e.g. Meggie and Father Ralph finally boinking their brains out because they love each other so much (maybe I'm oversimplifying). By this time, I'm over my fear of sex but not my love of romance. In fact, it's gotten worse. Who needs Faun and Devlin when you have that tortured passion between ardent Catholics Meggie and Ralph? These two make me yearn for my own burning love that transcends religion and time. It's bad that I love to read so much. There's nothing else to do over a long, sticky summer, waiting for sophomore year of college to start.

My first year at Oberlin was very enlightening—a warm-up to the ecstasy I will soon experience, I just know it. And what better place than the compact intimacy of Oberlin? There's not a whole lot to do in this small Ohio town, so one must stay hyperfocused on classes and social activities. The campus itself is a hive of majestic buildings and dorms—both old and new—and hosts as diverse a student body as you'll find with its hippies, conservatives, serious musicians, loud people, quiet people, activists, pacifists, nudists, fashion plates, goths, theater people, intellectuals, and, yes, jocks. Since prep school prepared me to live away from my parents, I take to college life quickly, shrewdly scouting out my bliss.

There were a few items, though, that I had to take care of my freshman year, some necessary rituals before True Love could descend: losing my virginity and getting drunk. For the first, I chose a sweet guy, Danny, who'd been in love with my roommate. After he cried on my shoulder for a week (psychiatry is an effective tool of seduction, if you just wait it out), our relationship shifted into romance. A double major in music and science, he had this soft sensuality—sleepy brown eyes and a quiet disposition, i.e., the perfect man with whom I could share that all-important, potentially embarrassing, once-in-a-lifetime penetration event. After this, I wanted to spread my wings elsewhere, and in an act of utter *Dynasty* recklessness, I hooked up with his best friend. Danny then hooked up with another girlfriend of mine. Then our friends, the ones we'd each hooked up with, fell in love with each other. During this dramatic cycle, I discovered beer. It could have been beer goggles and the roller coaster of my *Dynasty* emotions, but I ended the year by falling for Ben the Buddhist, then a junior.

Now that it's summer, I am isolated in my mother's house in Rochester, New York, with my large room in the very back and the most important piece of furniture: a television. One might call it an opportunity for reflection, which I do over a glass or two of Mom's dry sherry. At the end of the day, she and I have gotten into the habit of sitting on the porch and having a few nips of Tio Pepe mixed with girl talk. Who knew a parent could be so much fun? All I had to do was grow up a little before we could enjoy supreme Jane Austen sister moments.

When Mom's not around, though, I snoop around the house for paperbacks, the more decadent, the better. I'm not sure where I find *The Thorn Birds*—I suspect it belongs my stepfather, Don, a fellow academic who secretly reads bestsellers.

My reading begins on my bed until I fall back to sleep. Once my mother and Don leave for work at the University of Rochester, I throw myself on their bed because it's bigger and there's more light streaming through the window. Plus, it feels a little forbidden to read on their bed—like, nasty. By evening, I read on the couch in the living room, which is close to the kitchen. My mother wakes me up for dinner.

But Mom, Don, books, and sherry can only do so much to entertain a nineteen-year-old in the house, especially one who can't contribute to a discussion of "intellectual history" or "early modernism." They are hard-core historians and, as such, don't take many breaks to do Jane Fonda's workout or watch MTV with me, or discuss John Travolta movies, though they do recommend classics that I might enjoy.

My mother—a rising star in her field, European history and women's studies—toils in front of her typewriter, notepads, and piles of library books. Her office is a disaster area. My stepfather is the same way, only he looks the part of a historian: scruffy, grumpy, clothes from another decade, and bad haircut (my mother cuts it). Mom is glamorous, with her perfect face, warm brown eyes, nice cheekbones, dark trendy hair, and fashionable clothes. The two are like Beauty and the Beast. Love is crazy.

My brother, Patrick, and Don's son, John, who's been in my life sporadically for almost ten years, are off living adult lives. Patrick is in New York City, pursuing his dream of being an actor. A handsome redhead, Patrick has done theater his entire life, was even a runner-up for Timothy Hutton's part in *Ordinary People*. John is busy as a musician and getting his degree in Miami. A few years ago, Patrick and John and I lived in the house for a summer. While our parents were in Europe, we were total wastebags but supported one another through a season of demeaning jobs. Patrick went through a brief fat phase, which was the optimum time for him to get a perm. John giggled at him for weeks, but he chose to wear this skanky black leather vest as a shirt like he was Bret Michaels. I loved watching the two of them, felt blanketed in brotherly affection, which is lacking this summer.

My friends are scattered across the country, and for me to survive at Oberlin—without financial aid and without a job—I need to work like a dog, not pine over absent people. This is how people grow up—by themselves. During the day I sweat out twelve-hour shifts at the dry cleaner's down the street. I've been alone before, so at night I retreat into my secret world of Dagwood sandwiches, MTV, juicy paperbacks, and many hours dreaming of my future boyfriend.

Romance shouldn't be on my mind, especially since there are no prospects in Rochester. Ben, the soon-to-be-senior boy I'm in love with—my Father Ralph, his holy hotness—is a Buddhist. It isn't so unique to be a Westerner ensconced in Eastern philosophy at Oberlin, but Ben lives the part. He even went to India and came back all swaddled in sheets, smoking funky cigarettes. Love isn't foremost on his mind, which makes him an even hotter stud to me. We've never come close to being a couple, but that will change once the summer ends.

Because of him, I immerse myself in Buddhist literature, a.k.a. the greatest love stories of our time, because they involve the welfare of all sentient beings. Do-gooders deserve love, so I try to be nicer to people without keeping a scorecard (though I do anyway—like if the chain-smoking, toothless drunk I work with at the dry cleaner's makes one more mistake with the clothes and blames it on me, I'm dumping her omnipresent vodka Tang cocktail all over her).

Buddhism helps me endure the dry-cleaning job: Vodka Tang's endless coughing, the mean customers, and the jungle-hot store itself. All day long, wrapping and pinning clothes, I think, *Ben the Buddhist will love this, my burying myself in manual labor, chopping wood, carrying water.* I'm building character, even as Rochester's local weatherman—a total jerk—screams at me for losing a button on his precious shirt, the one his mommy gave him. So my blubbering in the bathroom isn't Buddhist, but I'm releasing emotion.

And then my detour with *The Thorn Birds* really messes me up. Did I think I could go a whole three months denying myself desire and ego? Buddhism never considered the majesty of Richard Chamberlain shirtless. I can't wait to see my priest again. Sure, he's never expressed any desire to date me, but now he'll take one look at me, transformed by enlightenment, and declare his love.

The day finally arrives when I return to Oberlin. I'm settled in my dorm with my same roommate from last year, Laura. We are so chill together, even look like each other, that we decide to continue our winning hand by getting another small divided double in the same dorm, the ideal setup. It is essentially two rooms linked by an adjoining door and with one entrance. Though we have no common area, we have privacy. If Laura or I brings someone home, there are no traumatic sounds and images to deal with.

For some reason (Ben), I'm giddier than usual over the start of this year. Now that I've had a few boyfriends—and have finally found my dream man in Ben—I know there are more exciting aspects to college than getting an education. While I easily fulfill the credits to be a Latin major and consider adding French, the idea that I'm here to study doesn't even occur to me. Bigger issues are at stake, like pitchers of beer and long walks through the quad with someone I adore. Grades are not that important. What is a grade, anyway, compared to that connection with a human being? I can't share this with my mother, who is footing 95 percent of the bill for my college education. She wouldn't understand.

I spritz myself with my latest perfume, Femme, and psych myself up to go reunite with Ben at the Tap House, the dive where Oberlin's coolest people drink. I am ready emotionally, physically, and spiritually for Ben. Plus, my hair is finally long enough.

Love at last!

This is like when adult, doelike Meggie comes down the stairs and Father Ralph sees her all grown up. He is tormented by how beautiful she's become. Ben will sense how I've risen in the ranks of Buddha consciousness.

In my gut, though, I know that my constant thoughts about him couldn't possibly lead to happily-ever-after. We've never even kissed. Or anything. In those books I still grab from supermarket racks, there is no heroine obsessing about her man like this. Sure, our dear Faun is mostly baffled by Devlin's strange behavior, how he keeps showing up wherever she goes. But Ben never shows up purposely to see me. I seem to be the one to follow him around, which is so not Harlequin-esque. Why is my gray matter focused on Ben and not my own ambitions? That can't be healthy. I try not to be negative since letting go of emotional attachment is an important tenet of Eastern philosophy. Ben has so much to teach me. I am eager to learn (and tangle in his bedsheets, though I'm not sure if he even does this).

My heart palpitates as he walks through the door. His herd of friends follows him, including a new girl who resembles Stevie Nicks. Stevie has this mellow look about her, with long, flowing hair and sweet brown eyes. We shake hands. I get a strange feeling but ignore it and do the standard pretending I don't see Ben yet even though he's right in front of me. A romantic heroine is always taken unawares by the hero's presence. Men practically have SEAL training and can creep into a room unnoticed. Of course, I've had SEAL training, too, along with years of experience reading and studying romance in books and on television. I'm fake-oblivious, delighted by everything I see. Ben and I acknowledge each other, but I try to focus on everything *but* Ben.

My friends and his rejoice over the beginning of a new year and we drink and talk for hours. When Ben asks to walk me home at the end of the night, I'm hopeful. Maybe my boy is a little shy and really does care.

We walk, the balmy air caressing us on this perfect evening. This is where my doubts are defied by true love's insistence. He secretly loves me, though, like Father Ralph, he can't give in to that love.

"Did you get my letters over the summer?" I ask.

He nods. Silence.

Oh God. Maybe I shouldn't have sent him stacks and stacks of letters. What girl does that? Now I'm embarrassed. All those pages. Well, boys don't write letters anyway, unless they lived a hundred years ago. I had rationalized that Ben didn't write back because he wanted to show me how manly he is. The thoughts swirl in my head.

"I can't run with you," he says as we reach my dorm.

Even his rejection is poetic, like we're horses galloping across a field. "I know you can't." I mean, duh. But my heart is still breaking.

"Do you?" He stares at me, his eyes sparkling. I'm not sure what color they are, even in daylight.

"I knew all along."

"Then you're a witch," he says, hands on my cheeks. He means it in the nicest way. Just how affectionate he is makes me want to cry. Usually guys reject you and search for the nearest hiding space. They treat you like you have the plague. Ben is loving, knowing full well that he hurt me.

"It's okay," I say, trying hard to be strong. There is a volcano of emotion that I push down. He's saying that he doesn't want to make out with me on our conjoined meditation cushions (though I can't fit my ass on one and he has no problem, which I find suspect), and it really hurts.

Ben kisses me, promises eternal friendship, and leaves. It's a little like when Meggie and Father Ralph make out for the first time— except in my case, there is no passion involved. I don't feel hope that Ben will change his mind. In fact, this is nothing like the vortex of lust that consumes Meggie and Father Ralph in their first joining of lips.

I discover a day or two later he started seeing Stevie Nicks on that first night. I can't be upset, because I love Stevie Nicks. She is gorgeous and I would have done the same thing. I can't blame Ben at all.

The worst part is that he is so kind. He tells me the truth, gives me a kiss, says we are meant to be close friends. It doesn't sound like a line. In fact, I feel enveloped by his love.

From that night, he doesn't disappear from my life. Though heart-broken, I know that everything I did—the meditating, the literature, the living-in-the-moment stuff—was positive. Ben was never supposed to be my boyfriend.

For fuck's sake, though. Now I have to find a new guy to love, because that's what college is: a dating party. My future husband is wandering around here somewhere. They say college is the place to meet your soul mate and make strong lifelong connections. I only have three years left—must act fast!

I am driven by an uncomfortable desperation. Family, friends, and therapists tell me that my parents' divorce caused all my emotional turmoil, so I chalk it up to this. Or maybe it's the culmination of moments I spent burying myself in books and television, moments where I avoided taking action. I want to show someone how amazing I am, but I'm not sure how to do this. And the more *he* walks away, the more infuriated I become . . . at myself and at him for not recognizing my greatness.

By chance, *Fatal Attraction* comes to Oberlin, and the buzz hits in a tidal wave. Though with a group of friends, I feel as if I'm in an empty theater and the only one who feels badly for Glenn Close. She's so unusually pretty and tenacious, but the people in the audience cheer when she's shot at the end. Why does everyone want her dead? Okay, she boiled rabbits and threatened the sanctity of Michael Douglas's family, but he participated, too. She just needed someone to love her, give her what she wanted. I feel as if I'm headed for the same kind of misery.

Having lost my Father Ralph, along with my purpose, I sit on the steps of the main building on campus and people-watch, witnessing the cascade of students across the steps and over the field. This is the central part of campus, with a quad in the middle and a circle of buildings: library, dining hall, dorm, classrooms, and central administration.

It's a gorgeous Indian-summer day when I first see Craig, who's been gone for a semester. Still sad over Ben, I perk up when Craig appears. He is the campus bad boy, the life of the party, the guy who stays out way past last call. He's starting his fourth year on the six-year college plan. I remember he and my roommate had a brief fling our first semester.

"Hi, Schuntzie," he says to me, smiling as he lunges toward the mailroom. The nickname tickles me. Usually people call me by my whole first name, or "Pay," "Paysh," or "Payshie." Craig takes the last part of my name and makes it his own.

"Hey!" I get the feeling he's coming back out to see me, so I wait.

Such is the tale of the instantaneous rebounder: I stare dreamily when he returns, thinking he's the spitting image of Michael Paré from *Eddie and the Cruisers*. Nici, my best friend from high school, and I spent hours discussing Paré's biceps, and now Eddie's here in the flesh at Oberlin College. The similarities are frightening: that dirty-blond hair that falls just right, the bright blue eyes, the rocker look. Craig is in a band, of course. He's the lead singer.

Suddenly, I'm a little smitten and ready for a diversion. If Ben is Father Ralph, then Craig is my Frank, Meggie's brother from *The Thorn Birds*. All wrong, potentially violent, worships at the altar of bourbon, and you just can't help wanting his company. Frank fits that other romance stereotype: the Bad Boy. He's a little too rough (and, um, is in love with his mother, but I'll overlook that). He lives by his impulses, runs foolishly into danger, and sort of commits murder, but I love that about him (since he's fiction). For now, I'll forget that Frank and Meggie are brother and sister. Boundaries are a mess in *The Thorn Birds*.

Craig joins me on the steps. We catch up on our lost summers, then unleash our sorrows. He mourns his Nordic, blond ex-girlfriend who started seeing someone else. I wail about Ben running off with Stevie Nicks.

Just the fact that he's still in love with Nordic Ex means that he's a good boyfriend. Craig's self-destructiveness comes from true love gone awry, which can't be his fault. How could Nordic Ex not see that he cared so much? Spending time with me will heal Craig. During our curative interludes, he will notice that I'm his perfect girl.

"You want to go for a ride?" he asks, referring to his new Yamaha motorcycle.

Craig's owning a motorcycle is sort of a bad idea. Even I can see that. Worse is my getting on the bike with him. But some people make you want to do bad things, *really* bad things. You know they're bad, but you do them anyway. Sort of like Father Ralph and Meggie. He helps raise her, tells her that girls get their periods every month, and then defies God by banging her. And he was like a father to her! How scandalous is that? So what if I hang out with the campus's most notorious bad boy and get on his motorcycle? Craig would never hurt me on purpose.

Since I'm so virtuous, especially with my recent Buddhism, I'm due for a forbidden adventure. It may not be with a holy man, but I'll make do with a lush. I want intensity, conversation, running through the streets screaming at all hours. I want to drink beer, dance at the college disco, play video games, do cartwheels across the quad, and go to psych class with a hangover.

I deserve this. Sure, I'll ride on his Yamaha.

Oberlin College is the perfect place for a girl to let loose. Everyone else is doing the same thing. There are patchouli, endless bar scenes, same-sex experimentation, liberal ideals, long floral skirts, breast fests, great bacon cheeseburgers at the main restaurant, no restraints on sexual orientation or religion, co-op dorms, musicians, and, of course, a fabulous academic curriculum (I'm pretty certain).

The idea of riding on a motorcycle scares me, but what's the worst that could happen?

He gets on his hog (if that's the right term), his gaze beckoning me to climb aboard and hold tight. He's wearing a gray striped shirt, which will soon be covered by the requisite black leather jacket all bad boys wear.

We ride around the town square and I bury my face in his back, laughing. Craig seems so confident on this machine. I know I'll be safe.

In a few days, I'm in over my head. Loving a heavy drinker takes work. Also, Craig and I spend too much time together. We sort of hate each other but can't stand to be apart. The hours I'm away from him are torture—like during my classes. It's of vital importance that my parents don't know how I'm pissing their money down the drain at another institution of learning, only this time I'm not wasting money on yogurt peanuts, vanilla shakes, and fries. I'm nearly flunking a class or two. But what's money when love is involved? I care so much for Craig's tortured soul. What starts out as a rock-and-roll love story, a saga of forbidden love through the ages, evolves into a Russian novel where someone will walk into an oncoming train.

Either that or I'm turning into Mary Carson, the crazy, white-haired rich landowner who holds Father Ralph and Meggie hostage, torments them out of sexual frustration. Because she has all that Australian cash, they're dependent on her. But even when they don't need her, she can't let go. Obviously, Craig doesn't need me one bit. All I have to do is dangle a bottle of bourbon in front of him and he's at my side. It's very clear I should run away fast, and yet I can't. I am that old lady staring at Father Ralph as he takes off his clothes after getting caught in the rain. Her love grows like a spore, as does mine. Craig is such a fine specimen of rugged good looks, freakish intelligence, and rough edges.

Like Mary, I have no real power over Craig. Just the opposite, and this infatuation is ten times worse than it was with that Buddhist. Craig is my new everything, except when he goes on about Trotsky, Hegel, and Marxist theory. I'm not sure what these things mean.

The night we officially get together, a windy September night, I wait hours for him to stop talking and make a move. In romance novels, the heroine never waits. Devlin just crushes his mouth to Faun's even before she finishes sharpening her pencils. There are no monologues, no conversations—just instinct. He wants her, he gets her. I wonder if other women go through this, waiting hours for the good stuff to happen, listening, trying to be interesting. Meggie did have to nudge Father Ralph a whole lot before his "little priest" gave in. It takes effort to keep up with my new man. *The Love Boat* and all my romance reading don't prepare me for *this* chatterbox.

I'm just sitting, listening, and waiting.

Craig and I stay out past happy hour at the local bar. He wears a maroon striped shirt and jeans, smokes his Marlboros. By happenstance, I turn to Marlboro reds and pick up chain-smoking. Who knew my voice could sound like Kathleen Turner's after forty cigarettes in a row? I smile nicely and nod at his forgettable comments. More about Marxism. Yeah, I have no idea. Twiddling my thumbs.

Finally, at four A.M., when the lights come on in the bar, he says, "Let's get out of here."

It's a line I later hear in movies to indicate the rerouting to an apartment for sex. Finally! We go to his small room above the bar, a dark place with no windows but with a mattress and disheveled blankets sitting on the floor. Typical boy space, I'm thinking, but he's a rich boy, or so I've gathered from all his stuff—the motorcycle, a nice car, trips here and there, many nights out on the town. Wouldn't he want a better resting place? No space goes untouched by mess, and I sit graciously on the mattress. He brings over a six-pack and sits down.

I'm not sure what's happening, though I pull my fourth beer of the night from his pack. I'm a little wasted.

For two hours, I continue listening, sipping lukewarm beer, and adoring him. I'm still confused by his monologue, wondering why an affluent guy would go to Oberlin and rant about communism. Something about the proletariat. I will definitely look that up in my dictionary.

At six A.M., with two hours until my first class, he finally kisses me. The sour beer breath hits me instantly, but I block out the unpleasantness. This is the legendary Craig, the fun boozy guy, lead singer in a band, well traveled, intellectual . . . and he is with me, a girl who a month ago would never have gotten on a motorcycle. Who thinks Karl Marx is just a guy with a cool name.

Craig is a great kisser, if I forget the beer breath. In fact, a lot of good things happen when you don't look too closely at the details. Craig is like a movie star to me. Our future together will fall into place. He will eventually graduate and I will, too—possibly around the same time. I don't mind if I have to support us, just as long as he whisks us off on a new adventure. This has been a whirlwind.

One more marathon date later—which involves a repeat of previous encounters—I learn of Craig's ultimate death wish. It's a shock to my system, that a perfectly healthy person would consider suicide not just to be dramatic. He even admits to it.

"All that's left is death," he says.

"But I won't let you die."

"You can't stop me."

A hero with suicidal thoughts? This doesn't happen—except in movies or police shows. The brooding men in my romance novels throw down a few scotches now and then, but not a single one fashions a noose for himself.

I remember when I was nine years old, upon hearing a scuffle outside, I looked out the window and saw my father in the driveway, helping a young woman from the neighborhood who'd slit her wrists. She sought out my father because he was dependable, a decent protector. Like the good Boy Scout that he was, he calmed her down, tried to stop the bleeding, and got her help. I wasn't sure what had happened until he explained it to me, that some people have real problems and want to leave this world. This poor woman. There was so much to live for.

This is my chance to save a life. I can make him better. It's my mission. All my energy goes into curing him.

"I can't get drunk enough," Craig tells me soon into my plan to save him. We're in the middle of our usual night, only this time he's on the verge of tears, empty cans from a case littering his floor. How could he be miserable with a nice girl willing to do anything for him? This doesn't fit into my romantic plan at all.

Still, I follow him around for a few more days. I see girls, older girls, more experienced girls, eye him knowingly. The gorgeous Hispanic girl. The blonde who could pass for Marilyn. The lovely, dirty-blond-haired brainiac who prepares her food so carefully that I wonder if she has an addiction of her own. The short brunette with the peaches-and-cream skin.

Turns out, he's had them all.

Sad, dirty mattress sex and booze. Puking off porches. No window in his apartment. Endless talk about governments. Overthrows. Coups d'état. Russia. Our romance reads like a tragic film about a rock star who dies at the microphone, choking on his vomit. It's still romantic. As a heroine, I must learn how to tame a bad boy.

My one escape from this dreary routine is the basement of the Oberlin library. I gather my Ovid, my textbook for economics (a course I'm flunking) and notes, my cigarettes, and an assortment of pens—and my diary. My other studious smoker friends work down there, and we sit in a large room, smoke, and stare at one another during breaks. I am productive during these moments and sometimes confer with my study buddies—mostly older men in Craig's class—out in the hall. They warn me that I'm demeaning myself, wasting time with a guy on a downward spiral. I take their comments to heart until Craig enters the room and I turn bad again for him.

Craig and I cut classes together, lie out on the grass of the quad, smoke endless packs of Marlboros, and talk about nothing. We notice the weather, the changing skies, and, at one point, he sees a burst of sun coming through a patch of storm clouds.

"You see that?" he says to me.

"Yeah." I note the gorgeous juxtaposition of storm and sun.

"That's pretty awesome," he says.

"I'm calling it Craig from now on."

He loves this. This is so *The Thorn Birds*. I've forgotten which characters we are at this point. But it doesn't matter—I've learned that love equals emotional torture. We may not wind up together since our destinies don't match: He wants to leave this world, I want to . . . well, I'm not sure yet. For now, though, I'm willingly stuck (obsessed) with him: how striking he is physically, that rocker edge to how he carries himself, his intellect, and that fine line between tenderness and volatility. We have long days that turn into even longer nights. I get tired of our routine, though I can't shake it. All I want is to be in his presence, keep idling with him in the grass, be wrapped in his vile comforter. But I know it will end. So much of his darkness rubs off on me. I slink from place to place, chain-smoking Marlboros, feeling low. It has to end, but I can't act on this.

Craig is especially sad one night, keeps looking at me as if I'm the most wonderful person on Earth. What should I expect? He doesn't seem to notice me much, unless I provoke him. But suddenly, he pulls me in close, looks deeply into my eyes.

"I love you, Schuntzie. But you're like . . . my sister."

Is there any greater aphrodisiac than this? Soon after this, he dumps me for Peaches and Cream.

I'm deeply insulted by the whole sister thing. It's almost as if *The Thorn Birds* predicted this fall from grace, the inappropriate love with a near-sibling. Part of me is relieved I don't have to deal with this lovable hot mess anymore. I can get some sleep, don't need to save him from himself. But the connection I feel to him continues. I miss his sweet face, his friendliness, his wanting to sit with me in the dining hall. He seems even lonelier than I am, and we tend to find each other at the end of the day, in the bar or in the library. I hate seeing him go through this torment, especially when one day, he walks into the cafeteria with a bleeding gash on his cheek from a motorcycle spill.

His friends assure me he's not an alcoholic. This is college and people drink. Just because my maximum is four beers and Craig's minimum is twelve with a few shots of bourbon doesn't mean he has a problem. I have this feeling they think I'm overreacting.

I wait it out, knowing he will come back to me.

A few weeks later I discover that he's broken up with Peaches and Cream. I find him staring ahead stony eyed in the snack bar. He smiles when he sees me. I can tell he wants to escape.

"Wanna go for a ride?" he asks.

He's drunk, I can tell. Winter has set in. The streets are icy, and it's a terrible idea for me to get on a motorcycle with a drunk person. If I get on the bike, I'll deserve whatever fate comes of this disastrous decision. There is nothing stupider than drunk driving, unless you're a willing, sober passenger.

Of course I go. Even as I get on the bike, I hate myself. Love him, hate the power he has over me. This might be the only thing I have in common with Meggie, Mary Carson, Frank, and Father Ralph— the feeling of powerlessness. It's tragic true love. I can't stop it.

He starts up the motorcycle and we ride along the country roads. The wind howls and it's obvious he's smashed because he's swerving. Usually quiet, I start screaming in terror, into his back, into the air, hoping somehow he'll make it all stop, have some regard for my life. But he doesn't care. There is no thought given to my welfare.

I regret not caring for myself, that I'd feel desperate enough to get on a drunk's bike, that I've gained all this weight from drinking. That I'm practically flunking two courses. That this person with a death wish wants to kill himself and take me down with him. I have so much that I want to do. I vow not to waste another second.

Until he slows down and we are safe.

As we stand near his apartment, he invites me up. It's decision time. I could either go home and cure myself of this sickness or keep up the destructive routine. I go upstairs, still hating myself and feeling like that tragic heroine. As Craig drops off to sleep, I go back downstairs, watch people returning home at four o'clock in the morning, and think, *This can't go on.*

The next day, I go back to my own cave again, start studying, staying in the basement of the library, going back home at a decent hour. Maybe I slip a few times with Craig, though we get no pleasure from it. It's like withdrawal—my hunger keeps getting reawakened and I feel as if I'll die if I don't have him again.

Maybe I have my own death wish, as I go through periods of drinking and lingering in bars until all hours, waiting for him to show. Then I'll buckle down and study again. When I do see him, I start vicious fights with him or I literally run after him—aggressive acts that were never in my good-girl repertoire.

What have I become?

One night, when Craig ignores me, I figure this is the end. Those images of death flash before me: that woman in the driveway; Craig lying passed out on his bed; a girl in high school who took too many pills but then changed her mind. Sad people who have lost their way—they're not just colorful characters in movies and books. Maybe I'm sad, too, since I can't do anything else to win him over—and why would I want to? My mission has failed, which prompts me to go out the door of the bar and sit in the middle of the main road.

Three things to remember: 1) At three A.M., the street is unlikely to have traffic. 2) I have great reflexes and can dive onto a sidewalk at the first sign of headlights. 3) I'm not Sylvia Plath. But it's definitely a moment of deep despair. I want Craig to see how far I've fallen—that I want a car to run me over (though I really don't).

I've only had one suicidal thought before this, on my fifteenth birthday, and it might have been food poisoning. While lying in bed sick I thought idly about running scissors across my wrist. Just the fact that this thought entered my mind scared me. This time, I want time to stop, to release this pathetic, fragile being I've become. I feel ridiculous, chasing after someone who doesn't want me. At least Father Ralph returned Meggie's love, cared for her well-being. Damn *The Thorn Birds*!

The light turns green, yet no car comes. I turn and look at the bar window to see if anyone notices I'm sitting in the road like a crazy person. Certainly not Craig. He probably doesn't even see me. The only person sitting in the window is Ben, and his expression conveys such compassion that I immediately stand up and get the hell out of the road.

This is absolutely not romantic.

I'm sort of fine after this until I realize my period is two weeks late. In my beloved romances, this moment is one of happiness, ending with a marriage proposal. For me, it's anything but happy. I summon abundant courage to approach Craig to tell him I might be having his baby. Worse, I *want* this baby. If I can't have Craig—and I shouldn't have Craig—I will raise his child.

"I might be pregnant," I declare when he's alone at the bar.

"I'm sure I have a lot of children running around the world," he says casually, his eyes cold.

It's easy for me to leave. Why would I stay for more? Craig isn't abusive. He's just living on a different plane from me. But a few days later I get my period and realize that, thank goodness, I am not with child. Still reeling from his casual dismissal, I try to keep my distance from him, though, as with addiction, I relapse one more time when I beg him to take me back, screaming at him in the quad (it's really attractive). He turns around and walks away from me forever. What's next, throwing battery acid on his motorcycle or sitting on his front stoop, waiting for him to come home?

My inner *Fatal Attraction* fades because it's hard to keep up 24/7. One spring morning, I'm sitting below an arch in the quad, absorbed in my Ovid translation. I've almost survived the year. Just a few more weeks before I can go back to long shifts at the dry cleaner's, get lost in making money for the following year, a clean slate. Everyone has a bad year, right?

Suddenly, I hear the roar of a motorcycle, and my stomach goes cold. As the motorcycle goes around the quad, I whip my head around to see Craig with one of my good friends on the back. It's nine A.M. No way were they up this early to go study. They spent the night together, probably didn't sleep a wink.

Tears run down my cheeks, my Latin work unfinished on my lap.

It's then that I decide to physically leave the school and escape Craig. Within days, I'm all signed up for a year studying in Paris, my childhood home. A girl can heal in a country with patisseries and Rodin.

Many years later, during a midlife torture fest of Googling exes, I look up Craig in the college alumni directory and his name has a black ribbon next to it, indicating death. I'm shocked and so very sad. He wrote letters to me about leaving this world altogether, but I figured he'd survive his dark thoughts and grow into the hero I'd dreamed he could be.

Every now and then, I think of him. When I see that same patch of storm clouds with sun bursting through, I think, *Hello to you, too, Craig.*

CHAPTER THREE

◆━◆◆◆━◆

When in Crisis, Go Party in Paris!

1988, Junior Year Abroad

Paris is a little better than anywhere else. The candy is better. You can buy a whole fish and gut it yourself instead of face the prepackaged lump of whatever you see in supermarkets. The produce tastes fresh. You'll find entertainment and culture on most streets, even if it's just you and a friend playing hopscotch. Kings lived close to Paris. Great movies were made here. Simple and complex fashions thrive in Paris, and pastries look like works of art.

I need to be in France again. Because my father started an exchange program in Paris through his university, this city was my home for ages five through seven, and a sprinkling of two, three, and eight. I ate like a French girl, spoke like one, and got to visit castles, museums, and mountains. Pretty rough stuff.

Now I have the good sense to spend a whole academic year studying abroad in Paris—and it's way cheaper than another year at Oberlin. Off I go. I blink and I'm back in my former home, living in the Twelfth Arrondissement, near the Bastille, which used to be a prison (the guillotine fascinates me).

It takes so little for me to immerse myself in Paris life, the cobblestone streets, the narrow sidewalks, the quiet way the French speak on the subways. The most amazing bread ever, like you buy a baguette and eat half before you get home. French mayonnaise is out of this world. It comes in a tube that you squeeze and it looks like a star, like frosting. I could eat it all day long! Tomatoes, which I normally don't like, are robust and delicious. I live on tomato and mayonnaise sandwiches.

The only American thing I miss? *Full House*, starring John Stamos. Oh, and nice people in the post office. French postal workers are abusive to us foreigners. If you ask for stamps in flawless French, they answer in English and scowl. But still, I love it.

I'm no longer that lovelorn sophomore girl who only cares about her next boy fix. I'm a college-junior Parisian for the next nine months, taking classes that are independently run by SUNY Brockport. The program has set up shop in the Latin Quarter, which is a primo party place for me. My hosts are the Chevaliers, friends of my parents, whose patriarch is related to a French prime minister. The Chevaliers have an extra room in their daughter's apartment. She is about twenty years older than me—or thereabouts—and seems amused by my girlishness. I am happy to have my own space and lovely and familiar people around me.

There are challenges to being an American in Paris—and a redhead. I get picked on constantly in the metro. I don't consider myself a supermodel. In fact, I'm sure it's the deer-in-headlights expression, the Howdy Doody coloring, and my white sneakers that arouse these pests. If there's a crazy person, he'll come over and scream in my face from one stop to the next. I get hit on a little too much, so I go out and buy a fake gold band and pretend I'm married. That's right, married at twenty.

Unfortunately, this attracts even more crazies, so I pull out my baggiest clothes and pretend I'm six months pregnant. I stick out my belly—made rounder with each *panaché* (beer mixed with 7Up or Sprite) and many stacks of almond croissants—waddle down the street, take extra care in sitting down. Maybe I feel a little guilty when people give up their seats to me, but I'm just trying to protect my virtue. The idea of getting mugged, swindled, overpowered, or raped in a foreign country scares the crap out of me.

Add to this that French men can be terrifying, as well as irresistible to a twenty-year-old. They have a reputation for being gorgeous scoundrels. Despite this, I'm entranced by the beauty of the French. The way they talk and wear their hair; the large, soulful eyes; and how they can converse for hours about trivial things. Seriously, three-hour conversations about a type of herb grown in a remote region of France, an abstract cube in an exhibit by an unknown artist, the ribbon worn by a diplomat's wife fifty years ago. I'm American; I speak in generalities: love, politics, bathroom humor, books, celebrities. But I start to notice little things and talk about them.

My fluency comes back within five minutes. My former French self returns with a vengeance, along with the rapid-fire Parisian way of speaking. Who wouldn't fall in love with the cute streets, the architecture, the feeling of history, the dizzying array of gâteaux, the devotion to art, the café culture, and running up and down metro steps? Women wear patterned panty hose, something I never would have considered if I'd stayed home. I soon buy hose with dots, paisley patterns, and stripes. French sizes are unforgiving for the curvy girl, so I can't buy too much in the way of clothes. But accessories I can do.

Soon, I'm ordering my sandwich *au jambon* like a French girl, though my white sneakers give me away. I am *l'Américaine* at my favorite hangout, Bar Monaco in the Latin Quarter, where I get my morning coffee and afternoon *panaché*. I read my Sartre and Camus, smoke constantly, and question my place in the world.

I notice again how French people are smaller framed, and mostly have amazing legs and a refinement we bumbling Americans can't begin to attempt. At the same time, I miss the vulnerable, in-your-face, melodramatic, talk-everything-out mentality of the United States. Can I love both countries?

My school-year-abroad program begins in September, when I will officially be attending SUNY Brockport, but in Paris. It's a one-semester program that runs twice a year, and I will be attending both terms. The program my father started twenty years ago through the university. Now it's run by close family friends, the Wallaces. Eric Wallace, a tall, white-bearded man who always wears a green jacket and smokes a pipe, lovingly shepherds us through landmarks, takes us all over France, and teaches classes. His wife, Eloise, the epitome of French elegance and joie de vivre, teaches the language classes.

I've known them for most of my life. They are like second parents. From the time I was yea high, I tried to climb up Eric's long legs while holding his hands and then flip over into a somersault. Eloise indulged me at every turn, laughed at my antics, all while wearing fabulous lipstick, her hair pulled back in a flawless French twist. Now that I'm fifteen years older, these divine Wallaces feed me culture, tell me about books, and get me sloshed on red wine. Too many times to count, I stagger to the metro and wake up at home with a mild hangover.

We tour the Loire Valley, visiting places I already saw many times when my father led the program, the glorious châteaux de Chambord and Chenonceau. Now, as a twenty-year-old, I'm mesmerized by the wide, stony trails and well-maintained greenery leading up to spectacular royal castles. As we roam through the châteaux themselves, the giant rooms, the intricate upholstery, the velvet, the embroidery, the short beds, the flatware, I wonder how lonely it must have been to live in such an expanse—but how awesome! Your true love could be on the other side of the building. I dream about the French counterpoint to our Harlequin hero Devlin. He's probably a European prince, a Louis, but a tormented one with amazing clothes and an effortless way of being elegant, as the French often have. Maybe he's being groomed for a powerful position in court and has to marry some hideous lady-in-waiting. Only she's secretly not hideous. In fact, she's hot underneath that scraggly hair. If you pinch her cheeks, she has a nice blush. Faun would be *Faune* in French.

At night, after dinner, my group-mates and I bunk up in our hotel rooms, sometimes three to a bed, and gab and smoke until we collapse. That's what you do in France. When you're hanging out with students from other colleges, so close together in one program, things happen. Crazy things. Good things. I came to France to revive my soul, surely not to have a fling with an American boy. Why wouldn't I date an exotic Frenchman, my Louis? Well, maybe I need to get my feet wet first with a known element. My zest for life returns toward the end of the first semester. I am so zesty that I forgive all transgressions and want to hug the world.

Enter Hal, the loathsome pretty boy in our program who thinks he's the next Gordon Gekko. From day one, I hate him, with his fussy tie and button-down shirts. He's arrogant, thinks Ronald Reagan is God. I call him "the Reaganite" behind his back. Why would Hal even enroll in a French program—to make his curriculum vitae slightly less boring? I hate his dark, perfectly combed and gelled hair. I hate his crystal-blue eyes and tanned skin, as he is the type to hit Fort Lauderdale during spring breaks and guffaw during wet T-shirt contests. Hal has terrible pickup lines, which show his innate insecurity—at least in my book. He plays wingman to his more gorgeous friend Bill. The Reaganite lurks around parties and looks for people to notice him. My loathing for him grows over three solid months.

Until I slip.

One night in December, I feel great—weightless, happy, enlightened. People are festive due to the change in season, the lights in the trees, and beginning of the holidays, though Paris is different in its celebration, with no tacky plastic Santas on the rooftops. All you see are cheerful lights.

The elation flares in my chest and spreads out to my body. Who cares about Craig and all the sadness back at Oberlin? Instead, my every cell shimmers with joy over the human condition. We are on Earth to live and love (and eat patisserie). That is it. I have to do just this and make my life important. This sense of purpose makes me float. It makes me buy these amazing French cigars and smoke at least ten of them in one night.

As I step out of my apartment, I *know* I look fantastic—big hair, pretty smile, brown leather jacket, and all rah-rah. Soaring over the sidewalks, my peers, those typically French awnings, the kids with their ice-cream cones, I think how great it is to be alive.

I attend a program party with a premonition in mind. I want to be bad, the way I used to be when I was with Craig, fearless, daring (but minus the drunk motorcycling). Not only that, but I *will* sleep with someone. Sometimes it isn't so much a goal as divine knowledge.

The party takes place in Bill and Hal's apartment, celebrating the last weekend of the exchange program. We spent three months together, about twenty of us, and have become a family. I open the door to their apartment and enter to a bustling group. My friends mill around the living room, sit on the foam couches, and drink wine.

For once, I see Hal, really see him, and don't want to ralph my brains out.

Wearing a white button-down shirt and pressed pants, he is over-dressed, as usual, ready to walk into a conference room and deliver a speech. Our eyes meet and he comes over to me.

"Hey," he says.

"Hey," I say back.

The conversation of champions.

"You look nice."

I know, I want to say, but thank him instead. We sit on the couch and talk for hours. Who knew we would have so much to talk about? For once, I don't delve into the morass that is my family dysfunction. My parents have been apart for more than a decade and were remarried five minutes after the divorce papers were signed. My stepparents are fixtures I accept and even feel affection for from time to time, except when my father's wife is easily irritated and I have to walk on eggshells around her. Then there's my mother's hard act to follow, my dad's growing absence, and how much I miss my brother. But I don't mention any of this. I keep it light and happy.

During breaks, we mingle, conversing with others but rarely

taking our eyes from each other. After midnight, people leave, and soon, the Reaganite and I are alone on his small futon.

You are mine, I think. How could I have ever hated him?

The air is tense and my heart skips when he turns off the light. He comes over to the futon and kisses me. I feel his stubble on my face. Thank God it's a weekend, since my skin is about to have a scary rash. Yet I hope it stays awhile so that I have evidence of this debauchery and can show my friends.

Within seconds, I have his clothes off but keep my boots on the entire time. It dawns on me that this is my first one-night stand where there's no hope that a relationship will ensue, since the semester is about to end. I don't even like this person. Well, maybe that will change. I am a girl, after all. And a night of passion while keeping on your boots does mean true love.

Around five A.M. I put on my clothes and leave his apartment. The victorious rush of leaving without being asked fuels me. I am such a strong, independent woman who doesn't need to linger. I can't waste a second since I have an entire day in which to spread the news of my whorishness. I want to scream across the Île Saint-Louis, *I just had my first one-night stand!* But I don't since it's five in the morning and the Parisians would give me constipated looks, since they have one-night stands, like, every day. *Quel est le* big deal?

In my fantasies, I imagine Hal wishes I'd stayed through breakfast. Of course he'll spend the day thinking of me.

Within a few hours, from his train station to my apartment, I concoct a love story with Hal. We could overcome the long distance. He might have loved me all semester. Women are frightening creatures and my intelligence might intimidate him. We could carry on a relationship; he'd return to college and I'd spend the next three months in France pining for him. Because he's committed to finance and always has the appearance of being rich, I know he'll amass a fortune someday. And I'll be there cheering him on as he realizes his dream.

I know better than to call him (especially since I don't have his number). Showing up at his place a few hours after leaving would be psycho, even for me. No, I'll let the love simmer from Sunday to Monday, when we'll see each other again in class.

I won't tell a soul. Maybe a couple people. Between Sunday morning and afternoon, I blab to most of my friends what happened. By Monday, I regret the entire situation. The fact that I can't stop thinking about the Reaganite means the relationship is doomed and I am officially psychotic and desperate.

The least I can do is look attractive in class, try to recapture some of that electricity I sported over the weekend. How could I fall under the Reaganite's spell?

On Monday, everyone smiles at the two of us in class. Our one-night stand has become *the* big news this last week of the program. Hal ignores me completely because I am a whore. As the days tick by, I lose hope of an eleventh-hour declaration of love. Why would he make one? I can't start baking him cookies after what we did.

When the program ends, I have to tape down my fingers to avoid writing a sappy letter to him. After all, no good comes from pining over men like Hal. Luckily, the beauty of Paris always outweighs the fleeting ecstasy of romance. No person can ruin the happiness I've found in this magical place.

———

I instantly forget my sad fling when Pan Am flight 103 explodes over Lockerbie, Scotland. This is the first time I'm alert to the fact that there are *real* crazy people who blow up planes. Some of the passengers are students going home after studying abroad. This sobering knowledge puts a damper on the holidays . . . until my mother and Don arrive to whisk me off to Sicily.

Traveling with family can be a special kind of heaven and hell. My mom and stepfather, Bonnie and Don, are both the best and the worst travel companions. They adore fine dining, seeing the sights, soaking up every fun aspect of a landmark. You just have to listen to them fight like cats and dogs while en route.

"Don, watch the road," Bonnie says, grasping the handle above the window. Her jaw is clenched. Like me, she must be carsick. Don drives competitively, which means jerkily. No one is safe on the road. If you pass him, he will speed up, race you, and then pass, sometimes flipping the bird. As he does this, he might also sideswipe you.

"Would you calm down?" he barks.

"Don, you're not staying in your lane. We're going to drive off the mountain."

And die, is what I'm thinking.

This is when I use my Walkman to escape. How did these two ever get married? I'm not sure. All I remember is that in 1978, my mother introduced me to this portly man with wild eyes and scary eyebrows. "This is Don." He flashed me a rare impish smile, and his eyes twinkled, like I was this cute little butterball. I sort of liked him and resented him at the same time.

Within hours of knowing him, seeing how they interacted, I wondered how they survived each other, except for the fact that they are both passionate historians—and workaholics. All day long, books, discussing books, writing about dead people.

Over the course of a week in Sicily, we arrive at our various destinations in one piece: Palermo, Syracuse, Agrigento, Taormina. A bird shits on my shoulder on my first day in Palermo, but I see it as good fortune. And plus, these could be exotic Mafia birds. With all my *Godfather* reading, I expect to be greeted by the mob in every restaurant. My machine-gun sound effect makes my mother laugh, which makes me laugh.

We suck down plates and plates of pasta and sip sweet vermouth martinis while sitting on a veranda and looking out at the sea. After driving for a few hours, we take afternoon naps. There's nothing like sleeping next to your mom. Our siestas are some of the best Zs I've ever caught. The only downside to this is that I accidentally see my stepfather naked as he's walking out of the bathroom.

Eventually, I return to Paris and prepare for a second semester with the Wallaces and a whole new batch of students. Eric excitedly tells us we're going to spend the semester seeing classic French films. Poor us!

Ever since *Jean de Florette* (1986), I keep wanting to run into Gérard Depardieu, a.k.a. Mr. French Actor. This turns out to be unnecessary since he is *everywhere*, like McDonald's. A film comes out at the end of my first semester in France and we all run to see it at least once. Gerard plays Auguste Rodin (of course he does) in *Camille Claudel*. Isabelle Adjani plays the tragic Camille.

The story goes like this: Camille is this genius sculptress—and so beautiful you can barely look at her. The saving grace is that she's covered in clay . . . but this only makes her sexier to Rodin, her new mentor. Because he's so famous and she's so pretty and they're sculpting geniuses, they fornicate amid these naked clay figurines. The problem is Rodin won't leave his longtime mistress—whom he eventually marries after decades. Once he stops calling on Camille, she goes crazy, stays in her room, takes in stray cats, and talks to herself (but always looks red-carpet ready). What comes of this mania? Moving, achingly emotional sculptures of women reaching out, the blind innocence of children, love found at last in a waltz. Camille's brother commits her to an asylum, where she stays for thirty years.

Poor Camille may have hit a dead end, but she still produced great art. Coincidentally, much of her work is featured in the Musée Rodin. I run to see it, wondering what it must have been like to witness these two—so doomed in love but creating these provocative pieces. For hours, I pine over the statues, think about what Rodin and his protégés must have endured to bring this brilliance to us.

How will I ever be the same?

So the moral of the story is that tortured love isn't all bad, as long as you have a hobby. My time with Craig wasn't a total waste since it brought me here. Hal was a learning experience, too. And this American-in-Paris lifestyle suits me. I don't even try to be the little French girl I once was. I am inquisitive, I am social, and, more important, I am all over the Paris bar scene. It's part of my new living-out-loud routine. If every great artist in France did it, so can I. This is romance, for sure, with its mixture of tragedy and exultation.

I begin my nights in the Palais Royal area, right off the rue de Rivoli, in a tiny Irish pub called the Flann O'Brien. I go there most nights to be with other Americans not specifically in my program. It's just refreshing to hear English after a day of French immersion. The bartender is true Irish and serves me Guinness, which I love. By the time I have a good buzz, my program-mates and I stagger across the Pont Neuf and into the Latin Quarter, where we hit up the over-priced, touristy Pub Saint-Germain. The many floors are filled with international clientele. On one floor, you may meet Swedes, another a pack from Italy. The waiters are all French.

My first time there, I'm with David, a boy who took me to my first formal dance at Taft, the one I hid from in the stairwell. David was in love with me, wrote me these beautiful poems in French, and I treated him like *merde*. Since I'm mature and in college and in Paris, I feel compelled to make amends with David. Now living in England, he comes to visit. When I meet him at his metro stop, we run into each other's arms. I'd forgotten how tall he was. He has a cute face, not conventionally attractive, but more like I've-been-beaten-up-a-few-times handsome.

We go to Pub Saint-Germain, to the top floor, which is empty. There we share our stories. I unload about the drunk I dated in college. He tells me about his father, who just died. It's all about the angst, isn't it? It brings people together in such a miserable way, like Camille and Rodin. Throughout our storytelling, I notice the speed with which David downs his pints of beer. It begins to worry me, as in *I've been here before*. For the first three hours, I give him a pass, figure he's mourning his father. But it's soon obvious that he could black out at any moment.

I'm traumatized and keep looking for an exit. Can I just ditch him the way I did at the dance? Glancing up, I notice the waiter making eyes at me. He can see I'm in a problematic situation, winks at me.

I've seen him before, with those French blue eyes, the kind that have magic powers. Now, how do I get rid of David?

By two in the morning, with no chance of doing anything except walking home—especially since I've spent all my money—I leave David at the table. I can't even worry about how he's going to get home.

"Sorry, I have to go."

"Where you going?" he asks, smiling widely, as if nothing's wrong.

"I need to leave."

Carrying my coat and purse, I make a quick Cinderella escape and literally bump into my waiter.

"Leaving so soon?" he asks in this adorable French accent.

"My friend is too drunk," I answer in French.

"Too bad." He smiles, then does the unthinkable: pulls me around the corner and kisses me. It's such a French moment—spontaneous, absurd, romantic. "When are you coming back?"

"I don't know."

"I call you."

"Sure." I scramble for a piece of paper, write my name and number on it.

"Ah, Patience." He grins. I often get this reaction to my name. "I'm Denis."

He kisses me again and takes my phone number. "Tomorrow, I call you."

"Okay!"

What fiendish luck! Though saddled with drunken David, Denis the Waiter saves my night. Waiters in France are not like waiters in America. Many of them are career waiters, in that they are well schooled in service and manners. They're not doing this so that they can go to auditions during the day. I'm sure some are planning a different vocation—but every time I go to Paris, I'm amazed by how waiting tables is an art. And here I've encountered one waiter who kissed me.

I wait an entire twenty-four hours for Denis to call. Seriously, watch the phone, don't take a shower, don't leave the apartment. The question is whether I should pull a *Fatal Attraction* and go back to Pub Saint-Germain. Of course I will. Camille Claudel was a crazy stalker—and an artistic genius. I will do as she did!

I enlist my friend Fiona in my mission to date a French waiter. She understands my crush since she has a French boyfriend of her own. She's eager to go along with me—the first time. But Denis isn't even there. I look everywhere for him. Did he quit? Oh God, how could this happen to me, just when my love life was starting to blossom (sort of)?

My insanity flourishes, along with my love for cheap red wine. I go night after night to Pub Saint-Germain, am a relentless French waiter pursuer. If I have a friend visiting, a buddy from my program who has nothing to do, we go to Pub Saint-Germain. Meanwhile, I'm hemorrhaging money that my parents don't have, withdrawing more dough for this overpriced tourist-ridden pub that is not in the least bit French. Love is expensive.

Just as I give up, Denis shows up. It's divine intervention, showing me that hope is alive. My heart palpitates. Did he think of me, the love we shared in those thirty seconds when he kissed me?

His face brightens when he sees me, and he winks. Those French and their winking! It says to me that I'm going to have a French boyfriend, like my friend Fiona. She gets to experience the ecstasy of French desire and lust—just like in the movies! Denis is an obsession in my blood, my Rodin.

When I see a lull, I go up to him. *"Bonsoir."*

We kiss on both cheeks, as if we're old friends. "Where've you been?" I ask.

"I went skiing," he says in French, then rattles off his itinerary. As I swim in those ocean-blue eyes of his, I know this is just an intense and passing fancy. I have no more chance of dating this Denis than this pub has of being French. Why would he kiss me and then ask for my number?

Because it was polite. Because he saw me in the hellish David situation. It was a nice thing to do. And now I'm back feeding more money into the pub, into his livelihood.

I've been played.

I go home at three in the morning, dejected. How could I come to France and not find a nice French guy? Well, it isn't my original goal, which involved getting away, feeling better, getting a life beyond pining over a boy.

So I spend the rest of the semester doing just that. A few places that capture my heart: Versailles, home of Louis XIV, who had the most rock-star hair ever. As a kid, I bonded with this Louis's audacious stance in paintings, showing off his legs and crazy hair. His palace is beyond luxurious with the pools, the statues, never mind the room full of mirrors—a narcissist's dream come true. After this, Giverny, the home of Monet, bewitches me. It's like living in a crisper version of one of his paintings, a riot of flowers everywhere you walk. I am speechless, never having seen this kind of utopia. Wandering around, I snap pictures that don't quite do the place justice. At one point, I see the Wallaces walking arm in arm, obviously in love, obviously enjoying every minute with each other, and I take a picture. This is how I want my love story to be.

The last few months, I continue touring France, guzzle more *panachés,* smoke Gauloises, eat as many pastries as possible. I stare at the fashion shows right in front of me—more dotted panty hose, short skirts, red lipstick—the graceful gaits, the French charm that renders most dullards breathless.

I fall in love with Paris but never find my French Louis—just the charming waiters. I figure that my true love is the city itself, which makes my heart feel full again. Well, there is this other waiter, Jean-Baptiste, also from Pub Saint-Germain, but he also wants me to hemorrhage money on tips for him, which I do for a couple weeks. Then he sleeps with my friend.

I leave France happy, poor in finances but rich in spirit.

CHAPTER FOUR

—◆—◆—◆—

Harrison Ford Isn't Coming to Cleveland

1991

There is a movie that plays in my mind as I graduate from college: *Working Girl,* a popular rags-to-riches movie from 1988 and an excellent guide for finding a job and a boyfriend. My senior year was a breeze because I focused on work and friends, and avoided drama. Days before graduation, I received a bittersweet letter from Craig, who's moved to Japan with his girlfriend. He congratulated me on my surviving college and wished me happiness. It was a sweet message, one I'll always cherish. I never answer him but appreciate the nice send-off.

Commencement at Oberlin went without a hitch. My parents mostly stayed away from each other and we all traveled in our different directions after unloading the moving truck to my future. Mom and Don returned to their new house in New Jersey, close to Rutgers University, where they were both just hired to teach history. My father went back to Brockport, Patrick to Manhattan.

Now it's my turn. Let the adult fun begin! I can already tell great things will happen to me. And since I'm the star of my own romance novel, I figure I'll land on my feet without a career track, especially if I follow Tess McGill's lead.

The idea of living in New York City is too overwhelming, so I decided to move to Cleveland as a transitional home—only thirty minutes from my college. Baby steps to my big dreams, which, at the moment, are as mystifying as my dwindling savings. Where does the money go? Most of my friends find employment in other cities or go to graduate school. Except for a couple college friends who live in my new neighborhood, I'm left to my own devices.

Thanks to a generous girlfriend, who spends hours helping me look at places, I find an apartment in the safe-ish suburb of Lakewood, Ohio, a thirty-minute bus ride from downtown Cleveland. This neighborhood is made up of families and Yuppies, mostly Caucasian. The city has invisible racial lines, which cause tension from one end to the other. To add to this, bigotry is everywhere. No sooner do I step into this city than I hear the N-word out of Caucasian mouths. It shocks me. Not exactly the harmonious environment of Oberlin, where all races are celebrated.

Despite the underlying violence of this city, my one-bedroom is enormous, with a giant living room, ample closet space, a full kitchen and bedroom. And cheap! My parents each donate old furniture and rugs, and setting up my new independent-girl digs is a blast.

The only outrageous part is that my parents expect me to make my own money. I am allegedly an adult. There is an exciting quality to this adulthood phase—that I *can* make my own money, decisions, and meals. This is also the worst part. To make money, you need to work—every day. If you're lucky, this work builds into a career. To get work, you need to make a decision about what kind of work you want to do. I just want to be famous or rich or married or . . . something, as long as I don't have to break a sweat.

The food part is fine, though it's painful to leave the luxury of the campus dining hall. How hard could it be to cook a meal? I know how to make rice and pasta and open a can. In a matter of weeks, I'm certain that my Prince Charming will whisk me off to fancy restaurants where we'll have five-course meals (I love going out). For now, I really want to try powdered potatoes—the forbidden fruit. My parents wouldn't let me eat them, so now's the time to try this awesome contraband. With potato flakes, just add water and milk—along with a stick of butter. Maybe Parmesan cheese. It's a delicious, easy adult meal! Ramen noodles are so cute and cheap, too, and I buy baskets and baskets of them.

Next comes adult employment. What helps me through the hurdle of being jobless with a BA is the idea that I could be the next Tess from *Working Girl*. In a nutshell, Tess, the eternal temp with big dreams, fights to crawl out of the job sewer and, in her quest, finds a great profession and a man with whom she can order Chinese while number-crunching into the wee hours. She is the quintessential romance heroine because she's special and smart. We all know that she'll get the job she deserves. In her spare time, when she's not being adorable at work—e.g., giving cartons of cigarettes to friends, just because—she secretly takes all these business classes. Though stuck working a temp job, she gradually outdoes her boss (who has a bony ass) and attracts the love of Jack Trainer, played by Harrison Ford. Jack is so hardworking that he stays at the office late to the point where he needs to change into a new shirt and start a new day. On the outside, he's a ruthless businessman. On the inside, he's a lovelorn puppy, offering to make herbal tea for Tess when she accidentally gets trashed at an industry event. Best of all, he packs her a high-fructose lunch for her first day at work at the end. Tess is multifaceted, brainy with the voice of a porn star. She may start at a less-than-great job, but she gets a better job and the guy in the end. I need to be Tess: a wage earner with the ability to seduce executives without even trying.

In fact, many romance novels begin this way—with the woman in a new job or situation. Now that I'm going to be making my own money, I can buy these juicy books with impunity or find them in my local library. Off I go, picking up my powdered potatoes, ramen noodles, and saucy romances at the supermarket. I never take notice of authors or publishers; I just grab the first book I can find with the hottest cover—heaving bosoms, long Cher hair, naked calves, and windswept clothing. I try to find stories that relate to my situation. There are so many Fauns out there, like me.

Faun usually works for her future Mr. Right at a less-than-ideal job. They say most love affairs begin at work. For me to reach this ecstatic destination, I decide to find a transitional job as a secretary, like Tess, like most heroines. There are several reasons why this is appropriate: 1) I type one-hundred-plus words a minute. 2) I love organization. 3) Eventually Melanie Griffith shows off her smarts and wins the heart of Harrison Ford. 4) I made absolutely no career plans while I was in college so I'm kind of fucked. Everyone says that Latin is so helpful in life, but it isn't. Translating Cicero and Ovid did squat for my SATs. Catullus's pathetic—and by *pathetic,* I mean totally awesome—love poetry to Lesbia helped not a whit in my job search.

I'm envious of my brother, Patrick, for knowing what he wants to do and going for it. He's doing a play now, *Tony n' Tina's Wedding,* and auditioning for everything under the sun. His life is about finding acting jobs. Perhaps like many of my generation, Generation X, I have a lot of potential but no real passion aside from watching television and reading. Well, that may not be true, and my circumstances aren't deplorable. I am fluent in French, I can sight-read Latin, I am a professional-level calligrapher, and I pick up languages easily. I've lived overseas and am presentable. Sadly, this doesn't translate into a lucrative profession right out of Oberlin (no one warned me about this, by the way), but someone will want me. A college counselor said I might like advertising or publishing. For three minutes, I chose advertising (because that's what Timothy Busfield and Ken Olin do in *thirtysomething*). When I asked what I'd need to bring to an interview, the agencies said my portfolio would be a great start. "Don't you have any boards?" one agency receptionist asked. Oh sure. Boards. So I made "boards," basically other brilliant ads pasted on cardboard and somehow engineered into my own work.

Secretarial work is easier than jumping right into a lucrative career. I love administrative work anyway. It seems so glamorous to work in an office. I fantasize about wearing my sneakers to work and changing into pumps, just like Tess. Being a secretary will give me time to reflect on what I really want to do. Maybe I could write an amazing novel in my spare time.

When my father asks me about my long-term plans, like when I am going to get health insurance, I explain about having a practical job before launching into a real job.

"What if something happens to you?" he asks. Ever since he married *her*—that woman who used to be fun but who now finds me disruptive—I am expected to follow a linear pattern.

"I'll try not to get hit by a bus. And if I do, I'll pay for it, don't worry."

"You need health insurance."

"It's hard to get a job out of college."

He doesn't seem to understand this until a year later, when he reads a *New York Times* article that states exactly what I said, that my generation is having a tougher time finding employment right out of college. Good thing I don't confide my real dreams to him. One of the few times I tell him I want to be a writer, he says that this would be like winning the lottery—i.e., don't even bother. Sure, he's being practical, but after *Working Girl,* it's hard not to dream.

Plus, romantic heroines often have side jobs as an outlet for their creativity. They work in an office to pay the rent, but in their spare time, maybe they bake muffins for their friends and this somehow takes off into a Mrs. Fields thing. Or the heroine makes her own candles and soap, which mushrooms into her own cute store with her name over the door. I once made a candle in Brownies. It was fun but uninspired, as in the Brownie leader provided the wax, string, and molds. We mostly just dipped the string into the hot wax. Where would I sell my candles anyway?

Temping is the way to go for now. In Cleveland, my new home, I go from company to company. I'm bound to gain valuable experience and meet Harrison Ford "at the office." The perfect career will make itself known. Perhaps my fairy godmother—every romance has one, an older woman with watery blue eyes and sage advice—will guide me on the professional path. In the meantime, I try to replicate Tess's wardrobe, buying a black skirt and cream-colored blouse. At my first job, in a law office, I change out of my sneakers and try to navigate my way in wobbly pumps. I wear a pair of my mother's pearls—though I'm not sure she's aware I have them.

As I answer phones at Temp Job #1, I watch the daily soap opera that is corporate America. I see the tragic love story between two lawyers. Lawyer 1 and Lawyer 2 used to be lovers until she ran off and got pregnant with twins by someone else. Lawyer 1 watches 2 run to the bathroom, heartbreak etched on his face. He wishes he were the one married to her now. It's been a good two years since they were together. Now they work in the same office day after day as her belly grows with children! I nearly cry watching Lawyer 1's pain, then type up his notes, swimming in the memory of his mournful gaze.

Just when I start to make some friends, the job ends. I pack up and go to the posh British Petroleum Tower, located in the heart of downtown Cleveland. It's a tall, clay-colored building—you can't miss it—and the second I walk in, I feel like I'm on the set of *Working Girl*, or, better yet, a Jackie Collins novel. I can already see it. A Hollywood director—they are all painfully good-looking—wanders into my building to meet with one of the executives on my floor. He needs BP's backing for his next blockbuster. On his way to meet Mr. BP, he sees me sitting there so innocently typing away. He thinks, *For months, I've been trying to find the star for my new movie and here she is.* Even though I'm not an actress, he casts me—turns out I'm Katharine Hepburn—and during filming falls in love with me. One year later I'm in my second trimester, an Oscar nominee, and throwing swanky parties in the Hollywood Hills.

Well, Cleveland isn't that glitzy. Still, my head spins as power suits swarm around me. This is where oil gets traded, the place Oberlin protested during the antiapartheid controversy. I don't broadcast where I'm working, especially since I secretly like the ambience and the people. The head honcho is on the fortysomethingth floor, and his secretaries have secretaries, and they all whisper, as if not wanting to disturb the master at work. It's like a little secret club up there. I love it.

Everyone is so nice to me as I settle into my cubicle, put my sneakers in a drawer. My two cubicle-mates are lovely women, sassy and full of wit. They take me under their wings, crack jokes throughout the day. What impresses me is that they type like demons, fingers flying over the keyboard. Transfixed, I watch them and try to mimic their speed, which must be close to two hundred words per minute. One of them just had a baby boy. Another is phone-flirting with one of the British traders from New York City. She's planning on flying down to meet him in the city—a blind date. They've only spoken on the phone, had this whirlwind courtship without ever seeing each other in person. British Trader is about to get the shock of his life since my cubicle-mate has this Playboy Playmate look about her, with intelligence to boot. It's a real romance happening right in front of me.

Aside from this drama, the work is easy and I mostly report to these women with thunder fingers. During my eight-hour day, I relay messages back and forth to traders using this electronic device that's sort of like a calculator with letters that makes noises. The memos I whip up come from deciphering chicken scratch on a legal pad, though I understand nothing about the business. I have ample time to read the *New York Times* from cover to cover. Might as well improve my mind while I'm at it. The traders are men, mostly cheerful, not the type to grope, which I find surprising. With the exception of my Playboy Playmate colleague and her long-distance-trader love, I notice no smoldering glances across the room, no drink invites or chatting up around the water cooler. I'm just the temp.

Honestly, it could be a lot worse. I never have a bad day working there, though it gets old. Simple office job? Not so simple if you feel like you're wasting your life, day after day, and returning to an empty apartment. I look forward to small things, like this new legal show called *Equal Justice*, starring Sarah Jessica Parker, Jane Kaczmarek, Cotter Smith, and this hot new actor Jon Tenney. After a long day in the office, I run home and get ready to watch, hoping that my new JT (John Taylor is on the back burner) will have more airtime. Because my brother is an actor and I have no exciting news to report (about anything), I tell him about my latest obsession.

"I'm so in love with one of the actors," I blurt out, forgoing niceties. You can do that with siblings. "Have you heard of Jon Tenney?"

There's this pause on the other end of the line before he blows my ear out. "Oh God. *Jon?!* You like *Jon*? Ewwwww!"

"Whaddaya mean? He's gorgeous."

"He's a good friend of mine. You've *met* him."

"What? He's my future husband is what he is."

The wheels in my head turn. What a twist of fate this is, just when I'm bored in Ohio. I could marry my new favorite actor on TV and move to Los Angeles, somehow slip into becoming an actress myself. I must use my brother wisely, though he doesn't seem excited about the idea of me and Jon (note to self: Brothers never help fix you up).

A couple weeks elapse, with me wanting to call Patrick and ask him more about Jon, my imaginary boyfriend. My mind races with what kind of wedding invitations we'll order, if I'll take his name when we marry. Imagine the squealing when I come home to a large manila envelope in my mailbox with the return address: J. Tenney. My hands shake as I open it and find a large photo of Jon Tenney and a real honest-to-God *letter*. I read it several times, looking for hidden meaning, using my book on handwriting analysis to dissect his psyche. Of course I compose a response, a long one, detailing my entire life, my problems, my upbringing, and my wish to come to California, and suggesting that maybe we could meet for coffee. Damn Nici and the Harlequins. My brain is abuzz with Jon and *Equal Justice* and our inevitable marriage.

My response to Jon goes unanswered, and, gradually, I come down from cloud nine. I will not be a movie star's wife—and I will no longer use my brother to further my love life. As the months tick by, I grow frustrated by the daily grind of waking up, getting coffee, doing repetitive tasks that don't tax my brain, eating the same lunch, going home, watching TV, falling asleep. This transition could easily turn into a permanent situation. Terrifying.

I take to drinking wine and scrawling in a notebook like I'm Hemingway. The "real world" is not the dating party of college, and I don't like it. This can't be how I end up. It seems outrageous that my suitors don't magically appear as I step outside on my way to the bus. My summer of hope evolves into a dreary January. Something has to change. Anything. I can only take so much red wine and ramen noodles.

Of course I should be careful what I wish for.

My life does change in one night, over the course of an hour and a half. I randomly become a traumatized crime victim. More on that later. It seems like a story one should tell over and over again. I'll only do it once. Suffice it to say, I come home one January morning from the hospital, disheveled. I can't bear to look at myself.

The positive: I'm very happy to be alive. The negative: Aside from the obvious, I regret all the energy I devoted to finding/keeping a boyfriend. Romance is a waste of time. There are bigger goals—such as taking care of myself, getting a better job. I don't want to be a loser, especially since I lost my latest temp job due to my little vacation in the ER.

I want to feel better, so I focus on the immediate things that make me smile:

Joan Rivers, who has her own talk show. I watch her every day and laugh my ass off.

Cigarettes and water. The perfect blend of dirty and clean. I need both.

Ice cream. It's the only thing I can stand to eat.

Pasta. Okay, that's delicious, too.

For now, I can't read romance novels. Because every heroine has a gritty backstory, I may fit even more into the mold, but it's a painful way to become my beloved quintessential romance heroine, Faun.

My mother cancels her much-needed vacation to Costa Rica to be with me. She pushes my hair back and looks seriously into my eyes—things she hasn't done since I was a kid.

I can see she's deeply worried, like I'm the bad-luck child who keeps getting into trouble. She feeds me, makes my phone calls, advises me on my next step, tells me everything will be okay, and takes me out for walks. Basically, this is the montage for regaining strength, going out into the world again. My mother pretty much saves me from rotting in my apartment. Frequent calls from my brother, Patrick, have their restorative properties, too. My mother and brother become the two people I call in case of any emergency. They are always there.

The bottom line is that adulthood doesn't begin as planned. My dream to be Tess McGill ends, and I pick up *The Bonfire of the Vanities*. No Harrison Ford for now.

———

A couple weeks later, when my mother leaves, I realize it's time for me to work again. Kelly Services, my temp agency, assigns me back at BP, that large oil company housed in that lofty downtown building of mauve marble. The edifice blankets me against the dirt and violence. I rush to my place of employment and lose myself in typing and answering phones, only this time on a different floor and for a different boss, a redhead, like me. Lindsay is stern, a female lawyer working in a mostly male field. Every day she is professional, discerning in her judgment. Now and then, she and I exchange personal information, but very rarely. I respect how she keeps boundaries with me. She knows about my troubles, gives me some leeway, but expects me to put in my time. Her expectations mean a lot to me, and I work hard for her.

This is the part of any romance novel that is never included, the mundane details, the forging ahead, the suffering that doesn't involve pining for a boy. I'm by myself and a mess. I desperately want to move back in with my parents, but that's not an option, so I put one foot in front of the other.

It is an absurd time for a boyfriend to appear.

For a boost, I sign up for a spring creative writing class. I took the fall semester and really enjoyed it, even wrote a couple of short stories. It meets in a school at night, a few blocks from my apartment. It's not the safest part of town, and I regret signing up for the class. Why bother with this when I could be lying on my couch and crying? The group will consist of retirees who want to crank out a book before the memories vanish—and maybe one cute guy sitting in the back, keeping to himself. What are the chances I'll find a sanctuary with this motley crew?

Turns out, it is the best decision. I slowly crawl out of my depressing hole. In a small classroom, with colorful collages on the walls, a blackboard, and those precious little desk chairs, I find some measure of peace—and distraction. Our teacher has spiky, fake-blond hair, that scattered aura of a busy writer homing in on her talent. She is a published author, writing children's books. I enjoy listening to her Australian accent for a few hours. We'll see if I learn anything.

"Okay, you're going to write a two-page essay, arguing a point," the teacher tells us.

My classmates, the motley crew, are the same types as last semester. The man who likes to play golf. The wig-wearing lady in the scooter who beat cancer a couple times and has more energy than I do. A few women close to my mother's age, looking to express themselves. And then there's the cute guy, Zack, who has signed up again. He sits toward the back, off to the side. I sort of noticed him a few months ago, the first time I took the class. We don't really talk.

During our short break, I go outside to smoke. A couple people join me in my nicotine refuge. Zack comes out, but he doesn't smoke with us. I have this sense that he wants to be social but isn't quite sure how, which makes me like him even more. Maybe he's that beta male I sometimes catch in a romance novel—the guy who doesn't treat you badly, who listens to you, wants to spend time with you, is tender when you need him to be. Okay, so maybe Harrison Ford *is* that beta male in *Working Girl*. Just nice, a total curiosity.

I learn that he works as a freelance writer and loves music. He has hazel eyes set close, a wiry build, a spectacular smile, and thinning blond hair. Generally, that boy next door you should marry. He is twenty-seven, so cute, with this halting way of speaking, as if he's working to get the words out. Shyness worse than mine.

These strange feelings take root, like actual attraction, and I'm ashamed of how I feel. How could this happen to me again? I'm supposed to be in hibernation, focusing on healing. But my hormones melt me like a fever and even though we don't have an organic way of starting up a conversation, I psychically command our romance to happen. I am just that powerful.

One Wednesday night, I return home to find a message on my answering machine.

"Um . . . I . . . uh . . . am leaving a message for Patience . . . Smith. She's in my writing classes at the community center. Um . . . so I was wondering if you'd like to see a movie with me on Friday . . . um . . . after work. . . ."

He's too amazing for words, so inept in the manner of an awkward, infatuated boy with rescuer fantasies. This rush of romance happens at the darnedest times, when I don't want or need it to. Lucky for me, during those awful periods, I tend to look fantastic. I'm super-skinny, like at a weight I haven't seen since the eighth grade. My hair is long and red. Who wouldn't want to date me, setting aside my currently gloomy narrative?

For our first date, Zack is taking me to see *Dances with Wolves*, which is a movie about Kevin Costner dancing with animals, I guess, and there's a romance and Native American lore. It's the boost I need, and I can't wait. When I get to Zack's car, I see flowers on the seat. Boys in college never do this, so I wonder if they're for someone else. I pretend I don't see them until I do.

"Are those for me?" I ask.

"Yeah," he says hesitantly, though I can see he's smiling in the dark.

This is typical beta-male behavior, the gift-giving with

follow-through in manners. Harrison Ford gives Melanie Griffith her own briefcase after she "forgets" hers for a meeting. That's beta. Maybe this is the kind of guy I should have been seeing all along. Alpha heroes don't give you jack!

Zack's little touches make me ecstatic—lovely flowers, cheeseburgers, cake just for me. From day one, Zack delivers these small items. Plus, he loves movies as much as I do. We see *Thelma & Louise* on the next date, then *The Silence of the Lambs* after this. It's strange to see these ultraviolent movies mere weeks after my victimhood, but I go with it. In fact, Anthony Hopkins's Hannibal Lecter makes me giddy with joy, even as I face a tumultuous year in and out of courtrooms and the ADA's office. Zack's care also helps. We make dinners together, keep seeing films, drive around the city, and listen to music.

In the spring, I go visit my brother in New York City, a scary trip for me given I'm still recovering and it's full of noise, danger, and people. I sit on a stool as Patrick performs in *Tony n' Tina's Wedding*, a hit off-Broadway show. It's one of those performances where the actors interact with the audience. Patrick plays a greasy wedding photographer, and, at one point, he comes over to me in character. His hair is slicked back, and he's wearing an ugly suit. But behind the costume, I can see he's happy that I'm there. It's the first time we've seen each other since my ordeal.

"Can I take your picture, young lady?" he says.

"Sure, because I'm getting married," I respond.

I can see a flicker of alarm on Patrick's face, but I don't let his reaction sway me. I'm certain I'm going to marry Zack, though he doesn't know this yet. Right now, he's back home, writing an article for some magazine, probably missing me. He's really the greatest. For the rest of the weekend, Patrick seems skeptical of my overflowing devotion (though if he were really concerned, he could fix me up with his movie-star friend).

Zack and I continue in our sweet vein, engaging in such normal activities that I slowly reclaim my groove. It's not lost on me how lucky I am to have found such an angel during a difficult time. We talk about new careers and ditching Cleveland forever. He wants to move and so do I, not necessarily to the same place. Though we don't speak about our future as a couple or apart, I start to wonder—and I think he does, too—if our relationship is meant to be long term. My marriage plans could be a bit hasty. While I only want to be with him, I consider that my first priority is finding a permanent job and focusing on myself.

With my skills, I make a short-term plan for a real career. Let's see: bilingual in French, nine years of Latin, decent typist. When in doubt, teach high school! I consult a map and pick the most beautiful places in the United States (that I know of). After careful research, I send out a slew of résumés to random schools in Maine, Colorado, New Mexico, California, Virginia, and Georgia.

In May of that year, Sandia Preparatory School, a private school in Albuquerque, New Mexico, contacts me for an interview to be a high school French teacher. They like my history as a Francophile and my boarding school experience, and my Latin training is icing on the cake. I have no teaching credentials, but what the hell, I hop on a plane and the second I smell the air, feel the peace of a slower life, I know this is the place for me. Private schools tend to like young blood, so I rely on this to help my chances.

I walk out of the airport and I'm instantly enchanted. They don't call it the Land of Enchantment for nothing.

The headmaster and dean of the middle school give me a tour of Albuquerque before my day of interviews. The school is a palatial, Southwestern version of my boarding school experience, with manicured lawns, cute one-story buildings, and a faculty that cherishes one another and its students. The headmaster, a bear of a man with red hair, becomes a paternal figure the minute he takes a chance on me. The fairy godmother of fate sprinkles me with magic dust, because I am hired.

After a long drive across the country with Zack, fast and furious apartment hunting, and an awkward car-buying experience (the salesman teaches me how to drive a stick shift and then I buy the car immediately), I settle into my small apartment with its hideous wall-to-wall carpeting and beige walls. I sort of love it. Zack helps me unpack and comes with me to orientation at Sandia Prep.

I live about a quarter of a mile from my new school, in a large apartment complex, on the scary first floor (with the apartment number I-69, which is awkward to say out loud). Even though I'm still worried about safety and afraid of living alone in a new place, I fall head over heels for the Southwest, the colors and lighting and sultry desert. I don't like Mexican food, know nothing of Native American culture, and find Southwestern art superbly ugly, but I love New Mexico. It's as if Cleveland never happened. I even grow to crave burritos. Before New Mexico, I avoided spicy foods. Now I go for the mouth-burning chili and jalapeños. As much as possible, please.

Since I'm all moved in, Zack decides it's time for his trek to

Denver so he can pursue writing and just have a change of scene. It's a seven-hour drive on I-25. Not quite next door, but we commute and pretend we're meant to be just a little longer.

The first time he leaves me, as school is starting, as I'm embarking on this new life, I start to cry, really bawl. It's a profound sense of loss. This good-bye is the end of a very long eight-month trip. Where did the time go? He really did pick me up off the floor, help me reestablish myself and believe good people are out there. How can I say good-bye to such a positive force? I am so grateful. Zack must smell the inevitable in that first Southwestern good-bye, too. We last six months after leaving Ohio. Maybe we aren't destined to marry. Some people just appear as angels and help you move on to the next gig. At first, I had hoped Harrison Ford would be my angel, pack me my lunch for my first day of work. He'd stay up nights to help me with a big presentation and crash parties with me, and we'd go merrily down the street, eating scary sandwich-cart sandwiches with white sauce. My Harrison stand-in just left. It dawns on me that my real boyfriend was even better than the movie version. And this one gave me the will to start looking again for that perfect someone for me.

CHAPTER FIVE

———◆◀◆▶◆———

If He Says He Doesn't Reciprocate Your Feelings, Believe Him and Run

1993–1997

New Mexico is an enticing place and I never want to leave. Now twenty-five, I'm about to start the third year of my plush lifestyle. As I lie in my regular candlelit bubble bath, I have a chilled beverage in one hand and a breakfast burrito in the other. My love of love has crept back in little ways: in the Sandia Mountains and then miles of sparkling desert outside my door; in the fascinating people I work with at school; and, of course, in those books I can't stop reading, such as a military-themed romance by Merline Lovelace, a spooky paranormal story by Heather Graham, and delicious tales by countless other names I'm sure I'll encounter again. Oh, and a whole bucketful of Harlequins.

Suddenly, I have this great and original idea: Writing + Romance = A Prospective New Career. In the one-hundred-degree heat, I get right to work and tap away on my typewriter.

It's highly inconvenient that the summer is ending, because my active inner world is just beginning to buzz with genius, with juicy love scenes for *Teacher's Pet*, a title that I doubt has ever been used before.

Teaching French is fun, but now that I've survived two years and have yet to go on a date, I need extra stimulation. I peruse even more romances (it's research)—a fabulous break from creating interesting lesson plans about Gilles's vacation in Nice and how to say *raincoat*. Fast-forward through many hours of Captain Steele bending his new sailor (really a woman dressed as a boy—how homoerotic is that?) over a couch after she gets through the seasickness. She's trying to escape an arranged marriage, never expecting anyone to find her in the captain's suite.

These inspired readings make me think I could write a Harlequin romance. How hard could it be? I have my whole plot set up. My hero is a new headmaster, though really an undercover FBI agent. He has dark hair and blue eyes, and speaks in a raspy voice. And the heroine is a red-haired teacher who spends a lot of time thinking and drinking coffee. Christine Laraby is pure fiction and, like any heroine, spends hours in front of the mirror, brushing her hair. I have to fill up the pages somehow.

The point is time is slipping away fast. I keep getting distracted between my reading, teaching, writing, and obsessive movie watching. I have to think of writing romance as a "hobby," like watching sports, for which I will develop a passion. Maybe I'll be like Susan Sarandon in *Bull Durham*, an eccentric woman whose gusto brings her to a bigger cosmic event: Kevin Costner. What I love in this movie is how Susan's this cultured, wanton teacher who thrives on baseball, seduces a young player, and helps him get to the big leagues (through intercourse). Over-the-hill-yet-gorgeous catcher Kevin is signed to coach the new pitcher, Tim Robbins. Sadly, Susan picks Tim to tutor (sexually) for the season, but she really should have picked Kevin because he's smarter, hotter, and understands what a lovable freak she is. Maybe the headmaster in *Teacher's Pet* should resemble Kevin Costner. It's easy to close my eyes and conjure Kevin. This takes up the last few weeks of vacation.

All too soon, the semester begins, and I drive over to the headmaster's house for a meet-and-greet party. He lives in a serene section of the North Valley on flat, more fertile ground, in a sprawling adobe house with an outdoor area for parties. Upon arrival, I greet friends whom I haven't seen all summer, like Lou, a fellow teacher (history, English, and creative writing) who's been a real mentor to me. We give each other the Look, loosely translated as: *I can't believe the summer is over.* She's around my mother's age, with salt-and-pepper hair and bespectacled green eyes. Like my mother, Lou has this deep wisdom, which she imparts at the right moment. I've come to rely on her, and I love listening to her talk because she always makes interesting comments with a fabulous Texas drawl.

After catching up, I go for a soda and a chair, wondering how this year will unfold. Each year has its own personality.

"Hi!"

I look up toward the voice. A sunny redhead leans over me. The cheerful woman standing in front of me could even be from my family, with her auburn hair and freckles.

I rattle off my identification. "Hi! I'm Patience. I teach French."

"Oooh la la, le français! Très romantique, n'est-ce pas? Hahahahahah! I'm Natasha!" The mysterious woman goes on about how she'll be

teaching middle school English, how she just got her master's in American studies, how she loves cycling. *Goodness,* I think. *These kids are going to have a blast with this one.*

"I'm throwing a party next week and you have to come. There'll be lots of hot cyclists there. You'll be like Cinderella," she says.

I sip the rest of my soda, trying to get rid of the lump in my throat. Any girl who wants you to be Cinderella is truly a fairy godsister. Most budding heroines prefer to play the role themselves. Should I trust this awesome chick who came out of nowhere? Of course I should, so I resolve to elevate Natasha to best-friend status. I'm ready to be her molding clay. This is my new hobby and, I suspect, where any good romance begins.

On the night of the ball—or Natasha's party—I call out my mice to pull together my Cinderella wardrobe: a black lacy top with blue jeans and high heels, increasing my height (I'm not tall).

I nervously stumble from my blue Honda Civic hatchback, questioning the good sense of leaving my bed. But life often happens in those moments when you say *What the hell* and do it anyway.

As I walk up the driveway, my mouth drops.

Over two years in New Mexico, I've wondered, *Where are the boys?* Walking up to the party I realize they've been at Natasha's house all along. It's like an ad for *Men's Health* magazine right in front of me, a flock of spectacularly athletic men, most of whom wear bright uniforms and tight cycling pants as they mill around Natasha's driveway and the grill.

Hidden treasures at my new BFF's house. This is definitely a scene from *Bull Durham*—just a different sport.

Natasha breaks through the crowd, her sunny smile visible from space. "Pay Pay!" she yells, her hips swiveling as she approaches me. She takes my arm and starts introducing me right away.

"This is Patience. She's our fabulous French teacher. *Oui, oui, magnifique, n'est-ce pas?*" Natasha purrs.

I say hi to as many people as I can, remembering no one's name. More fascinating than the idea of dating an athlete is that this energetic, appealing woman would want to bring me into her social network.

"I give good party, don't I?" she says quickly, passing by with a wink.

I love her instantly and watch her work the room.

The presence of so many cyclists unnerves me, until I have a flash of insight. In my secret romance reading, I know that the athlete is never a desirable specimen. Sure, he seems like he could be the cat's pajamas in bed, but there's narcissism involved; he might be more into his body and groupies than lasting love. Then again, Kevin Costner falls in love with Susan Sarandon. He's not just a dumb jock but a good guy who learns from his early mistakes. He appreciates a seasoned woman who likes slow, wet kisses that last for days—oh my. As for Susan, she bathes in baseball testosterone— and is unapologetic and interesting, the kind of woman I'd love to be.

This is my chance. The athlete with the heart of gold—like Kevin—could be the one for me. Except Susan starts out with the younger guy she can tutor into being a successful athlete, not Kevin. I must rethink my strategy.

"Hi, I'm Chris." The mighty cyclist in front of me has a buzz cut, greenish eyes, and a long, lean, tan body. He reaches out his hand

and we shake. He has a sexy, raspy voice, like what you'd expect from a seasoned athlete hero, like the voice of my hero in *Teacher's Pet*. Chris does some mysterious work at the local university and races as a Category 1 pro. Very Kevin Costner. I might just die on this concrete patio.

"Patience."

Because he watches me too closely, those eyes roving over every twitch, I want to hide. The universe is giving me a gigantic sign—it's almost too overwhelming. Chris appears as if he knows me, every molecule, every fear, every piece of me. He is familiar to me and must know how awkward I feel, how alone I am. Must regain control over myself.

"Hahaha, your name is Patience. You must have a lot of patience. Hahahahaha!"

How original.

"We must seem like a bunch of weirdos, huh?" He smiles, big teeth.

"Lots of bright colors," I say.

"Good that you came, uh, I hope to see you again," he says before someone starts to drag him away.

I smile and look down at my shoes, and a deep flush washes over my skin. He seems so perceptive, *a trait every romantic hero shares*. The cosmos is no mystery to him. I wouldn't be able to hide my super-secret qualities from this person, and it scares me.

Maybe I should stick with another beta hero, like Zack. Someone nice.

Natasha pulls me aside to report that I am a hit. Everyone is in love with me. "Who do you like?" she asks. I can take my pick.

As I look around, I notice this dark-haired man sporting a Yale sweatshirt. He keeps staring at me. Something tells me he didn't go to Yale.

"What about him?"

"Oh yeah, that's Ivan! He's really nice," Natasha whispers loudly. "I'll introduce you."

She brings me over to Ivan. He smiles warmly with these bone-melting brown eyes. Though the instant he speaks, I feel his education could be remedial at best. According to Tash, he's a cycling machine. By day he is on the bike. At night he buses tables for money. He's been pegged as a promising athlete destined to ride with the likes of Lance Armstrong, a budding superstar on the cycling circuit. A little past his cycling prime, Chris is his mentor. Wait . . . this setup sounds familiar.

Five minutes later, Ivan and I are a thing. We go on our first date to an Italian restaurant on the northeast side of the city. When we walk into the large, airy eatery, his eyes light up. It's as if he's at the Four Seasons, about to taste caviar for the first time. I enjoy being the worldly one, which is so very Susan. This is the young superstar I'm supposed to build into a strong, successful athlete—my Tim Robbins, which will lead me to Kevin.

This year does have a personality—me dating cyclists. I tell Lou about my new love life, since I do want her approval on all matters.

"Is he a good kisser?" Lou asks. Doesn't she have a wicked streak, now? But I do confide in her and she gives me the encouragement I crave. When I start to have doubts about Ivan as my future husband, she encourages me then, too, sort of like that wonderful older female auntie in many romance novels, the one who says, "Faun, dear, you're doing okay. Don't be afraid to love again." Then they both pull out hankies, drink their iced tea, and munch on homemade shortbread.

Lou is also an advocate for my pushing through the writing process. She's a writer herself and we often discuss our struggles with getting words down on the page. *Teacher's Pet* becomes a burning priority for me, so much so that I break up with Ivan in December. He's a distraction, and I have a book to finish! Christine Laraby is done drinking her coffee but then is kidnapped by the school's embezzler, the assistant headmaster. ShKevin ShCostner somehow finagles a rescue and then announces his desire to marry me—I mean Christine Laraby—in front of the whole school. Wild applause.

So I do wind up finishing my dreadful novel during my extra free time and don't think of Ivan much at all. But as April swings around and students fully rub up against one another with their crazy hormones, I wonder, *Is there anyone else out there?*

Years before the online-dating storm, this strange thing called "the World Wide Web" comes into being. I only hear about it in the spring of 1994, but it has been around since before then. By sheer coincidence, I remember Chris's mention of this project on which he works, dealing with this mysterious cyber-invention. It's crazy contacting Chris just to ask him about this neat new World Wide Web thing and a new phenomenon called "e-mail."

Sometimes Prince Charming is that guy you overlook the first time, the one who's a little too much. Chris is now the seasoned hero who understands me.

My one e-mail exchange with Chris quickly turns to a first date.

Then a second. The evenings are sunny, with light cascading off the mountains, and we are chatterboxes about living in the Southwest, the genius of salsa, how important it is to exercise, and his average caloric intake before, during, and after his rides. Sunsets in Albuquerque tend to be red-gold, and a slight chill makes the air electric. Perfect landscape, perfect situation for me, and perfect hero who takes care of his physique.

"I am very happy," he says.

"Me too."

A strange yet familiar feeling comes over me: passion. I notice where I am when he's with me. I see every line on his face. How his eyes sparkle when I say something funny. He likes to provoke me, so he often repeats himself just to irritate me. When I realize what he's doing, I poke him and tell him to stop. He laughs. "I do it on purpose."

I haven't felt passion in a long time, maybe since Paris, when I ran around like a headless chicken after those waiters, after Rodin and my next Gauloise. It's humbling to discover you've existed without such a vital force. Colors seem brighter and I'm excited for each day.

I have passion again. Chris is my passion.

A few days later, when Chris is away on one of his races, I look over at my single bed—the one my father bought me for graduation—and decide to trade it in for a bigger model. Adults sleep in big beds to facilitate sprawling or welcome other adults. Getting in the mood, I buy candles, incense, and new clothes for Chris's return.

He does come home and appraises my new exotic furniture. His expression goes from lighthearted to stern. I can see him looking around and thinking, *This is a little much.* It *is* a little much. Now all he has to do is eat my cereal and ravish me on the kitchen table, just

like Kevin Costner. But he claims fatigue and we forgo most romantic activities.

Just as we are about to go to sleep, my cat, Jack, jumps onto the
bed. He's a friendly animal who loves everyone, but Chris grabs him
with one hand and throws him off the bed.

"I hate that cat."

"Oh." I can't think what else to say. This should be the deal-
breaker.

My new bed, the incense, the floating candles in the bathtub, all
for him. This is how you create romance. He must appreciate it since
I think I bring out the same passion in him. He cares about us, I
know he does, deep down.

"I'm not sure how much time I can devote to this relationship," he
tells me the next day on the phone.

"Oh." It's a temporary condition. In love, you can't skip through
fields of daisies all the time. I'm almost happy for his cold feet since
it means our relationship is deepening. If I play it cool, he'll realize
how lost he is and come back to me.

"Okay, take whatever time you need," I say cheerfully.

Though when I put down the phone, I worry that our days are
numbered.

A week later, I attend another Natasha party, only this time the boys
are off at a race near Juárez.

But in the middle of dinner the phone rings.

"Phone for you," Natasha says, handing me the receiver.

Excited that Chris would call me from the road, which feels so couple-y, I take the phone.

"I can't do this anymore," he says, straight off.

"Oh," I say once again. I didn't quite plan for this breakup to be so soon, like three weeks after our first kiss on my stoop, under a full moon. Only three weeks. Twenty-one days. That's not enough time for me to fall in love, but my emotions are bone deep. This despair doesn't feel right. I'm too scared to admit it may have little to do with Chris and more to do with that awful empty feeling I keep having when someone leaves.

"Okay," I say distantly, hoping that once he gets home, he'll change his mind.

A few months go by. I turn twenty-six, which seems ancient. The breakup with Chris is always on my mind, an agony that disrupts my visions of the perfect romance. Chris was perfect for me—smart, adorable, abrasive, handsome, self-aware, and sensitive (but never showed it). This romance added up. It was supposed to work out.

"You have got to read this Venus-penis book." Natasha hands me *Men Are from Mars, Women Are from Venus*. It's the big book of the past two years, detailing how men and women are different, which will help the sexes get along.

"This might explain Chris's behavior," she says soberly.

Because I'll do anything, I devour the book in one sitting. Here's what I discover: Chris isn't rejecting me at all. He's *in his cave*. Secretly, he may harbor a deep love for me—which I suspected all along. Chris just needs to be alone. Giving him space is the best possible thing, so I go about my business and sign up for the French master's program at the University of New Mexico. When Natasha tells me about Chris's new girlfriend, I stop talking to her and focus all my attention on my degree.

Lucky for me, small private schools tend to turn over with young staff, and Ashley, the new freshman English teacher, soon stands in as my BFF. A year younger than I am, she's new to town and starting her life over after a string of bad boyfriends. I can relate. I'm reading depressing French novels after a bad romance.

As for Chris, my love is still there, and it feels like an illness, growing stronger with each month. My disease reaches a fever pitch on New Year's Eve 1994. Ashley and I decide to bar-hop, knowing we will run into Chris at some point. In my intel-gathering, I notice he has befriended another over-the-hill cyclist who spends most of his time yelling in bars. The two men hit my favorite haunt, Gecko's, regularly, so I know they will be there on New Year's Eve. This tells me that he is single again, has nothing else happening. It's time to strike.

Within an hour of my arrival at Gecko's, Chris and his loud friend enter. My heartbeat echoes in my ears. I can't bear that he's not with me, but I play it cool, waiting for him to come over and talk to me. In the height of celebration, my ultimate wish comes true. Chris asks me out again.

"Maybe we can see what happens, huh, Patience?" he says, emphasizing my name. "I can't make any promises. You can be patient, can't you?" He laughs.

I'm shaking with joy. "Sure. I can be patient."

———

During this time, I feel so benevolent that I forgive Natasha and we become fast and furious friends again, on the phone constantly, laughing in the halls at school. I've missed her energy, that spontaneous friend who wants to go out for Thai food at a moment's notice.

Natasha seems happy that Chris and I are getting back together, but I know they kind of hate each other. She's so supportive that she shows up to help five minutes before the long-awaited date. She wants to "prep" me, approve my makeup and wardrobe. Maybe she'll say hi to Chris and everyone will be friends again.

We wait. And wait. An hour goes by.

No Chris.

By eight o'clock, he's officially a no-show. There's this sinking feeling in my gut. I know why he bailed.

The next morning I check my e-mail: *I saw her car,* he wrote. *This isn't going to work.*

My last resort is bending Chris to my will in another way. The Wicca way. Yes, I'm going to try witchcraft. If it worked for Samantha on *Bewitched*, why not me?

It seems so crazy. Maybe I am going nuts. In a crowded gymnasium, right before morning assembly at school, when I should be taking attendance, I *pssst* Lou and whisper in her ear, "I'm doing a love spell."

She looks back at me and smiles. "Good for you."

Oh, okay, so I'm not crazy if mentor-goddess Lou is approving. I am going for the gold, taking an active role, fighting for love, even if my methods are not traditional. I'm not praying, getting a makeover, or doing another drive-by of his house—just a spell. I consult books, gather ingredients, and ponder my desires. I scratch his name into a black candle and make fervent pleas to the universe to grant my wish. I want to be the Bride of Chris, i.e., Mrs. Chris Cyclist.

In doing the spell, a strange thing happens.

I open up to what could happen, though I have no control over my future. I let the universe take over. I can't do anything else. I have to let go, let him go, love him despite not being with him. I may never be with him. As I do this universe-opening, candle-scratching, flame-gazing ceremony, a serenity comes over me and it has nothing to do with Chris.

I begin to *see* my wedding.

It is winter, a small ceremony, candles, lights, and a groom. He is standing there, a mystery groom, waiting for me to come down the aisle, waiting to marry me. An eerie calm takes over my body and I just *know*. I will get married someday. I won't even have to do anything. He'll just be there. No more obsessing, okay?

This kind of event isn't covered in romance novels. The worst part is that I can't give up on Chris as my romantic hero. Despite this, I'm grateful that Chris made me feel passion again. Two years before, I felt depleted. I wanted to stay under the covers and let each day pass uneventfully. Chris made me excited to go out and live life in a big way.

But still, I should have walked away when he threw my cat off the bed. A real hero would never do that. Just for that, I get Jack a brother and name him Antoine.

The era of Chris fades, and I figure I'm doomed to be Marianne Dashwood, the girl who runs after her gold-digging lover during a storm and contracts a deadly cold, almost dying from her sensibility (and she's poor).

That's right, I'm reading *Sense and Sensibility* finally. I should be more like Elinor, i.e., Sense. Stay in your parlor, do embroidery, and don't go bananas over the whole marriage issue. I'm also knee-deep in my master's program, anyway, reading amazing books about post-colonial theory, postmodernism, and naturalism. I can't be this fix-ated on my love life anymore—unless by secretly reading romance novels.

It's an especially lonely time since my brother, Patrick, has just left, returning to his bank job in New York City. Because acting isn't exactly lucrative, he's found a more practical job at a bank, which results in a greater need to blow off steam on vacation. When Patrick and I weren't indulging in a movie marathon, he occasionally had to use my e-mail account to correspond with his colleague Gunther. They had work to discuss, a pain for Patrick since he loathes Gunther but was grateful the guy covered for him during his visit with me.

Now that Patrick is gone, Gunther becomes this intriguing forbid-den fruit to me. He lives far away in New York City. What if I befriend Patrick's rival? It's a little what Marianne would do, though if I keep things simple, talk about the majesty of the Sandia Mountains, I might be okay. My new, restrained Elinor nature is within reach. Gunther is merely a potential long-distance stranger-friend. We've never met before so this makes our interaction exciting.

I concoct my plan and coyly answer an e-mail Gunther addresses to my brother. Patrick's nemesis latches on and one e-mail turns into several, just as Patrick is landing in New York. It sort of feels like cheating, which only adds to the insanity of why I would write to Gunther in the first place.

How were your holidays? Gunther writes via e-mail.

Dreadful, I write back, tempted to unload all my troubles onto him.

Gunther, if you only knew, I want to write. Finally, I do. And he seems so nice! Everything Patrick told me about him is wrong. Why would my brother hate sharing a cubicle with such a warm guy as Gunther? The man allegedly screwed over Patrick's friend: He slept with her and then treated her shabbily, then dumped her and slept with her again. Patrick heard the story and relayed it to me even before I started writing to Gunther. It's so confusing now and must be far from the truth. The woman must be a terrible person, otherwise why would Gunther be so mean to her?

I could cheer you up, Gunther responds.

I'm sure you could, I want to write but don't. I giggle at the light flirtation. With five years of teaching under my belt, my restlessness is growing. Isn't there more to life than watching cyclists and teaching the *passé composé* in a mostly Spanish-speaking area?

Inevitably, by January 1996, a couple weeks after our first e-mail, I hit that somber time when I remember what happened to me in Cleveland, but Gunther's e-mails wrap me in a warm cyber-blanket. Since I've never met Gunther, I ask my brother for physical details. Patrick describes him as "interesting," which means "ugly," but he has unreasonably high standards. So what if Gunther's eyes are dark brown, beady? I think they're sparkling. He wears sexy serial-killer glasses, has a voice-over voice that would make a grandma's panties moist. Though ten years older than I am—another thrill—he takes all my problems seriously, answers my e-mail, and "validates" my agony. Gunther quotes Jung, talks about me as his anima.

Gunther is my Colonel Brandon, the old soldier who whisks Marianne from her obsessive chasing of Willoughby. Though I convince myself nothing will come of this, I run home every day to check my e-mail and spend hours checking and rechecking my messages.

I feel so much for you, he writes during one exchange.

This comment makes me insane with joy.

It turns serious near Valentine's Day 1996. I go into school on February 13, expecting nothing. Without a thought, I pass the receptionist's desk.

"Uh, missy, you've got flowers."

I stop, eyeing the enormous yellow bouquet. "Really?"

"Those are for you," the receptionist says with a wink.

"Who's the boyfriend?" the librarian asks as she passes by.

"Just someone I'm e-mailing." I grin and rush off to teach.

That night, my pen pal turns into a phone pal. Our lengthy conversations set my hormones afire and I replay the scripts in my head. I wake up cheerful and ready for a new day.

Booking a flight to meet Gunther in the flesh is easy, plus it coincides with my tenth high school reunion.

After I make an appearance at my high school reunion, barely acknowledging anyone or noticing my alma mater, the taxi buzzes me from LaGuardia, over a bridge, and through much-loved neighborhoods of New York. How I love this city suddenly. I belonged here all along.

Hell's Kitchen comes into view and the taxi stops in front of Gunther's building. I walk up the five flights of stairs. The door opens and there he is.

My beloved Gunther. My mysterious pen pal of the past five months.

For an instant, we stare at each other.

"Hi."

"Hi."

And then I run into his arms. No kissing, no speaking, just hugging. He really hugs me, squeezes me tight and absorbs me. As I peer over his shoulder, I notice the shower is in the living room. The living room is an alcove, no cable TV, and there's a hallway into the kitchen against the wall and a small cavelike bedroom covered with books against brick walls.

It's the New York I never thought I'd see.

"For twenty-four hours, you're mine," he whispers into my hair.

It's a little creepy, but I ignore it. You'd think a line like this would make a girl swoon. It should.

"I have a present for you," he says a few minutes later, eyeing my clothes, probably to get a sense of what lies beneath.

We sit on the couch, and he hands me a small box, the present for coming so far to visit him. He consulted a friend to find the appropriate gift to get a potential new girlfriend.

Victoria's Secret.

A present from Victoria's Secret is a little weird, implying instant, skeevy sex. I am still a good girl. I undo the ribbon, open the pink box, and find three slinky undergarments. One navy thong. One set of ivory bikini bottoms, another ivory thong.

How did he know my size? (Insert creepy shudder.)

Marianne Dashwood would relish the silky lingerie and try it on immediately—thong first. Because this gift makes me feel a little Elinor-ish, I laugh awkwardly and put the underwear away quickly.

For the next twenty-four hours, I am his. I do fall hard for this caring, sensitive, semi-strange guy.

Gunther accompanies me to LaGuardia Airport the next day. On paper, I've had a one-night stand with a thirty-seven-year-old man I've only met once. He's a temp. Not that nice, according to two people, but I don't believe them.

"I feel sick," he says as we sit in the airport restaurant.

Colonel Brandon was sick with love for Marianne. I share his nausea. In fact, I am now so in love that hurling and laughing are my two impulses. I just keep looking into those dark eyes, finding warmth, and running my fingers through his shaggy auburn hair. I want to throw up my joy. Chris is such a small speck in my rearview mirror. No more cycling and—soon—no more New Mexico. I might be thoroughly, nauseatingly in love with Gunther.

Manhattan or bust.

When I read about arguments in romances, they always go something like this.

"How could you try to take over my father's business and blackmail me into marrying you, you pig!" Louisa Toner-Cartridge tries to smack her boss, Lars Corporateraider, but he catches her delicate hand in midair.

"Ah, but you like it." Lars gazes down with his smoldering, dancing, coal-black eyes, then crushes his mouth to hers (crushing, it's always crushing).

A month after our twenty-four-hour lovefest, Gunther is visiting me in New Mexico. This new relationship is . . . well . . . I'm not sure what it is, but this is how our fighting goes:

"You're having issues with your father complex," Gunther declares in the midst of our first argument.

Yeah, duh. "I know. I'm not sure why my father has such a hold on me." Maybe because he's my father and he used to be a great dad. I've told Gunther all about my father. How years ago, he was a loving father, and I worshipped him. I could go into his office and bother him. He spent time with me, encouraged me, and showed me endless possibilities for adventure—mountain climbing, swimming anywhere, riding roller coasters, going on long road trips—and giving me endless advice about school, vocation, and matters of the heart.

Starting when I was nine, my parents newly divorced, I lived with him and we were like two heartbroken peas in a pod. We made burgers, went to stupid movies, and played catch. Because he'd turned into an exercise junkie, he and I would run laps around the track and watch the sunset. As I grew tired, in that last lap, he would yell from across the track, "One more lap for Wonder Woman!" Later, in my teens, it was "One more lap for Duran Duran!" And then I'd sprint.

Not only was he that funny dad who embarrassed me by doing the Steve Martin King Tut dance at our eighth-grade roller-skating party, but he was also the dad who prepped me for soccer by watching me kick a ball into a wall, remarking that I had a powerful foot. So many times, he told me I was special.

In sixth grade, I prepared myself for utter mortification when Dad was invited to give a talk about mountain climbing. A hundred kids crowded into a classroom to watch the slides, which I thought would be deathly boring. I sank down in my chair and blushed like crazy, until Dad started talking, showing stomach-churning heights, Indiana Jones–type rappelling down mountains, and his own remarkable tales of the great outdoors. My classmates thought I had the coolest dad ever. So did I.

I try to think of those times, not the other ones when he stopped looking at me after what had happened to me in Cleveland, the endless discussions we had of his wife's rough life and how no one suffers more than she does, how the divorce ruined everyone's lives, of our tortured family dynamic and how the world sucks in general.

Though he drifted away from me starting when I went to college, my father showed rare moments of affection, such as when he recommended I watch the 1995 version of *A Little Princess*. My dad and his wife are huge movie buffs, so I figured it had to be good, probably containing subtitles.

In the story, a father sends his daughter to a private school while he goes off to war. There, she creates a rich life for herself until the day she learns her father is missing. Because she's lost her fortune, she is forced to do menial labor around the school—sort of a reverse Cinderella. Despite this, the daughter makes the best of life, imagines new worlds for herself, and builds a network of friends, never knowing that the old man next door has taken in an unknown soldier, injured from the war and suffering from amnesia.

As events escalate and the daughter is about to be placed in an orphanage, the soldier hears the girl's voice crying out in protest. He knows his daughter instinctively, and they are reunited in a moving scene. Every time I miss my father, I watch the movie and cry buckets.

My father's recommendation of this movie seemed like a way to convey love. Or so I like to think.

But even though I've explained it all to him, it doesn't stop Gunther from harping on my sadness over losing the dad I once knew. "It's all about your father. And it makes you highly manipulative, Patience."

"I know. I can't help it. I'm sorry I denied you the option to order veggie pizza instead of pepperoni." And this is where I start crying, because I can only stand confrontation for about three minutes. I always cave.

"You understand that my dream about eating meat comes from a very deep place? I don't think you listen."

"I know. I'm such a bitch!"

He doesn't come over to comfort me but goes into his corner to consider my transgressions. I retreat to the living room to wallow in my inferiority. It's only a matter of time before one of us has to speak. All I want to do is lie on my couch and read the latest Miranda Lee novel, *The Bride in Blue,* where a quivery bride has to marry her fiancé's asshole brother, who turns out to be unbearably hot. I'll also eat.

An hour later, he finds me weeping into a bin of yogurt almonds.

"It takes a while for me to shift. I can then forgive," he says, smiling a little.

"Shift?"

He takes me into his arms. The fight is over. Somehow I'm redeemed—from awful schemer to quivering, vulnerable new girlfriend.

One morning we attempt to drive to the top of the Sandia Crest. The mountains overlooking Albuquerque are my majestic old friends. When you fly into the city, the mountains greet you. They sparkle at sunset and shoot off brilliant light on the sprawling city. I love them. Until I try to drive up them. The road is winding and steep and as we ascend the peaks, my knuckles grow white.

Gunther finds my trepidation amusing. He even fake-vomits—one of my phobias—out the window, which is the last straw. I turn the car around and, with a shaky leg on the brake pedal, navigate down the mountain. Funny how a week before, when my father was visiting, I was slightly more able to drive up this damn mountain but mostly wanted to jump off it.

"Your father's wishes are more important than mine," Gunther says sullenly, looking out the window at our tragic descent.

Well, duh. Who wouldn't drive their father up a mountain to win his approval? But Gunther is traumatized.

Love is supposed to be painful. This is what growing up means. Gunther is a tough customer, but underneath his criticism is the real deal. That's love.

"I thought about getting a ring," he says as we drive to the airport.

"Really? Wow." Just what I was thinking.

"But then I decided to wait."

"That's probably smart," I said.

"One of us will have to move. Maybe you can spend the summer with me," he says.

Time in Manhattan. Time with Gunther to see if we're compatible. My ticket is booked.

June begins on a high. I'm done with school for the semester and off to Manhattan for my first experience of living with a romantic partner.

I set down my suitcase, Gunther and I hug, and we're off to the races. He temps during the day while I do research on my master's thesis (though mostly lie on the couch and read), and then he comes home, cheerful to see me.

But our happily-ever-after takes a vicious turn on my birthday in July.

Gunther is angry at me from the moment we wake up on my special day. But he has a surprise.

"We're going to the Upper East Side. A nice restaurant," he says.

Actually, I was hoping for a crappy restaurant, and the instant I see the menu I start to feel nervous, sick. Where are the mashed potatoes? The beige foods that bring me such comfort? What about pasta? A little mac *et fromage*? I don't know what to order in this fancy joint. There's salmon, but I'm not that into fish. Gunther would approve of my eating fish because of its health benefits.

"I'll have the grilled vegetables," I say. Well schooled in fake eating, I can move things around on the plate, pick at a shard and take a bite of a leaf on a twig of a broccoli branch.

Gunther stares at me, his face turning red. "You're in an upscale restaurant. Why don't you order something better, like the salmon?"

"I just want the vegetables." Maybe there'll be cake. That'll offset the pain.

"I can't believe this. We could have just gone to the Japanese place around the corner." He gets more and more frustrated.

"Okay, I'll get the salmon."

We order and I am dreading that damn fish. I can't really stomach the idea of eating a whole piece of orange fish. I figure I'm destined to puke my guts out by the end of the night. At least if I run outside, Gunther won't have to witness it.

The dishes arrive, and Gunther watches me closely. I am positioning my fork so that it picks off the least amount of salmon. I put a fleck of fish in my mouth and want to die.

"You look like you're going to vomit," Gunther says.

My legs start to shake under the table. In a rare moment, I have to flee a scene—not to barf, but to breathe out in the open air, to get away from the salmon and maybe end up in . . . I don't know . . . Connecticut.

I wait for Gunther outside and he exits carrying a birthday cake with my name inscribed. "I took a cab ninety blocks to get this cake and bring it to the restaurant, for you!" He's yelling like Al Pacino in every movie.

"I'm sorry." I'm openly crying on a city street. So embarrassing, so New York.

"You should have said you didn't want the salmon!" he shrieks.

"I did! But, I don't know, I should have insisted. I just wanted the vegetables."

"You won't let yourself be you and that's what I object to," he says a few minutes later as we get into a cab.

There's some truth to this, but how can a girl be herself when she's wrong all the time? I don't feel I can argue. Now I understand why Elinor Dashwood is so understated when it comes to love. After watching Marianne's failed passion, Elinor wouldn't want that for herself. I have to be more like Elinor.

The summer ends two weeks later. By this time, Gunther convinces me that working out our problems brings us closer.

A new school year starts. In addition to reading as many romances as I can, my master's work helps me think about making responsible decisions. I can't give up everything for a guy. Even with the misgivings, my correspondence with Gunther deepens. We send chaste videotapes back and forth. In one, he mentions he has a Christmas present for me, "a little box."

I start to imagine myself as an engaged woman, like that heroine at the end of the romance novel. Finally. A few years ago, a psychic at a dinner party told me I'd meet Prince Charming much later in life. Well, that psychic was wrong. I am marrying Gunther, and I prepare myself mentally for opening that little box and finding a diamond sparkler. Even though I've started having panic attacks every day since hearing about that "little box." Shaking legs and hyperventilation are normal.

The holiday break arrives, and not a minute too soon. I pack my best clothes and fly to my new home, to New York City, where I am destined to move . . . as Gunther's wife.

He doesn't meet me at the airport this time. I can take a cab or the bus, he says. Don't I understand how taxing it is to meet a person at the airport? Of course I do. He must be nervous about proposing to me. Maybe he'll surprise me anyway on bended knee at the terminal!

But when I don't spot him at the meeting place or baggage claim, I'm crushed. Thirty dollars later, I trudge up the five flights of stairs and knock on the door. He barely kisses me. I start unpacking and put my presents for him underneath the tree. Of course I check for a ring box. Not there. But maybe he's saving it for a special moment. I prepare myself for the big event.

I wait and wait. Days go by and it's finally Christmas Eve. He hasn't even touched me, which worries me. What's happened to my Gunther?

Finally, we exchange gifts and he brings out the pièce de résistance: an ancient teapot (I don't drink tea) from China. He found it at a flea market in Chelsea. Maybe we can brew his favorite tea together.

Inside the pot sits a long, eloquent letter on fancy paper all curled up, explaining his love for me, that we need to get to know each other, and that it's too soon for marriage. The missive has all the earmarks of a rejection, and I take it to heart. I am thoroughly disappointed. Gunther is officially drifting away on parchment.

It seems like the end of the world to leave Gunther on January 2, 1997, but when I get off the plane, the relief floods me.

After confronting him, Gunther says I misheard about "the little box." He claims he never intimated that he'd purchased an engagement ring and it must be my imagination, my desperate desire to marry him.

A few days before Valentine's Day, a year since I received those bright yellow roses, Gunther breaks up with me over the phone. I saw it coming when he yelled at me over the birthday salmon.

The idea of moving without Gunther saddens me, but at the same time I feel weightless. At least I made it through to the end, didn't run away when it got too difficult. In fact, most of my time with Gunther was difficult. I start to understand the truth: Gunther isn't the one. He is a complicated person. So am I. He would leave me to die in a cave (the way Ralph Fiennes does to Kristin Scott Thomas in *The English Patient*), weep bitter tears of regret over my beautiful corpse, then find another redhead.

On the edge of thirty years of age, I am moving home, with or without the promise of Gunther. Starting over yet again isn't so bad. My mother and brother will be thrilled. My father and stepmother maybe not so much, but they like it when I come over to mow their lawn or help them clean windows. If I'm good, we'll also have frozen yogurt. My family is worth a move back east.

Saying good-bye to those desert sunsets isn't easy. Those quaint one-story adobe buildings, the ridges of California-esque homes, and even the strip malls. My friends have a party for me. Chris and I reconcile for two seconds and bid each other a fond adieu—meaning we will never talk again.

Gunther resurfaces around Christmas, a year after our terrible holiday break. He is desperate with love for me. I know I should delete the gushing e-mail, but my loneliness wins out. We make plans to see each other after our long separation. But when I see him again, I remember how he wasn't there. Not for any of it—the master's thesis, the master's defense, the packing, the moving, the full-time teaching load, the three graduate courses I took, the lonely Valentine's Day, the two-week Christmas disaster.

Then again, he did give me a great gift. I would never have moved back east if not for him. So many things wouldn't have happened if not for him.

My desire for true romance evaporates as I focus on a fresh start in my career and an improvement in my surroundings. Dating duds is a huge waste of time—at any age. Though by this time, I've heard the whole "You have to kiss a lot of frogs . . ." thing enough to feel a little jaded. I don't even want a prince right now. It's perfectly fine if my love life is on the back burner, because romance is far better in books and movies.

And besides, it's all about me now.

PART II

Some people are settling down, some people are settling
and some people refuse to settle for anything less
than butterflies.

—Candace Bushnell, *Sex and the City*

CHAPTER SIX

◆▶◀◆

Romance on Paper Can Help a Girl Through a Long Dry Spell, and It's Not as Messy as the Real Thing

1997

What a difference a few months make. Gunther is gone, I've moved from New Mexico, and now all my dreams are coming true. I'm almost thirty, overly educated, unemployed, and living with my parents in New Jersey (about forty minutes from Manhattan). My two cats have already ruined the upholstery. What more could I want?

I'm excited to start over, spend more time with my family, and find a career more in line with what I love: reading. Going into publishing would allow me to read full-time. There's something to be said, too, for being home and having parents fuss over you. Mom and Don do what they've always done: teach, write, argue about history or who's taking out the garbage, and throw dinner parties every chance they get. This is comforting to me since I've just uprooted myself. The only missing pieces are my brother, Patrick, who's in

Manhattan, and my stepbrother, John, who moved to Texas a few years ago. It's just me and the parents.

I adjust to the move quite well until full-throttle humidity sets in. I forgot how gross the tristate area gets in the summer! Every day it saps me of energy, but I stick it out through June and July. By August, I'm barely conscious, resulting in this conversation at the dinner table.

"How about more potatoes?" My mother starts putting them on my plate before I even answer. I know she's worried about me. And frustrated because I've lost about ten pounds since moving back east.

"It's too hot to eat," I answer. This is a hint for them to turn on the air-conditioning. Apparently, old people enjoy sweating like dogs. We've had this tug-of-war all summer.

"Don, would you turn on the air-conditioning?" Mom asks.

The man argues for about two seconds, then does her bidding. They both don't like the artificial air, but the ultimate goal is to fatten me up. Don draws a cartoon of my mother handing me—a string bean—a hamburger with a caption: "Bonnie's Patience Is Wearing Thin." In all of his drawings, my mother is wearing a pink bathrobe. You have to wonder what he's thinking.

But seriously, how can I eat when I have a job and apartment to find? In Manhattan, no less? This is scary stuff. Can't I at least have a moment of flipping out? No, because the sooner I get a job and apartment, the sooner I won't live with my parents. On the whole, we get along and they are very generous, but taking the train into the city is a drag.

I read the papers, sift through the want ads, looking for jobs in publishing. I'll take anything, even though I want to work in the romance genre, or fiction, at least. Those early days in Cleveland come back to me—looking for temp work, finding work clothes, feeling giddy about a new beginning. Manhattan is frightening to me. There are too many people. How will I find a job even remotely suitable, especially since I'm not sure what publishing houses are available to me?

One morning, I dress in my old graduation dress, which looks corporate, and head out for the train to go "pound the pavement." This is where you cue the *Saturday Night Fever* music, with John Travolta walking the streets in his disco clothes. There's nothing remotely glamorous about what I'm about to do. And these days, you don't exactly show up at the office and apply. But I need to do something active. My mission is to stop in at a few temp agencies and register in person. I haven't had to do this in a long time.

At the train station, just as I finish buying a ticket, a wave of stomach-plunging panic hits me. How can I go back there? It's such a big city. I'm going to die. If I were married, I'd just go home into the loving arms of my husband. Why didn't I marry someone rich and good-looking? I'd have no problems whatsoever.

Oh God, how will I get home? I can barely move. I'll be the lady in the middle of Penn Station having a nervous breakdown. This is when I stand on the train platform and start crying. The sunny sky feels oppressive. I can't move forward physically, much less emotionally. This is no way for me to look for a job. What would I say to these temp agencies? They'll know I'm in crisis. Moving from New Mexico to Manhattan was too drastic a change. Why did I think I could start over in such a big city?

I turn around and run home, sweating in the awful heat, feeling dizzy. My mother is in her office on the second floor. I'm completely out of breath, falling apart.

"What's wrong?" she asks calmly.

"I can't do it, Mom." I'm sobbing. Mom has only cried once in front of me. I, on the other hand, feel no shame blubbering my face off repeatedly. It's not even an issue.

Sadly for me at that moment, Bonnie Smith is not a "there, there" type of mother. She won't rush up and hug me and tell me it's going to be okay. She did that in Cleveland, but not now. I'm too old now. This is not a near-death situation. I've lived six years as a full-fledged grown-up person.

"Why can't you do it, Patience?" Her eyes are stony brown, not a shred of warmth. I know she loves me like crazy, but she's kicking my ass.

"It's too much." I cry even harder. My corporate outfit feels like a clown suit. Teaching French in New Mexico was such a good gig. Now I've screwed it all up for this desolate stinky place that has garbage on its streets and noisy, crazy people. Dogs piss everywhere, at least judging from what little time I've spent in New York City in the summer. Oh yes, my summer with Gunther.

"So, you're going to stay here and be a big baby," Mom says.

Can you believe she said that? I know she's right, but would it kill her to be gentler? Gentle is the wave of the future. If your student gets a D in your class, it's okay. He's not "feeling" right about learning French. How will it help him with his big plans to be Donald Trump? Oh, little Ainsley can't make it to class. She's having some issues since not getting invited to so-and-so's party. I've heard many excuses and requests for indulgence over the years, and now I'm giving one to my "old-school" mother. I've been through so much, I should take extra-good care of myself, spend a few days relaxing and reading magazines.

Every heroine needs a push, and my mother is usually mine. Then again, I am her daughter, so I push back.

"I'm not going in to New York *today*." My voice is a little stronger and I go back to my room with my furniture-destroying cats. The strong thing to do would be to rush right out and catch the next train. But screw it, I do feel like a total mess. By the time I got home, it would be night.

I know Mom is disappointed in me. She's aware of that mantra I have flowing through me, the one from seven years ago: *You've been through so much. Give yourself a break.* She teaches students like me every day, ones who ask for a paper extension because they have the sniffles.

I've given myself plenty of breaks and pity parties. It's easy to fall back on trauma—though it is valid to some degree—and not advance. But do I want to stay in this house, watch my shows, and put off my dazzling future? If I were a character in a Jane Austen novel, my options would be limited. I might be able to attend a dance, maybe take a trip to London to visit my aunt and uncle. Not so for me. My choices are limitless, and it's paralyzing.

I'm afraid of being mediocre, even though on some days it's fine to wallow in an average life. Otherwise you might die from the stress of being so amazing. I'll push past this bad period. So I don't make it into the city today. But I am on the train the very next day. I don't find a job that day, but it's a start.

Going to my first Smith family reunion since my return east is difficult. The Smiths are a fabulous breed—friendly, loving, and they all have a dry sense of humor, as well as a large appetite for starches (cookies, potato salad, macaroni salad—it's one of the many reasons why I love them). Since my grandparents passed away, our family functions are more sedate. It's up to the aunts and uncles to keep us together and organize reunions.

I want to show everyone that I have my shit together, even though I don't. Showing up counts for a lot, doesn't it?

We meet somewhere in Connecticut, out in the boonies. Most of all, I know my father will be there, and his approval means everything to me. The vibe I get is that he wishes I'd stayed in Albuquerque. Why would I give up a good teaching job to come east when there's nothing here (except family)? He would love for me to marry and settle somewhere far away—at least this is my sense. How did things between us change so fast? One day, he was telling me what a special person I am, the next, I'm this foreign element disrupting his landscape.

This only makes me try harder. If I am a mess, I make sure I have the appearance of a beauty queen. My hair is lush, chin length. I'm wearing white shorts (how confident is *that*) and a black shirt, makeup flawless. Basically, I'm dressing for my father. The reunion turns out to be a golden afternoon of chatting, mingling, eating. At one point, I corner my father.

"So I'm back!" I say.

"Good, good."

I can tell he's not buying my faux-cheerfulness. It's a bummer when someone knows you're treading water. "I'm getting into publishing, sending out résumés. I was dying in Albuquerque."

"Oh, I thought it was a good place for you, nice school."

"I couldn't do it forever. I'm not a teacher."

I try to emphasize this, but he's still not hooked into my façade.

My mother would at least pretend that all was well and say, "Good for you!" He's eating a potato chip, which is a rarity since he's given up junk food.

It dawns on me that he doesn't expect a lot from me anymore. I could stay in Albuquerque in a job that doesn't suit me, and that would be ideal. This whole striking into new territory seems rash and neurotic. In some ways, he's right. My life would have been just fine, teaching French, gradually losing my Parisian accent, not seeing my family all that much, dating more cyclists, eventually marrying someone who worked at Intel.

But now I'm here, along with all my possessions, my cats. I have bigger plans. As with college, I'm just not sure how they will materialize. In the meantime, at least I care enough to haul myself to the reunion. My greatest fear is not that he disapproves, but that he just doesn't care anymore what I do.

My cute white shorts and I make it home somehow, more determined than ever to prove my father wrong—or surpass whatever path he may have laid out for me.

I blanket the New York publishing scene with cover letters and résumés. It is starting over at its finest, with me trying to convey that I am worthy enough to start at the bottom, which is where I belong. My experience in publishing consists of having read several books on how to edit, devouring countless romance novels and French literary fiction, and grading students' papers, as well as doing my own writing. I learn about copyediting and network with publishing contacts. One person leads me to another person until I get a temp job in the publicity department at Simon & Schuster.

On my first day, I'm whisked to my adorable cubicle (just like in the movies!), where I type and ferry around covers for initials. My boss is this blue-eyed blonde who loves to curse. She gets so impassioned that I think she'll have a heart attack. But I love her feistiness. In fact, New Yorkers tend to be witty, I discover. Everything moves at a faster pace, even the humor.

I know from the start I won't work permanently at Simon & Schuster. Publicity is not my goal, but my fascination with the romance novel blossoms as I study industry magazines such as *Romantic Times* and *Affaire de Coeur*, both of which give reviews of the latest titles—and there are a lot of them. At my local Barnes & Noble, I pick up as many of these little nuggets as I can, along with a few thick ones by Jackie Collins (I'm a superfan) and Danielle Steel. I even join Romance Writers of America and go to a few of the New York chapter meetings. It is a supportive, nurturing network with a definite feel of "us versus them" (with "them" being the editors). I'm not sure where I fit in since I did write my masterpiece, *Teacher's Pet*, and yet I'm trying to get a job in publishing. Which side am I on? Hanging out with both sides can't hurt, right?

From the beginning, I make friends with Tanya, a sassy historical-romance writer, who seems to have a wealth of knowledge about the romance world. Over the phone, we have a long conversation about my background, how I came to love reading romance, and what I plan to do. I tell her that I want to write romances, to which she chuckles, since, of course, I must have been bitten by this special bug. She tells me who's who and what's what, mostly from her long experience as a writer trying to get into print. You gotta watch those publishers, always trying to mold you, always trying to be marketers.

Okay, that seems typical. But still, you want to get published, right? So what other options are there?

For about a month, I commute to work and gather information. Each day is another step forward. I'm moving away from that crying girl at the train station. And then I get a call I never expected. It usually takes a girl a few transitional steps to get to a desirable plateau, but not this time. The call is from Mecca and Disneyland combined into one giant ice-cream cone.

"Harlequin would like you to come in to temp for them . . . ," my agency informs me.

Are you kidding me? *The* Harlequin? As in the biggest romance publisher in the universe, home of those cute books you can hide in your purse, the books that got me through high school, college, and finishing my depressing master's thesis? I practically run to my assignment, breathless and excited, ready to read these suckers full-time.

Someone up there is definitely looking after me. So it's only a temp job where I'll read "slush" and give my opinion, and also do tasks typical of an editorial assistant, i.e., transcribe notes, call authors, type up forms on the typewriter. Maybe by the end, I'll either quit reading those novels for good or never leave. Either way, I choose my side. I'm a "them."

The elevator stops on the sixth floor in a midtown-east building. My first view is the receptionist's desk, and this perky older woman with dyed red hair welcomes me. Two redheads in one place. Sounds good to me.

I sit on the couch and wait. So far, this feels like a tranquil place. Quiet, no rushing around, books featured behind a glass showcase. All I want to do is sit in an office and read, learn about these romances I still devour during candlelit bubble baths.

My new boss, Tracy, comes out to greet me. I recognize her instantly, with her red corkscrew curls and youthful features. What could be better: a third redhead in the same company. I read about Tracy during my extensive research on the company. She was often profiled in industry magazines and in books about how to write a romance. Meeting her in the flesh, and having her as my boss, is like working with a movie star.

She is incredibly nice, and it's difficult for me to believe that she's my manager. On my first day, I sit with her in her office, where she goes over the structure of the company. Harlequin is based in Canada with offices all over the world, mostly in the UK, Australia, and New York, but with satellites in a host of other countries. The offices in Canada take up several floors, with full marketing, art, production, and editorial departments. In New York, there is one floor with roughly forty employees, comprised of editorial and a handful of production staff.

As one might imagine, I discover that there is a romance for every kind of reader: racy, historical, light and fun, a more classic story, suspense, creepy verging on paranormal, home and family focused— essentially, whatever you can imagine, there's a romance for it. I gasp when Tracy tells me how many books the company publishes a month. Over a hundred? Really?

Each line gets piles and piles of submissions. As I walk down the hall I see mountains of unread manuscripts on shelves. No wonder my services are needed, especially when Tracy tells me that Harlequin prides itself on the mandate that each submission be read.

These submissions are where I come in, albeit temporarily. Since one of her editors just got promoted, Tracy needs a set of eyes to read for the line that she manages, Harlequin Historical, which boasts some stars of the genre: Ruth Langan, Margaret Moore, Carolyn Davidson, Merline Lovelace, and Cheryl Reavis.

On the first day, she hands me some manuscripts. "Just read these and tell me what you think." Exactly what I want to do all day long.

That seems simple enough. I taught high school and middle school, which involved high energy for eight hours, plus all the after-hours preparation and grading. This assignment—sit and read—is a piece of cake.

As I go through the manuscripts, I wonder about the people who work here. Where did they come from? Later, I hear that Tracy's background was in film and then she moved over to publishing, winding up here. Now she's a senior editor. Maybe her letting me work for her isn't so crazy at all.

In her department is Margaret, the next editor I meet. She's basically a supermodel—tall, blond, willowy—and if she wasn't so interested in what you think and fun to be around, you'd have to hate her. Not only is she perfect, with the perfect children and perfect husband, but she also displays high levels of enthusiasm for her job. She is funny, intense, and savvy—on the other spectrum from me right now, but I like her instantly and she helps me settle into my temporary position. Everybody is pretty darn nice.

I'm put in this large, recently vacated office with a window, which is pretty plush for a temp. The editorial assistants sit in a bullpen, these half-walled cubicles with no privacy. It's one of the rites of passage to endure before promotion to assistant editor. Though my office is good reason to resent me, my new coworkers are friendly. So it's me, a bunch of manuscripts, and the feeling that I could belong here. As I walk around the office, I notice it's lived in, with weathered carpeting, cubicles, and offices, and a close-your-door-if-you're-going-to-smoke policy. I smell some kindred smokers in a few of the offices. Mostly, though, the employees seem serene—overwhelmed with work but happy because it's fun work.

A few months later, I love my new job even more. Since I'm working on historical romances, I dash to my nearest bookstore to pick up some other samples, finding Julie Garwood's Clayborne Brides series: *One Pink Rose, One White Rose,* and *One Red Rose*—about three brothers in the West who find their special "roses." What fun to get lost in another time period, and so much more enjoyable than my American history and world civ classes (I always got a C). It seems like a special kind of heaven to read romances all day, but I'm given the submissions from the outside, the manuscripts called slush, which I find offensive since *Teacher's Pet* would be considered slush. Every writer thinks she's sending in a gem. But now that I'm a "them," I don't fight the term *slush.* Some of it is real slush, which I go through at a faster and faster pace. I learn that I don't have to read the entire manuscript to know if it's a dud. There's no time to be nice. You can be a little nice and send a personal rejection letter, but the only way to make the pile go away is to keep reading and evaluating.

I find a few stories that I feel are Harlequin-ready and pass them to Tracy. She rejects all of them and explains why. Over time, I learn more about what Harlequin readers might like, and one afternoon,

Tracy asks if I'd like to apply for an assistant editor position, which is one rung up from entry level. So I would be skipping over the editorial assistant level, which is way more than I expected. This is that moment in *Working Girl* when Tess goes in thinking she's going to be Philip Bosco's secretary, but instead is given her own office and a better job than she'd imagined.

Maybe this move to New York is the best idea I've ever had. I apply for the job, and by some miracle I get it.

"Don't you think we've watched *P and P* too many times?" I ask. After dinner, my mother and I retreat to the TV room and plop in videotape one of the BBC version of *Pride and Prejudice*.

The last version I saw was the *Masterpiece Theatre* version with my grandmother, back when I was fifteen, which made me want to read Jane Austen's book, which compelled me to read the rest of her books.

Here we go again. Jennifer Ehle, Colin Firth—our newest obsession. My mother claims she loves the meddling Mrs. Bennet most, because she has the serious job of marrying off her daughters and she goes about it expertly. But I know my mother is secretly in love with Colin Firth also. Massively in love. Once, we watched the five-hour miniseries twice in one night, fast-forwarding through less interesting scenes and rewatching others. Suddenly, it was two in the morning. . . .

A woman on a mission, Mom keeps rewinding to watch Colin as he acts, reacts, then displays emotion.

"You see how he just stands there in the distance?" she comments, then rewinds again. As the carriage pulls away from Pemberley,

Lizzie whips around and sees Darcy, ramrod straight, watching her. Romantic goose bumps.

"I do."

I'm surprised she doesn't make me rewatch Darcy's emerging from the pond, shirt clinging to his manly breasts. That's the scene most girls want to see again, Darcy being sexy, because the sexiness is far more subtle in the book. The BBC lays it on thick. Diving into the pond indeed. There's a lot of crap in the pond. It's not a pool in Beverly Hills. I doubt very much Darcy would really dirty himself like this.

"I can't believe they kiss. It's just terrible. Jane Austen never wrote that," Mom says at the end. Though she keeps watching.

"It's the nineties, Mom. We want the kiss."

At moments like this, I'm sad to be moving into my own place. There's nothing more precious than being a girl with your mother and enjoying Colin Firth. I just pray that he does another movie. Otherwise, I'm going to hate him. For now, he's my imaginary dream man—and my mother's.

The question is: Who wouldn't love living in Manhattan? There is so much to do, so many stars to run into. Your parents can't cook for you or make you watch *Pride and Prejudice* forever. Apartment hunting in Manhattan is a grueling process, and I do cry on the train home to my mother's a few times. For my price range, I look at studio apartments that are a third the size of my apartment in New Mexico. Some don't have kitchens or private bathrooms. I know for sure that I'll be living on my credit cards for a good year so that I can rent a tiny Manhattan studio. And you can't just drive up to a sign outside a building and inquire within—or maybe you can, but I wouldn't want to. Instead, I look through want ads and don't contact the landlord directly so much as the "broker," who charges a fee. On top of the months of rent ahead of time, I have to pay extra for someone to show me the apartment. There may be an easier way, but in my desperation to get my life on track, I don't find it.

I go from place to place with a perfectly nice broker, who eventually takes me up six flights of stairs in a reasonable, safe building on the Upper East Side, close to where rich people allegedly live, at least from what I see in the movies. Six flights, up to what is advertised as a one-bedroom but is actually a studio with a deep corner.

I know I won't find anything better than this unless I pay more or go to another borough. The idea of moving to yet another foreign place freaks me out, so I take this tiny apartment and build muscle going up those stairs. My brother tells me that no one will visit me. Ever.

"Wow, I get an apartment and a real job, all in one week," I say to the broker.

"That's how it is here. Sometimes your life can turn on a dime," he answers.

Just a few months after my giant meltdown on the train platform, I'm now a resident of the Upper East Side, on York Avenue in the high seventies. The more I walk around the neighborhood, the more I see young families, lots of women my age (I'm told later this is the "girl ghetto" since rents are cheap-ish), and the occasional celebrity if I walk farther west.

The first time I see Harrison Ford in my neighborhood, my "girl ghetto," I drop everything—coffee, bag, jaw. The man may not live in Cleveland, but he's sure in New York. He gives me that one-cornered smile and keeps walking. On another day, on my walk home, I see this tall, elegant woman sauntering past me. She has actual hips, wears sunglasses—nothing out of the ordinary from other women in New York. At the last second, I notice the mole under her eye. I know that mole. I just walked by the real Julia Roberts! Before I can digest this and keep from fainting on the sidewalk, I walk into oncoming traffic and almost get hit by a car.

These kinds of sightings help offset the strangeness of living in Manhattan. This is no longer the City of Gunther, my tormentor of last year. I am home. But who wouldn't feel a little off-kilter going from wide-open spaces in New Mexico to cramped quarters with little sunlight? The lack of brightness adds a somber edge to my transition. Luckily, my mother and my brother live nearby. And given that we're still on decent terms, I can hop on the train to see my father, in Connecticut. I have family close, and they keep me from hiding in my cave-apartment.

The great part about Manhattan, I soon learn, is that it's full of people just like me—big messes, getting to work, trying to survive. As I walk to and from work, I go from nervousness to feeling a deep compassion for my fellow walkers, workers, city dwellers.

With so much on my plate, it seems natural to take a three-year hiatus from dating. After Gunther, I can't even think of romance, not even Mr. Darcy, who, as I learn from working at Harlequin, is the quintessential romantic hero. We love him for his flaws and his secret perfection. At the same time, real romance seems completely gross to me outside of the novel. There is no one from my past that I miss. No visions of Chris turning up on my doorstep or Gunther declaring he wants me back again. I'm just another single girl in the city—one who is not looking for complications.

By winter, I start to wonder if I've gone completely frigid. But I realize I work in an office of women. Ladies all day long: married, single, nice, some less nice, fun-loving, boisterous, sedate, energetic, neurotic, sane, compassionate females, all working for the cause of romance and love of books. And my colleagues read everything, from literary fiction to the most obscure nonfiction you can find. Many of them have had marathon tenures with Harlequin, which bodes well for my wanting to stay.

I'm suddenly a romance editor (well, assistant editor, but still), within six months of moving to New York. Maybe I'm not dating because I get my fix all day long, plus we don't have an influx of XYs on the floor. I'm all about romance on the page.

Lucky for me, my time at work couldn't be more enlightening. I read historical romances mostly—sneaking in a few contemporary romances—plus, Harlequin has branched out into Christian romances (no sex, but yes on the hand-holding), a booming market, which Tracy manages within our walls. Some of the stories make me cry, as do the historicals. A gorgeous preacher helps a woman regain her faith after a death in her family. A medieval lord sleeps with his late brother's wife, then must marry her when she's with child. Neither is looking for real love until it just happens. These stories appease some of the loneliness of living in Manhattan.

One of my early jobs is to clean out the library and rearrange some of the books. Imagine about 70 percent of the Harlequin books written in the past twenty years in one room. The shelves are packed with those precious thin volumes, along with bigger books by rising stars in the genre. While the room is mighty dusty and I sneeze everywhere, I marvel at the vastness of romance. As I move books around, I get to look at covers from several decades and see how the genre has evolved. From the long-haired Fabio to short-haired heroes. From mustaches to that sexy stubble after a long day of espionage in a war-torn country. Every now and then comes a weird cover, a hero with a rainbow above him or a tornado behind him, perhaps indicating time travel. Some of the heroines seem like damsels waiting to be saved as they dangle off a cliff. Over time, these damsels turn bold and are able to pull themselves up from the cliff.

In the middle of all my research, there's a name I hear often, with glowing praise. I don't go too long without someone saying how much she loves Nora Roberts. This author's written for years, and her name has raced up the bestseller charts in a major way.

Reading her is almost a cliché, one I resist for months until I oh-so-subtly slip *The Fall of Shane MacKade* into my purse. Maybe I'll just read a chapter or two. That can't hurt. When I'm done, I'll just slip it back into the library.

Five chapters later, I'm a total goner. It should be called *The Fall of Patience*. The author hooks me from the first paragraph, and I'm totally smitten by this Shane hero. He's a player but somehow manages to stay on good terms with all his conquests. And then he falls in love with a bookish girl (like someone else we know!) who conducts scientific experiments. His passion for her is beyond his control. He can't stop sleeping with her—they have super-orgasmic sex. How does Nora do this?

I read the rest of the books in the series, my heart holding a special place for Shane. It becomes clear that writers of this genre are firmly grounded in the art of storytelling. You're not liable to study symbolism or foreshadowing in a romance novel, but without knowing why, you want to read on. By the end, you may be swept up in a whirl of happy images, joyful thoughts, hopes for the future. At least that is what Shane does for me.

Not too long after falling for Shane, I get to meet Nora Roberts. We're waiting outside a conference room. She's about to speak, I'm about to listen.

"Have you met Nora?" our mutual friend asks.

My breath freezes in my chest. She looks fabulous. Armani suit. Perfect hair. "No." I try to breathe again. "I'm Patience Smith."

"That is an *excellent* name," Nora says.

"Thanks!"

We both whip out our tins of Altoids at the same time, then the workshop starts.

With all these accomplished people around me, I forget to obsess about my own lack of a love life. Or at least about having a relationship. True love is not what I'm after, though I'll go out on a date. How could any real-life hero compare to the countless Darcys I read about every single day? I'm not saying I'll never look for Darcy again—he's fun to visit with in books—but I just don't need him.

CHAPTER SEVEN

———◆◀◆▶◆———

A Hero for All Seasons

2001–2008

No sooner do I finish *Bridget Jones's Diary* than I decide to date again. Bridget Jones and I have so much in common, aside from a neurotic obsession with our neuroses. She works in the editorial department of a publishing house and surely knows that the publishing calendar is the most important one there is. Poor Bridget falls for her handsome yet toxic boss, which costs her a job. She reinvents herself before stumbling into an even better romance with a man she's loathed most of her life. Well, the only qualities she and I share are our profession and our commitment to self-improvement. As I read a local magazine, I notice an article about online-dating, that everyone's doing it, like it's the most efficient way to connect with potential suitors. Meeting someone online seems the perfect solution for the shy girl who wants to date but doesn't know how.

Why not?

I'm ready to pull out my short dresses and heels, get my hair blown out, join a gym, and date in earnest. It's time for me to find a companion who is not my brother or one of my girlfriends at

Harlequin (though they are excellent plus-ones). My brother, Patrick, and I resemble the titular characters in *Will & Grace,* calling each other constantly to comment on what we're eating, who's cute, how great Julia Roberts is, how many times we've seen *Notting Hill,* whether *Sex and the City* is as good as Julia, where you meet cute guys, whether Mom really soaks all her food in a stick of butter. (The answer is yes.) Because Patrick and I spent much of our lives in separate places, we make up for lost time in New York.

We set up a time for him to take a picture for my online-dating profile: at Mom's special July Fourth family dinner. The Fourth of July, our nation's birthday, is not so amazing in the city. I generally see this celebration as a small-town thing, with picnics and fireworks. In Manhattan, you try to find a roof where you can see fireworks, though you usually wind up watching the show on television.

Good thing my mother and Don invested in a weekend West Village apartment with roof access. We have an amazing view. For the occasion, I get dolled up in a tan miniskirt and a flattering yellow shirt, get my hair blown out, and put on red lipstick and skyscraper heels. I stumble to my mom's place on the other side of town.

As I enter the apartment, my stepfather, Don, barks hello and goes back to his book. Mom is cooking dinner (in a pot full of butter) and I give her a kiss. I sit down on the couch after getting myself a glass of red wine.

Patrick enters the room and sees me. "Wow, look at you!" he says.

"It's the new me."

He sets up his camera and starts taking pictures.

"So the new you is a nineteenth-century French prostitute?" Don says.

I flash him a look of utter contempt—which, sadly, resembles my come-hither look. Click. My brother captures the expression and this picture gets me dates for the next few years in Manhattan.

I should thank my stepfather. Who knew that the thought *You're being a dick* would enrich my social life? Over eight years of online-dating, I learn a few lessons:

Manage Expectations: The person you meet won't be as gorgeous in person as in his picture. Though neither am I (unless I devote a couple hours to it). Every once in a while, I am pleasantly surprised and he is who he says he is. Do as Bridget does: Smile anyway. Reward yourself with a glass of Chivas and an éclair afterward.

Obvious Agenda: If you choose to date online, you're admitting that you want something: marriage, babies, security, sex—something. Know what you want and don't dial down your desire. While you're only shopping at the beginning, don't lie on your profile by saying you want "friendship" when you really want marriage. If he feels you're trying to trap him, then he's a jerk.

Hasn't It Been Called Buffet Dating Before?: When you're at the buffet, you think you want the roasted chicken with almonds. Then you see the ginger-encrusted trout and choose that instead. But then you catch a glimpse of the shortbread and chocolate mousse s'mores. You know, I get it. Being the roasted chicken, though, is not so great. In New York, there's a strange mentality of dating for the sake of dating while always keeping an eye on the better dish up ahead.

Pack-Dating: Some guys date in batches. Use a condom and cover it with Purell.

Vanishers: With online-dating, promising dates can appear, then disappear, like magic! He contacts you for a rendezvous, sets it up, then doesn't clinch the deal. Or he goes out on one date with you, then never calls you again. It happens all the time. Enjoy as much as you can before his untimely disappearance.

Resurfacers: Resurfacers come back after they've vanished once—and they keep resurfacing until you tell them to go away. Resurfacers are bored Vanishers, but they're never satisfied and need quick fixes. If an ex or ex-date comes back, you're better off pressing the "delete" button, unless you're prepared for another vanishing. Then again, if you're really, really bored and want to stir up drama (I've been there!), go for the gusto.

The best part about online-dating is the practice, especially if you're not used to going out and meeting people. Each date is unique. While my potential heroes have distinct attributes, they aren't a good match for my inner romantic heroine. The more I read, the more I can't help linking my guys to these particular storybook heroes. . . .

The Enchanting Earls (with Accents!)

The Romance-Novel Hero

Hugh Westingham, Earl of Buttershire, wakes up with a nasty hangover. After his wife died in a freak carriage accident, he hasn't been the same. To keep his fortune (according to his grandfather's will), he must find a new bride, and the idea of marrying again renders him positively beastly . . . but really sexy and rich, too. All the *ton* is abuzz over which lady he'll choose. It can't be the plain-Jane third daughter of a modest family, the little chit standing in the corner, talking to no one. There he goes, about to ask this fragile creature to dance. . . .

The Real-Life Version

Charles Middle Name Middle Name Willingham III, a Brit who once played tennis with John Taylor (my old crush, who by now is divorced from Amanda De Cadenet and remarried to Juicy Couture's Gela Nash—not that I keep careful track!), requests the honor of my presence in the isle of Manhattan, chez Starbucks, Murray Hill.

He's my first official online date, and British accents make my knees buckle. I wait a good five minutes before he arrives, sporting khaki shorts and a T-shirt. We smile and wait in line. Here comes the saddest part: After ordering our coffees, I whip out my wallet and insist on treating. Did I just inhale too much rubber cement?

"I like that," Charles says.

"My mother taught me always to pay my own way," I answer smugly. As if this is the coolest way to win over a future husband. According to his profile, he makes six figures doing something lucrative in the art field. The way he dresses, though, I have this feeling he might be incognito and married.

Charles and I talk for an hour before I have to return to work. He says he'll call me but doesn't until a week later. My phone rings at eleven thirty P.M., just when I'd given up on ever hearing from him again.

"I just saw *Bridget Jones*. It's bloody good," he says.

"Oh, really?" I pretend I haven't seen it twice already. After this, the conversation fizzles and Charles vanishes . . . until he resurfaces two years later, then two years after that.

Right around the time Charles leaves my dating sphere, 9/11 happens. It's one of those times when I am grateful for my life. Like the entire city, I am horrified and thoroughly heartbroken. My insomnia returns with a vengeance, to the point where I start popping Tylenol PM, trying not to fall asleep at my desk. The great part of online-dating is that everyone is going through the same thing. We talk about our shared experiences.

Secret, Temporarily Penniless Earls

The Romance-Novel Hero

Aidan O'Sullivan is the bastard son of Duke Lindsay Buckingham of Taliashire. After a tryst with a maid results in a son, Lord Lindsay sends her back to her native Ireland and cuts off all contact with her, never acknowledging paternity. Aidan grows up bitter (and gorgeous). He's determined to amass a fortune and destroy his dear old dad. Without revealing his identity, he becomes close to the dying Lord Lindsay, who recognized him all along. Aidan feels a magnetic pull to his dad's nurse, a wholesome woman who knows the truth about Aidan and teaches him to do the right thing—and they make passionate love in her attic room, after which Lindsay's evil wife tries to kill them both so he won't inherit anything.

The Real-Life Version

Lesley is articulate, Irish, and, from his profile, could be the little brother of R.E.M.'s Michael Stipe, as in he's adorably hairless. We make a date to see *The Royal Tenenbaums*. I spend three hours washing, drying, and blowing out my hair because I have to be as beautiful as in my picture. I throw on my red sweater, heels, my Little Black Riding Hood coat, and shiny, sleek black pants.

Standing out in the cold, I wait for Lesley, and finally, this short man walks by me, eyes me questioningly. He smiles, twinkles the way Irish men do, and says my name. Lesley is not what I expected, but then they never are, dear. It's cruel that I'd rule him out based on one second, but suddenly I am grateful for the movie date, that I won't have to pretend to be attracted to him.

We do the pre-date chitchat and I find myself enjoying him more and more. He's literary and high up in the advertising world but doesn't reek of affluence. He's not psychotic. He seems almost poor (takes my ten dollars for my movie ticket).

I accept a second date. Then a third.

Am I crazy? Not at all. I'm under the spell of that guy who's not classically attractive but grows on you like a virus. You can't get enough. The baldness. The charm. The ever-so-slight walleye. Add an accent to this, and I'm absolute toast. I even tell him I'm not that into him. He smiles, nods, and waits for me to fall into the hole, which I do. I don't just fall; I dive in, *Fatal Attraction* and all.

While I love his company—even as a friend and café companion—I know deep down the minute he asks me to read his novel that he's mostly interested in free editorial advice, which I'm happy to give since he is, in fact, a talented writer.

It's wise to steer clear of this kind of guy as a lifelong mate—and he would agree. I wish I could take my own advice. It takes me five years to get Lesley out of my system. We remain friends.

The Secretive Hero (Who May Be Hiding Something Really Bad)

The Romance-Novel Hero

Rafe Blackstone roams the earth, taking on dangerous assignments that could get him killed. He is tormented by guilt because he killed his father. When Dad went after Mom with a broken bottle, Rafe stepped in and beat him to a pulp. As a result of his adolescent rage, Rafe keeps to himself, secretly fearing he may carry the same violence within. He's reluctant to take on his new assignment, to find the heroine's kidnapped sister in a South American jungle. But within a few days, Rafe discovers a wild attraction to her and exposes his vulnerability as they swipe mosquitoes. The heroine assures Rafe that he's not his father.

The Real-Life Version

Terminal Illness meets me at Joe Allen, a cute establishment on restaurant row. TI resembles a young Michael York and hints that he has some terrible disease. Prepared to be Florence Nightingale, I gently ask him what's wrong with his health, but he turns his face away as if to swallow the emotion. The conversation is pleasant enough that I drop by his office with him that same night to "pick up a folder." We make out in front of a weird painting and I never see him after this.

Dangerous and Sexy Alpha Male Heroes Who Are Supposed to Have a Heart of Gold

The Romance-Novel Hero

Business tycoon Cutter Vance has a reputation for being a playboy, perhaps even driving women mad. His last girlfriend threw herself off a cliff, or maybe she was pushed. No one knows. Cutter lives on the edge and doesn't care whom he insults. In the boardroom, he is vicious, causing his employees to cower. Only his new assistant—the only one who's lasted more than seventy-two hours—suspects her boss has quivery Jell-O insides from years of neglect by his withholding mother (who died in a car crash). She learns that he secretly donates to children's charities, but when she confronts him on it, he turns her away with a brash word. Of course, he can't resist her and shows up on her doorstep with an indecent proposal—marriage in name only, which unexpectedly turns to true love when they kiss at the altar.

The Real-Life Versions

I accept Wife Beater's invite to meet him in a sketchy neighborhood. Maybe I am brain damaged, since there is very little about him that doesn't scream RED FLAG. In his profile, he looks totally cute in that raw, sexy way. I'm not sure if he has a job. "Self-employed" often means "unemployed" or "drug dealer," so I try to be cautious.

When I go to meet him, I see he's wearing a wife beater and jeans, a tad informal, but maybe he's the Stanley to my Stella. Ironically, this is the wardrobe heroes often wear on the cover of romance novels. They are bare and primal, waiting to ravish the heroine. While I love my primal on the covers, in real life I like to see a shirt.

We go to a bar to have a drink.

"When you first saw me, did you get a sexual vibe?" he asks automatically. "Like in the first thirty seconds?"

It's like *Looking for Mr. Goodbar*, only real! It's all uphill from there. I summon my inner ice queen and somehow make it through dinner, then dash home and triple-lock my door.

By 2005, I've been online-dating for four years and am no closer to finding Mr. Right, but I keep trying. After reading *He's Just Not That*

Into You (loving it but not taking it in as I should), I pursue Nathan the Spanker because his online personal ad is hysterically funny. He is very tall, is bald, and possesses an abundance of sexual charisma—the bald sexy guy who comes into fashion in New York around this time. They multiply in front of my eyes, and he is my fourth one in a row. We arrange to meet at an Italian restaurant in my neighborhood.

After a great first date, Nathan vanishes, as online dates often do. It's so typical that I don't get upset. He's *just not that into me.* Or, if you go by the romance formula, men need time to process their feelings of incredible love and devotion. I have work to do anyway, and the lessons of previous romances prove to me that another one will come along and true love is a low priority.

Just as I start to forget about him, he requests a second date. Because he waited so long to contact me, I am wildly attracted to him. Off we go to a spicy restaurant in the East Village on the stickiest day of the summer. At the end of this second date (which ends at 2:13 A.M. in Union Square Park, amid a few drug deals, I'm sure), he walks me home.

"Have you ever been spanked?" he asks as we get within a couple blocks of my apartment.

"Sure," I answer. Twice by my father for 1) eating the babysitter's chocolates, and 2) saying "fuck" at the dinner table when I was five. But I suspect he's talking about something else, so I conjure my trusty imaginary boyfriend, Jason. With Jason comes imaginary experience, so, yes, I have been spanked. A lot. Red welts on the back of my thighs, like, every day. Jason was born with a riding crop in his hands, and did I mention he comes from Cape Cod?

I know nothing about New York's S & M culture. It hasn't occurred to me, but I realize right then and there that this culture is real, not just in movies. I start to respect his interest in it. Why not? I really, really love knitting. The pleasure I get from finishing a hat is almost sexual (maybe not). I love knitting so much that I pulled a muscle in my back and had to go to physical therapy (and I kind of liked it).

Nathan is deep into spanking, an activity he shares with all his exes, who sometimes come over just for a paddle. Maybe everyone in New York City spanks one another and I've been living under my romance rock for too long.

Life is all about experimentation, which is what I tell myself the six months that Nathan and I date. It's never too late to learn new things, especially as you're edging closer to that scary forty-year-old milestone. The end of our affair is kind of ugly but perhaps merciful given we have *different interests*. As we start to unravel, I keep wondering how it will end but don't have the will to end it myself. I start canceling dates with Nathan because I can't deal with the inevitable, that I will be alone again, searching for more online suitors. Suddenly, Valentine's Day is coming up fast.

"Here's an idea. I read in the paper that it's more popular to go out the day *before* Valentine's Day. Whaddaya think?" he asks me on February 10.

My keen spidey sense tells me he is dating on the side. To add to his pre–Valentine's Day request, he complains of a pain in his . . . well . . . his spanker, and we wonder if he has an STD, which he would have gotten elsewhere. This prompts a quick trip to the doctor after the blade falls. It's easy to leave someone who orchestrates such a brilliant exit. There *was* someone else, but faking an STD was a bonus in case I didn't put two and two together. Never date someone who is leagues smarter than you are.

The Beta Hero (Who Cooks and Isn't a Tool)

The Romance-Novel Hero

In another life, pediatrician Brad Hanson was happily married and about to become a dad. No sooner is his daughter born than his sweet wife dies in a car crash on her way to meet him for lunch. Wracked with guilt, Brad must care for three-month-old Daisy and keep up his thriving practice. For two years, he mourns his wife's death, never noticing how his new next-door neighbor, Brenda, pines for him. The two strike up a friendship, with her bringing him casseroles, sharing meals, and babysitting when he's on call at the hospital. They listen to each other, and after a night of spilling their innermost woes, they kiss. Can Brad move on from his tragic past and risk his heart once again?

The Real-Life Versions

There are those online dates that go nowhere, but your hero is such a nice guy. He listens to you and contributes fascinating nuggets to the conversation, and you know he'd be a great partner . . . for someone else. Beta heroes (with an edge) are my favorite for real life, though at this juncture, I don't seem to be winding up with them. Then again, you never can tell who's going to surprise you and be the perfect match.

 Beta #1: Weird Haircut Lawyer is completely wonderful, but we have no romantic interest in each other. A year later, I find him and his new wife in the "Weddings/

Celebrations" section of the *New York Times*. I like to think that my role was instrumental.

Far-Too-Beta #2: Still lives with his mother—not because she needs help but *because he never saw a reason to leave her.*

Beta #3: Feeling that pressure to settle down, I date this sweet prince for nine months long-distance. If it weren't for my breaking up with him twice (over the holidays, cruelty itself), I might be Mrs. Beta #3.

But then the ultimate beta arrives. Ten months after Nathan, when it seems safe to go back into the water, I'm wooed by Barry the Teacher, that nice guy who screams Perfect Husband and Father Material. Handsome but not too much so, good job, virtuous, kind to his friends, kind to me. Not even remotely the type to cheat, treat me poorly on purpose, or vanish.

We get along well, despite our many differences. He likes doing things (why do I always find this person and not the couch potato?). His friends are mostly female. I work with all women, so I seek out boys as much as possible. He doesn't like my crappy TV choices. I'm not into bird-watching in Queens.

But we both agree that weddings are truly joyous occasions, and the best man's girlfriend could have an especially amazing time. That's me. After dating Barry for almost a year, he asks me to attend his best friend's wedding with him in Austin, Texas.

I am on the cliff, about to dive into the Land of Forty. This trip is an investment, one I hope will pay off. So it's with great pleasure that I arrange my schedule to attend the affair. How better to hint that I am ready to marry him? Barry has his imperfections: He is uptight, has intimacy issues, possesses a fleet of female friends who are nice but so obviously want to bang him, and he enjoys the attention a little too much.

Barry is the one who puts up pictures, reaches containers on the top shelf, and carries home Christmas trees for his friends. They are nice to me, too. I meet them all, and they never hiss or play vicious games with me. On the contrary, I am included in their activities: the hikes in upstate New York, the ice-skating in Central Park, the Easter celebrations, the museum-going, the long walks along the river, the Coney Island adventure, and the bowling—all with Barry's girl entourage.

His small apartment is cozy, filled with just the right amount of stuff. Barry teaches high school and is like one of those teachers you see in a movie—feverishly committed to helping young people learn, especially the illiterate student in the back who's been passed through the system. Affable, witty, and kind, he is an inspirational teacher and mentor. He even looks like a teacher, with his glasses and the earnest expression in his eyes.

On paper, he is a dream. Goes on the requisite two dates before leaning in for the first kiss. Drinks just enough alcohol. Has the earring and tattoo, which doesn't quite hide the fact that he is a square (but then so am I). I love this. It's so my speed.

Fairly early on, he pulled me into his arms and said those three little words (though I said them first during a bout of the stomach flu). A month after our Austin trip, he starts to backpedal, hinting that he isn't ready. That one-year anniversary approaches and I notice the fear on his face. I convince myself he just needs time. We are a good match—him with his height, nerdy glasses, and graying hair; me with the red hair, sagging under a too-heavy bag full of manuscripts. A cute middle-aged couple, that's us.

I don't regret most of my time with him, just the last six months. I could have passed the year anniversary on my own, rather than sitting next to his female friend and him during an Americanized performance of *Cyrano* (Jennifer Garner was fantastic!) on Broadway. Barry arrives with a bad case of hemorrhoids and is in such a lousy mood that he can't send me flowers.

We start seeing each other once a week, instead of twice.

One random day, I ask if he wants to go to Madame Tussauds wax museum. He agrees, though I sense his reluctance. This isn't on his approved list of activities. An hour before we're supposed to meet, I cancel because I can smell what's coming. I remind myself that only the week before he told me he wants to be with me forever and father my children. He comes over instead and we lie on my bed. I feel frustrated over this shaky future.

"So, are you renewing your lease?" I ask. It's the question I've wondered for months. Will he stay in his tiny cubicle of an apartment or are we moving in together?

He puts his hand on my inner thigh and breaks up with me.

I accept the breakup, just not the hand on my inner thigh. I am one pissed Bridget Jones. The second he leaves, I throw out everything he left at my place (including a $40 book about Hitler) and jump back into the dating pool.

CHAPTER EIGHT

Never Discount the Power of a Birthday Wish

March 2009

The romance novel of my life begins here, twelve years after moving to New York and going to work for Harlequin. I'm now a senior editor, managing a romantic suspense line. I've moved from the sixth-floor walk-up on the Upper East Side to a box in the Chelsea neighborhood of Manhattan. My life has improved drastically. Well, except in one area.

I'm sitting next to Superman for two hours on Amtrak, headed back to Manhattan after a weekend at his house near Albany. We've been dating for the past five months, and this was my first time seeing his second home.

Total disaster.

We met online last August. Newly brokenhearted from Barry the Teacher's vanishing, I searched for a hot rebound guy and found Superman. Not caring about rejection, I boldly sent him a note of introduction. By sheer magic, after landing in San Francisco for a

Romance Writers of America conference, I checked my e-mail and found that he'd responded. Needless to say, I floated on air throughout the conference and did my job twice as enthusiastically. A month after this, Superman and I met in person and embarked on an ecstatic new romance.

Five months later, we're stuck. He never promised me a rose garden, but now we're not speaking at all. I'm confused. All I did was ask, "Where is this relationship going?" He's now about to break up with me. This will be my third painful breakup in a row after Barry the Teacher and Nathan the Spanker. I'm so startled by it all, I can't even eat the gooey chocolate doughnut I bought myself at Dunkin' Donuts as a little pick-me-up. And I can always eat dessert.

I thought this would be a romantic weekend. Instead, we went to his house, I helped him clean for his new tenant, and he took me to the Olive Garden. He said he loved how I "keep him organized," which pleased me. Organization is my thing. The most beautiful man I've ever dated—resembling that superhero of my dreams—and he's slipping through my perfectly manicured fingers.

What did I do wrong?

I look down at the doughnut again, thinking I might eat it once we've finally and officially dumped each other.

I had so many fantasies about Superman. . . . Our beautiful children, his devotion to me, our continued appreciation of Judd Apatow movies and ice cream, the endless parading I would do on streets, showing off my GQ-model boyfriend . . . I feel too old, at forty, for this dating stuff now. Superman will just disappear—stop calling, stop e-mailing. In a year, he'll become a Resurfacer by contacting me and acting as if nothing happened. I love attention, so why wouldn't

I let him come back? He's cute and amusing. We'll casually date once more, have sleepovers, and then break up again. It's the circle of life, as I've learned over the past ten years or so.

At least the scenery out the train window is beautiful: sun sparkling on the river, quaint towns, and the beginning of spring. This makes me smile. I'd like to live in the country someday, plant a garden. I'll save up for a house, go to suburban book clubs, and drink wine again. That would be fun.

More pretty landscape along the Hudson. But even this doesn't erase the gorgeous problem sitting next to me. I can't even muster words.

In a romance novel, the weekend away cements the love bond. Usually the weekend away is an accident—the hero Jake Hunter's grandmother is having bypass surgery and he needs his assistant, the lovely Cassie McBride, to come along so that his billion-dollar business will stay afloat. Only she can help him. Naturally, all the stress over Grandma—the woman who raised him after his parents died in a car crash—compels him to repeatedly remove her clothes and his clothes. There's no Olive Garden in sight. Unbridled and constant sex ensues, followed by emotional intimacy and surprise pregnancy and marriage proposal (that doesn't happen *because* of the pregnancy, but who are we kidding).

Superman and I started out as Jake Hunter and Cassie McBride. Our Chemistry.com chemistry was immediate, and he is Mr. Alpha (which I love). Superman wears dashing suits to work and probably does fly over skyscrapers and rescue puppies and kittens from the subway tracks. The man never sleeps, which makes me suspect that he fights crime at night. As time passes, though, I note we are on different wavelengths. We don't exactly fit. Also, he displays no interest in my life (which in Jake Hunter–speak means he's secretly in love with me, but it's too painful for him to communicate this).

I need to wake up and stop sniffing Sharpie pens. The romance of this relationship is mostly in my head.

In a novel, it's so easy, because Cassie and Jake literally run into each other. She is walking too fast with a stack of papers and rams into his hard chest; he stops her from falling by grabbing her shoulders. They both feel the electricity of attraction running up their arms (rug burn?). He just happens to be the boss (and there's a large conference-room table on which their love child will be conceived). These two lovebirds can't help but meet.

In real life, you have to make the encounter happen. I think about the stack of Brenda Novak novels sitting on my bookshelf, waiting for my perusal. She's one of my favorite romance and suspense authors, to the point where I can barely talk to her at conferences. Her editor slips me her books, and I've hoarded them for the perfect emergency time when I can lose a weekend with her stories, a bag of Cheetos, and some Kit Kats. I will recover this lost weekend with Brenda.

My mind sifts through memories of ecstatic times with my past Jake Hunters, though none resembles the intensely driven, likeable heroes of Novak's stories. Nevertheless, my dating history contains a few dizzying love scenes. Some passionate kisses, but not under a full moon—more like in a sketchy park at two A.M. with Nathan, outside a deli with Barry, under scaffolding on a rainy street downtown with Rich but Still Worried About Money, all colorful in their own ways. There are a million restaurant moments, awkward silences, and great conversations that go on forever. So many apartments, some furnished, some not (See Charles the Brit), some messy (Nathan), some freakishly clean (Superman). An array of wardrobe preferences, from the grunge look to gorgeous custom-made suits. Some flowers delivered at work (Barry, Superman, Vanisher #342 who skipped out right before my birthday—I wound up secretly dating his brother) and the occasional present, just because.

The Jake Hunters I've experienced tend to have non-damsel-rescuing jobs. They mostly worked with numbers, but not in the glamorous Richard Gere–in–*Pretty Woman* way. Many of them had side passions, such as music (I saw a lot of shitty bands), bird-watching (oy), food (with finger bowls), skiing (love the gear, hate the falling down), and hiking (a little afraid of heights). They each showed me entertaining sides of themselves. With Barry, I went places that had trees and slopes. With Nathan, I learned about wine and *macarons*. Superman taught me to enjoy stupid guy movies and unapologetically eat a pint of ice cream in one sitting. Gunther helped me appreciate classic movies and the finer points of filmmaking. Thanks to Zack, I started the healing process and immersed myself in simple pleasures. With Craig, I started to appreciate my life as a gift. Chris inspired passion in me, and he was that alpha male in many Harlequin novels.

My real-life heroes had imperfections, too, which I appreciated since I'm, well, a tiny bit neurotic myself. There were nervous ticks, bad haircuts, eating-with-the-mouth-open stuff, hygiene issues. On the page, Jake Hunter has no bodily functions, so real-life dating was a rude awakening for me, especially French kissing (WTF?) and eating in front of a guy. With my three-dimensional suitors, I got used to their long vacations in the bathroom.

As for sex, who am I to complain? Sometimes it was great.

Sometimes it wasn't (Jake Hunter never takes Viagra). Real men are very sexy—and human, especially if an ex or a dead mother is plaguing the libido. I could relate to this, since I'm haunted by events in my past, too. A bad moment will flash in my mind and I'll have to go "somewhere else." On the outside, I may be hitting all the right notes in the love story. Inside, I could be a mess. Romance novels don't always examine the complexities of swapping bodily fluids—or even mention these fluids.

But enough comparison. Only half an hour left on this train with Superman. It's hard not to keep looking over at him, because when am I ever going to date such an Adonis again? I'm a little embarrassed that I can see myself married to him, mostly because we'd lead separate lives and come together to watch Judd Apatow movies—not a bad life. Some marriages are made on less. I went out with physical perfection and several "soul mates" and none of them worked out. Do I have to start over again?

That nagging voice urges me to take a few weeks off from dating and then get back on those sites, the way I always do. There will be hours spent watching television, editing my beloved books, impulsively buying makeup at Duane Reade, and crying while playing computer solitaire. A month will go by and I'll get the urge to meet someone new.

But I can't envision another date or boyfriend. I don't want to. These heroes are almost repulsive to me. Maybe I need a serious break, like forever. This crazy thought enters my head: *I don't ever have to date again.*

No laws will be broken if I stop dating. No one will mourn my love life. My family has long given up on my walking down the aisle and procreating. I don't need to find Mr. Right. Not now, not next year, not ever. Maybe it's time to love my forties as is.

I can return to my own schedule, no primping or carving out those three hours for dinner, packing overnight bags, answering texts and e-mails. The idea of a break used to make me anxious with thoughts of how there's not a lot of time left, what Mom will say, who will go to parties with me. Now the idea of free time makes me giddy. What a relief! I can knit all the time and run for my own enjoyment, not to look svelte. No more hiding that I love *The Real Housewives* (and the Kardashians).

I should be sad to lose this gorgeous man. A part of me is. And for the last leg of the trip, I try to tune out sleeping Superman, only faintly wishing that he'll say, "Let's stay together, Patience. Romance does exist. You're the prettiest and most interesting woman I know. We belong together."

This would be nice—a hero who tries to woo me back into love— but usually this hero reactivates his dating profile immediately. Superman can't possibly be dateless for long. I will savor these last few minutes. I steal glances at him, snoring away openmouthed as the train whisks us along more breathtaking vistas. Even in deep slumber and with a hint of drool off the side of his mouth, he is hot. Thick fisherman's sweater. Jeans. Perfect hair. Towering over me even in a train seat.

I hope I'm dodging a speeding bullet and not giving up the fight.

As the train comes to a stop, Superman's eyes open and he stares straight ahead. I like to think he's in agony also, over the disastrous weekend, what he could have done differently. Maybe he'll have second thoughts and come back. Romantic heroes do that after the I-can't-live-without-her montage.

We walk side by side up the escalator, each carrying our bags.

"Which way you going?" he asks, hair adorably mussed from the train ride.

"That way." I point toward the Seventh Avenue exit. He, I know, is heading toward Eighth. The message is clear. We are going in opposite directions in Penn Station and in life. He walks closer to me, gives me a quick kiss on the lips, and speeds away to the other end of the station. That's it. No fuss.

On the walk to Chelsea, I can't even summon the will to cry over another failed romance. Sandra Bullock would wail like a banshee—and she'd look so pretty. This time I'm not going to wail (and I know I wouldn't look as good while I was doing it). This time I'm completely stoic, no tears, no whimpering, no self-pity. Just tired . . . and excited about my no-dating policy. Romancing Superman was fun. Every heroine should date a gorgeous god.

The minute I return home, I put up my feet, order my favorite takeout—cheeseburger, fries, cookie, no salad—and start Brenda Novak's creepy romantic suspense novel *Watch Me,* which happens to be my new theme song in life. I relish this alone time and settle in to live the "single girl" cliché: television, cats, junk food, books that help you forget where you are.

Maybe there is one weak moment when I smell Superman's shirt, the one he left, the one I washed, starched, and ironed myself. But that's it. I'm done with romance, let alone love.

Two hundred and twenty pages of a Harlequin romance don't cover these kinks. From now on, I intend to soak up my independence. Cassie McBride would totally do this, too.

I throw the gooey chocolate doughnut in the trash.

It boggles the mind that four months could go by in such a blur. Suddenly, it's July, my forty-first birthday, and my family has congregated at a table in a fancy French restaurant around the corner from me. I've long grown out of wanting birthday fanfare, but I know my mom would be unhappy if I stayed home, ordered takeout, and worked on knitting projects. For her, I muster up an appetite and wear a dress. When I don my usual jeans and shirt, she winces and thinks I'm depressed, which is not the case. She's a little scary, like the all-knowing mom who yanks you out of bed when she senses you're in a funk. But I'm doing okay, I assure her.

Cassie McBride doesn't have to deal with an overbearing mother because she's an orphan (her parents died in a car crash). If anything, she's raised by either animals in the woods or a kindly grandmother who then kicks the bucket and leaves Cassie a huge house with a wraparound porch and fully stocked kitchen so that she can whip up cookies to bring to her neighbors or the office. Also, given her natural tendency to be beautiful, Cassie would never wear her college clothes. Cassie is all about the sundress.

Luckily, I'm wearing a sundress, too.

"I'm fine, Mom. Really. It meant nothing." Superman is a distant memory. I even sent his shirt back. Three Brenda Novak novels later, and I'm cured. Perhaps Mom had a little crush on Superman. He came close to Colin Firth's godliness. She and I will salivate over many romantic comedies in the future. There will be more birthdays like this, with her worrying about me, me telling her I'm fine.

It occurs to me that a year ago, I was sitting at this same table, fresh from another breakup, on that scary precipice of forty. Now I'm turning forty-one—yikes, can't go back now! My situation hasn't changed much. I definitely feel better about my life. Same job. Same apartment in Chelsea—at least for the past four years. A few more gray hairs. Who am I kidding, Cassie McBride would never be this old. Plus, she embraces all moments with family—that is, if she has one, usually long-lost brothers who own a ranch and have long-lost male half brothers who have an even bigger ranch.

I decide to embrace this moment even though I would rather be at my own studio-size ranch. Being out with family is probably a good idea for me.

"We're going to party!" my mother says excitedly. She's really into this. You can tell by her hip phrases. It's kind of funny, actually.

There's a new addition to the table, my brother's adorable boy-friend, Carlos. He is a dark-haired, brown-eyed Peruvian man, both an intellectual and a comic book geek, who is getting his master's degree in nonprofit management. Patrick is happy, relaxed, more active than I've ever seen him. For as long as I can remember, Patrick has been my rock, the one who helps me make big decisions, who drives people to the hospital and protects us all from evil. He's be-come our true patriarch. I thought I'd be jealous when he settled down, but his boyfriend had me at "I have Kylie Minogue on my iPod." Carlos has brought sunshine to our family. He encourages Patrick to cook instead of eat at restaurants, to visit family as much as possible, and to soak up life. As I see it, my family has expanded.

My mom, of course, continues to be the queen bee over all events. This doesn't fade one iota, though I notice how much I rely on her for my entertainment, even if I hate going to restaurants. There are the little things I crave seeing, like how her nose flutters when she finds something hysterical, or the way her head swivels if she eats some-thing particularly delicious. I tell her everything, and she listens, even if it's a bit of an overshare. Then there's her work ethic, as in work until you can't stand it anymore; I get that from her. Everyone loves Bonnie. In the past few decades, she's given up her dark brown hair for a short pixie style, frosted, like she's trying to be a blonde. Basically, my mother is still a goddess. She's also a mother and, as such, sometimes calls me five times a day to remind me of absolutely nothing. I'm not sure how I'd cope if she stopped doing this.

Don remains unchanged, continuing his role as the smartest one in the room, along with his penchant for making cutting remarks, rubbing his beard, and walking away in the middle of a sentence. Since spending more time in Manhattan, he's also taken to barking at dogs on the street. I remind myself that he's allegedly famous in his field and one of the world's great thinkers. Mostly now he's eyeing the red wine, his forbidden lover since he experienced some health problems and retired from academia.

Because forty-one is no big deal, I proposed staying home on my birthday, having a *Queer as Folk* marathon while I sink a fork in birthday cake topped with peanut M&M's and Cool Whip. My mother wasn't having it, though, and she's the boss.

So here we are: out in the open, muggy July air at a French restaurant, me popping an Ativan just as the waiter brings us our menus. Family dinners make me a little nervous and so do restaurants—something about the cluster of tables, an imposed time frame to sit still in one place. It's just how it is. My appetite dies slowly as I review the list of specials.

"Ooooh, look, they have kidneys!" Mom shouts. She loves to read aloud every item on the menu. "Beet salad! Look at that delicious salmon terrine. What are you having, Patience? Maybe a little duck confit?"

"I'm not that hungry. Maybe the hanger steak." This is my typical response.

Mom winces. "You'll get an appetizer, too. A little salad?"

"It's my birthday. No appetizer." I know full well she'll order an appetizer for herself and give half of it to me. This is part of the routine. Now that we live so close to each other, it happens a couple of times a month. But the people around this table are my family, and I love them desperately. The banter is the same as it's always been. Our dynamic is one I'm used to and it comforts me. I still need a tranquilizer. It's my birthday.

"Hey, I'm a prime number this year," I say.

Patrick and Carlos raise their eyebrows. They don't quite get my *A Beautiful Mind* obsession with prime numbers. Only Don does, because he's insane.

"That's right!" my mother says, playing along, though she doesn't really care about numbers. "It's going to be a *great* year!" She loves the word *great*. Everything is *great*. Did you see how Bessie organized her flower beds? They're *great*. The percussionist who makes so much noise next door, she's *great*.

The waiter comes around and takes our order. The bottle of wine goes fast. My mother orders a Sauvignon Blanc, telling the waiter that if he brings her Chardonnay, she "will vomit." I watch the waiter to make sure he fully digests this information, since if my mother vomits later, I might hear about it the next morning as I'm stuffing my face with pancakes. Though I love it when my mother confides in me, I can't let anyone ruin my dessert foods.

"And now I'm going to tell the story of Patience's birth," my mother announces, like clockwork.

Apparently, I was an easy birth, though a month late—for which my father was probably thankful since he didn't need to miss the '68 student riots in Paris—and I had to be induced. I didn't want to come out. Imagine that.

As I look around the table, I'm content. I could easily devote the rest of my days to social events with my family. They are wonderful people. Nothing needs to change. I'm in a good place.

And yet, all the books with their happily-ever-afters are ingrained in me. There's a better way to live, isn't there? I am allowed to dream. Maybe I can do that again, even though I'm exhausted right now. Cassie McBride would never indulge in this BS. She's up to her eyeballs in customers at the diner where she now works as a waitress (the knitting store was not lucrative). She has no idea that Jake Hunter can't stop staring at her, that he comes in for black coffee and a slice of pie every day. No, Cassie goes about her business, doesn't expect more, doesn't even want it. I should keep doing what I'm doing, which is work and family.

But when the cake comes, I do get this sudden wild yearning for more. More doesn't seem possible, especially at my age, especially after what I've been through. It's too late for me to start a family of my own. The men my age want someone younger, which makes me not want them.

But wouldn't it be amazing if I experienced magic of some kind— a romantic windfall?

That usually happens to Cassie. Just when she thinks her life is over, Jake Hunter appears out of nowhere and declares his undying love. I'd love for it to be easy, just this once. Let me just do nothing and have my soul mate show himself with a big neon sign. Would it be too spoiled of me to ask for this? I've worked so hard for so many years.

The cake emerges with a sparkling candle, the waiter singing "Happy Birthday" in French. Everyone sings.

The cake sits in front of me.

"Make a wish, Payshie," Carlos says. He's so cute.

Hmmmm. What do I really want? A backstage pass to a Duran Duran concert. Yes, still, my obsession with this band frightens most people. Maybe I could have lots of money—of course. Something bigger? I could wish for world peace (though that's a little boring). My mother wants me to be a high-powered executive—but that doesn't suit me. I could wish to open a yarn store like Cassie McBride. But not in this economy, and besides, that's her dream (was her dream).

No, this one is all for me:

Let me be engaged within a year.

Huh. Where did that come from? A romantic windfall would be nice, but *engaged*, like with a ring? That's way too much. Oh well, I can't take the wish back.

I blow out the flame and dive into the cake, forgetting the wish entirely. Though I keep the candle, just in case.

A few weeks later, August 10, begins as an ordinary Monday. I take the 1 train to the office, edit romances, and come home eight hours later. A sense of elation fills me. My year is basically over. No more conferences, family reunions, or trips. I only have to edit books. It's been almost six months since Superman, and I'm happy to not be fixating on a boy. There is no one.

When I go home at night, I watch movies and read tabloids. My cheeseburger and fries are a phone call away, so I never need to cook. My Chelsea apartment is worth the kazillion dollars I pay in rent. The credit card debt accumulated in my twenties is at an all-time low—just in time for me to discover the Anthropologie store two blocks away. I have a cat who is not an asshole. I am peaceful and have everything I need.

Of course, it takes one moment to ripple these calm waters forever.

Like most, I check e-mail and Facebook every five minutes. I won't lie: Notifications and "likes" boost my self-esteem. It's early evening, and this intriguing friend request appears.

Sam Something-or-other.

Familiar name. I recognize it but not the context. I get a good feeling when I read his name, like *I know him*. High school and college friends have merged in my memory. Foggy brain or not, my curiosity is piqued and I accept the friendship. Who is this cool person again?

An instant message appears.

"Hi!!!" Sam writes.

He's one of those—the three-exclamation-point kind.

"Hello!" I write back, a little eager to get back to my tabloids but still intrigued. I love his enthusiasm so far. "Where do I know you from—high school or college?"

"High school."

"Are you older or younger than me?" Might as well be complimentary and play dumb. I'm not stupid.

"I like that question. Older."

It goes on in this vein until I have a flashback of a brazen, husky boy with curly brown hair entering a school cafeteria. The entire room breaks out into applause. He is both mortified and pleased, as if, yeah, this isn't the first time. The smiles in the hall. The feeling that he liked me. That dance.

I *do* know Sam. He's the boy who swung me around the dance floor. He was the daring Evel Knievel of our bucolic prep school. Here he is friending me, the wallflower from high school.

But why? I guess it doesn't matter. My high school self would go bananas, analyzing this to death. Cassie and I don't give it too much thought. We dismiss the interaction as unimportant. He'll go away or find another special friend. I've been through this before. You're not fooling me, Jake Hunter. You're a mirage, and I've fallen for you too many times. This Jake is just being polite, doing light socializing so that his friending me doesn't seem so impersonal. He is probably in a bar, feeling lonely, reaching out to the little redhead from high school. He will seem amazing to me at first, suave and self-assured, so complimentary, more handsome with each e-mail. But with every step forward, he will crumble, lose interest, and then disappear. I'm so ready for this to be a big pile of hot air.

But then Sam does the unthinkable and asks for my phone number so that we can "catch up." Catch up on what?

For once, my usually cautious self takes a coffee break and I consider giving him the digits. What do you know? I didn't have to do anything to get this attention . . . and from a legend. How weird.

I'm fairly sure this will come to nothing, but that's okay since I have *The Real Housewives of New York City* and a whole host of guilty pleasures to keep me company.

CHAPTER NINE

The Voice from Five Thousand Miles and Twenty-Six Years Away

August 2009

It's a not-so-leisurely work-at-home Wednesday for me. Because I have at least two books—usually three—to edit per month, there is no shortage of work for me to do. I also have to gather information for the insides of the books, the dedications and the author bios, and then approve the back-cover copy (a.k.a. "jacket" copy on other books). I could work ahead on cover ideas for the next month. Should the couple be in a clinch or can I have a studly-hero-alone cover where he's wearing a black leather jacket, staring hungrily at the female reader? There is an endless pile of reading: of slush, of manuscripts authors have just turned in (August is a busy time, by the way), of proposals for new contracts. I could be writing articles for genre newsletters. Tomorrow I have a big meeting for which I'd like to be overprepared. More on that in a minute.

Usually, I have focus, but today I just want to stare into space. I can do that, right? No one will know. There is no child for me to chase around the apartment. No reason for me to get out of these pajamas. The idea is so satisfying, that I could lounge and stare without detection. But I do have my mother's voice in my head. She's telling me to make myself get dressed, become a whirlpool of productivity, crush those deadlines, go beyond my limits, create a new blog, impress my peers, work until midnight every night—be that sick workhorse who never ever buckles under pressure (like her).

But I'm not that girl. I don't need to be that girl. For twenty years, I've been a diligent worker who's given up many nights and weekends to her job. I have oodles of time yet to be a perfect worker, especially now that love is no longer a priority. I'm a free agent, delirious to not have a husband, a boyfriend, or, best of all, another bad date. I will just enjoy peace on this one little Wednesday.

Then I spy on my night table the next-best thing to having a social life: the books of Emily Giffin, which is how I meet the dastardly Darcy Rhone of *Something Blue,* the new heroine of my life, the voice I'd like to have in my head along with my mother's.

Darcy goes after what she wants and gets it. She lives by her impulses, ignores that she might upset people. If she sees a pretty scarf in the window, she buys it, using her ex's credit card. The words that come out of her mouth are cold, hard truths. No nice-nice from her, though she's easily the most fun person at a party . . . until she sleeps with the guy you're in love with. But that's not why I love Darcy. Her bratty princess attitude is refreshing to me. Having been a pushover my whole life, I'd love to be a brat for a while. Buy me that dress. Now. Get me that chocolate, like, yesterday, expletive.

In *Something Blue,* Darcy finds herself pregnant and, without other resources, goes to England to mooch off a friend. She winds up falling in love with her friend, who keeps showing her how there's more to her than her bitchiness. How does Emily redeem such a loathsome—yet somehow easy-to-love—character? Even though I love my virtuous characters, I treasure those flawed heroines who showcase a spectrum of traits. A little sass to go with the nice. I could learn a lot from her. No more wasting time on people who waste my time. The only obligation I have is to please myself. And torture myself just a little.

For the millionth time, I go over to my computer and stare at *his* e-mail:

> I saw Along Came Polly and it reminded me of you. By the way, your hair looks great!!—Superman

That was three weeks ago. Imagine, six months go by with nothing, and *poof,* the ex-boyfriend resurfaces, just as I predicted. And I'm still staring at the e-mail . . . because I must be bored.

At least Superman remembered my forty-first birthday and still checks my Facebook updates. Now that nearly a month has passed, I accept the fact that Superman wants to drop me a note, not get back together. I wouldn't even want to be with him. But why now?

And then that Sam guy friended me a couple days ago.

Crazy things have been happening to me for weeks now, ever since I made that birthday wish. Last week, I went on a surprise train excursion (sort of like what Darcy might do). I took an Ambien and, in my delirious haze, booked myself a trip out of town to visit friends—embarrassing, but not the worst thing I've done on Ambien (e-mailing subtle hints about my sex life to my father; writing haiku in the voice of Charlotte from *Sex and the City* and sending them to my longtime gay boyfriend Langdon, a bleached-blond radio personality in Los Angeles; and eating the contents of my refrigerator). The Ambien helped me press "Order Ticket." So I went, soaked up this leisurely visit, and returned home, revived. It was my Darcy moment of acting on impulse.

But impulse doesn't always pay the bills, so I edit throughout the day, taking Facebook breaks every half hour. By the afternoon, I feel spent, just in time to hear a *ding*. Someone is instant-messaging me. I wake up my computer.

> Sam: Hi!!!!
> Me: Hello to you too.
> Sam: Can I call you, Red?

Hmmmm. Can he call me "Red" or can he phone me? It's all about comma placement. This Sam person from Taft seems a little psycho. Why would he want to talk to me on the phone this early? We've been Facebook friends for only two days. Is he that drunk and desperate? He told me he lives in Israel—maybe if I lived five thousand miles from home, I would want to connect with all my friends, too. Poor guy. What would Darcy do?

> Me: It's a little soon in the relationship.
> Sam: But I'm in Israel. This is the land of aggression.

I laugh out loud. I don't know anything about Israel, just that there's some conflict with the Palestinians. I'm not sure what the conflict is, though. Very Darcy of me indeed. But this boy says all the right things. I find out he speaks French fluently, just like me. This Sam might not be gainfully employed; maybe he's writing a book.

People e-mail me all the time for publishing advice. I would do the same thing and I don't mind this. It's just nice to know up front. The bottom line is that I need more information since my memories of Sam come only from that bird's-eye view in high school.

> **Me: How about we talk this weekend? After I get to know you a little better.**
> **Sam: Okay!!!**

I get this happy feeling when I see all the exclamation points, the *okay*, like he's willing to wait until I feel comfortable. It makes me sad, too. Maybe he wants a friend. There's something sweet about waiting to talk to me. Sam might not be a pest after all. How could he bother me if he's living in Israel? It's possible he's sitting in his apartment, feeling the same sense of solitude. Because I'm now Darcy, I push thoughts of Sam out of my mind.

I remember that I have a meeting tomorrow with handsome middle-aged model/dating guru Tarken (this isn't his real name). For a second, I'm tempted to call the whole thing off, but I can't. This could be progress, and I need to do things differently if I want change. Though I work exclusively on romance novels, Harlequin has launched a new nonfiction line. I adore nonfiction and celebrities, so what better combination than a book written by a celebrity? Some of my alone time is spent perusing celebrity memoirs—Star Jones, the Kardashians, Jackie Chan, Joe Torre. You name it, I want to read it.

Tarken's work and profile immediately capture my attention. How to date more effectively, like the world doesn't have enough dating how-to books, but what's one more? Why am I the one reviewing this proposal? When I first thumb through his work, I see the guy I grew up dreaming I'd marry: white, gleaming teeth; one of those guys who rolls out of bed and is red-carpet ready, probably has his hair brushed by vestal virgins. It tickles my cockles that he wants *me* to buy his project. And the timing is strange.

With the teachings of Darcy Rhone in mind, I prepare for hours to meet Tarken the next day. Should I wear a pantsuit? No, that might be too formal. If I wear too-tight clothes, I'll look like an unprofessional tramp. My mother always dresses impeccably, and she taught me not to slouch when it comes to work events. I can hear her voice telling me, *He's just a guy. Do your job.* Maturity wins out as I select boring semiconservative attire—black pants, blue button-down, heels. This guy will appraise me based on what I'm wearing, so I go for bland. I need to be that forty-plus professional—except for the hair. For three hours, I straighten the long red mane into submission. It's what Darcy would want me to do.

The next day, my questions are ready, attire perfect, nails manicured. If this were ten years ago, I'd have stayed up the entire night playing out the scenario, concocting ways to be charming, like that romantic-comedy girl. Tarken would experience overpowering surprise at how beautiful I am. We'd start dating, because celebrities often date quiet editors.

This time, I don't lose a wink of sleep. I do, however, overprepare, research Tarken and the market of readers who might love his book. I'm the perfect editor for this project since I was that single girl looking for love. I've dated too much. I've made so many mistakes. If I'd had a stud model/dating expert at my elbow telling me how to play it, my life might have turned out differently. For the meeting, I write pages and pages of questions. This is very unlike Darcy, who would wing it.

Now it's time. I'm barely even nervous, just happy to have a new editorial experience. Maturity is a great tranquilizer.

I get that phone call from the receptionist saying my guests are here. When I go out and get that first look, for an instant, I feel that rush—a new person. Tarken comes over and gives me a hug. My shy wallflower self rejoices, mentally deeming him more beautiful in the flesh: dark eyes, rugged and tan, a movie-star smile. Then he hugs the receptionist and my colleague. The pheromones are flying in the office, which is hilarious to witness because, well, there aren't a whole lot of guys on our floor (though the ones we have are phenomenal gents). It's obvious to me that Tarken isn't remotely related to my Prince Charming. I mean, let's be serious. How nerve-wracking would that be? To play the part of his girlfriend, I'd have to share him with everyone. Plus, I'd need to pull my shit together—like all the time. No panic attacks, ever. No hanging out with grubby hair and pajamas. Can you imagine? We'd go to a restaurant and everyone would look at him, not me. I made that mistake with Superman. Plus, I'd have to wear a bikini, like everywhere! Even going out to dinner with Superman tried my patience, since waitstaff ogled him and ignored me. Plus, Tarken is the type who'd send back his steak three times—I can just tell. That would drive me nuts.

Honestly, I feel like I deserve a big hot-fudge sundae since, for once, I'm not eyeing someone as a future romantic partner. There are no insane dreams, no feeling that I could be happy with him. It wouldn't work.

I have no romantic prospects. None. And it feels pretty great.

We go toward the conference room. I'm just a woman walking

down the hall. Happy by herself, fine with the buzzing inner world she would rather keep to herself. I look back at Tarken, who's chatting up everyone around him like he was born in a litter of women.

The woman of Tarken's dreams is probably a more laid-back kind of girl. Like Darcy, she jumps on a plane to Fiji and laughs uproariously amid the rollicking waves. She gets trashed doing tequila shots, loves exotic shellfish, and glides down the street in skyscraper heels. Her leopard-spotted bikini—she has several—comes off at a moment's notice. When she tans on his yacht, she doesn't think about seasickness or the fact that out in the middle of the ocean, *there is no escape*. *Titanic* and *Jaws* didn't traumatize her one bit. Waxing is her middle name, too. In fact, female maintenance is a priority for her. She has fabulous eyebrows and eats lots of fresh vegetables, referring to them as "veggies." She might read one of the books I edit, but this is all we have in common—except I'd probably enjoy her company and adventuresome spirit.

I wouldn't even want to be Tarken's type. The idea of learning from him and his imaginary girlfriend excites me more. So here goes. I will soak up any new knowledge.

We talk for at least an hour—his entourage, my colleagues, back and forth with a lot of laughter. I forget to be nervous, which is to Tarken's credit. He is educated, too, which is a nice surprise, along with charming and funny. My neuroses drift under the crack of the closed door and I just smile. *You are not my future boyfriend. That's okay. I tried wearing a bikini once. Maybe I will again, but now I want my cheeseburgers.*

The meeting adjourns and I walk with the group toward the exit. My day goes by normally after this. I keep remembering the gist of his project, which is to put your best foot forward (and your boobs).

Even though I don't wind up working on the book, I keep the lessons with me.

Suddenly, it's the weekend. With nothing on my schedule, I am ecstatic to spend two and a half days alone. I will eat pancakes, watch television, knit, and edit. Doesn't this sound like heaven? No one will interrupt this schedule, and I'll return to work all refreshed and ready for another week. On Saturday morning, I crawl to the deli to get breakfast. Then I crawl back home to eat it. After movie #1 and pro-posal #1, I crawl back to the deli to get lunch; this time, though, I'm more conscious of the people spilling out of restaurants, couples in-dulging in a meal post–night of passion.

That's not me at all anymore. With my lunch, I go back to my apartment, ready for movie #2, then manuscript #1 to start editing. Maybe I'll clean my apartment, too.

What I won't do is think about where I was a year ago. Or two years ago. Or three. My situation is not uncommon. People are alone all the time. I go through periods of running home to my haven, feel-ing crazy joy that no one is intruding. But after twenty-four hours now of working and watching television, living within the four walls of my studio, interacting with my cat, maybe sending an e-mail or two, I retreat to that sad place, in front of my computer playing solitaire.

It's a bad sign when I pull up the solitaire. Definitely not Darcy Rhone behavior. She would throw on a sexy dress and find someone, anyone, and create a party. I don't know how to do this, where I could go. Within minutes of this repetitive game-playing, the tears flow. I cry for the missed opportunities, the sheer boredom, my father's dis-tant behavior, the fact that I gained ten pounds the second I moved into an elevator building, the sadness of having a knitting injury, the relationships I didn't want to end. Maybe there's lost potential somewhere. Why did I leave New Mexico? Maybe Chris wants me back. Someone might want me back. More tears spill down my cheeks. I feel pathetic, though I know that I'm not really sad. It's the drawback of spending *all* your time alone.

The sky outside turns gray, with light rain against my window. I turn to see it, interrupting my solitaire game for a moment.

What a miserable Saturday afternoon, I think.

Ding!

The sound of my computer calls me back. Brushing away my tears, I abandon my game and see the instant message:

Hi!!!!!! Red!?!!!?

Holy Jesus. This guy doesn't give up, does he? I start to laugh as more tears roll down my face. The lengths to which the universe will go to get me to stop playing solitaire.

"Hi, Brown!!!" I write back.

Can I call you now?

It's difficult to describe that feeling of gratitude. Someone's been waiting for me. He's not waiting for that girl standing next to me or the better buffet dish who comes after me, but me.

Why wouldn't I talk to Sam on the phone, if he's willing to call me?

Sure, okay.

I refuse to feel badly that I'm home on a Saturday night. This might be a stigma to other people, like Charlotte from *Sex and the*

City, but I'm okay with it. Sam and I are just going to talk. Considering my ability to converse with a celebrity stranger, I can talk to Sam. What would Darcy do? She'd absolutely pick up the phone.

I give him my number. My phone rings about thirty seconds later. "Hello?"

"Hi . . ."

"Sam. What a nice surprise."

We both laugh. I don't think we ever spoke more than a few sentences to each other during or after the dance. And now we're gabbing away as though we have twenty-six years to catch up on. What about our whole lives? I had no idea that he loved France, that we wrote our master's theses on the same French author (Zola), that he's been married and divorced, that he was a chubby kid and is now thin, that his mother died before he came to Taft. After high school, he went to graduate school and got his PhD at Columbia, wrote his dissertation on Proust. He was teaching at the University of Haifa, took some time off to go to law school, hated that, and is returning to academia, starting with a stint in Switzerland teaching high school for the fall semester. A wandering man, I think, definitely not the same route I chose.

As the content of our conversation lengthens and deepens, it's more the voice that turns me from a woman in mild distress to an attentive listener. I love how he speaks and what he says. There's some self-awareness in his narration and view of the world as slightly ridiculous.

The best part is that his voice makes me feel good on a rainy Saturday afternoon. Is this yet another soothing sign from way beyond? Someone to tell me I'm okay, that this route I'm taking is the right one? Sometimes a phone conversation is just a phone conversation.

I don't consider that my interaction with Sam will go further than this.

The funny part is that usually I avoid talking on the phone. It's not that I don't like people or can't maintain a conversation, it's just that I don't know what to say when I can't see my phone partner. My father is the same way. I can time our conversations to two minutes, tops, with the habitual how are you, I'm fine, what do you want to do, come up this weekend, okay, when should I pick you up, 11:55 A.M., done.

With Sam, though, I forget about that nervousness, the feeling that our conversation should end as soon as possible. I am relaxed in my chair, feet up on my desk, a smile on my face. There is nowhere I have to be. The phone—and instant messaging—is all we have right now. It's all we'll ever have. We are just two people who went to the same high school, having two very different experiences. And sometimes it's just nice to talk on the phone. Doesn't mean it will be a big romance. I'm not looking for that, remember?

By the time we hang up, about two hours later, it's dark outside, and I hear noise outside my window. The evening is starting for some people. My night is ending, and it's one I thought would end with me crying over computer solitaire for a few more hours.

I feel light. Happy. Talking to Sam gives me a boost.

It's an interesting turn of events. In just one week, so much happened. The Tarken meeting, the Sam friending on Facebook—ending with this one phone call. I won't wind up with Sam—how could I since he lives all over the place—but I like how these people keep popping up and giving me new lessons to learn.

I'm still on track, keeping to my own schedule, with this one little break to talk to an old friend. If I were Darcy Rhone, I'd jump on a plane to Israel, casually find myself in Haifa, close to Sam's place. But let's get real: It takes a village to get me to fly anywhere, and I've impulsively taken too many trips for romance. For now, I'll stick with the heroes on the page. For now, Sam is merely a friend who showed up unexpectedly on Facebook.

But then I get nervous when I don't hear from him. It must be because I sound like Marge Simpson. That's why he vanishes after our first phone call. There's no other explanation. My voice grates on the human ear. Or it could be that Sam has other things to do, like move from Israel to Switzerland.

No, it's totally my voice. But whatever.

At first, the dearth of Sam doesn't faze me. Since my expectations are low, my hopes for ecstatic love with the Popular Boy from High School are not dashed. I don't run for the king-size Snickers—just the regular size, and then I go for a run to stir up the endorphins.

We share a few e-mails after the call, but I can feel his interest waning. I try to lure him back with references to French personalities. I even start reading Proust just because he's a Proust scholar, but that's just stupid. I close the book on *Swann's Way* . . . and Sam.

For a boost, it seems only logical that I revisit the list I made right after my birthday, with that crazy wish. Now that I'm no longer dating, what can I say about my life? I read very carefully, soaking up each word:

If I died tomorrow, I'd be proud that . . .

1. My loved ones know I love them.
2. I enjoy my work.

3. I survived that.

4. I got to live in New Mexico and Paris.

5. I've loved with all my heart.

6. I've never made a really terrible decision.

7. I'm good.

8. I have seriously great hair if it's blown out right.

Do I wish I'd gotten married? I don't know. I've seen far too many bad marriages. Not many good ones. I can't regret something I haven't experienced, what I can't control. Maybe I wouldn't even be happy as a married person. Another human in my space might drive me bananas.

I can't waste any more time.

In restaurants and on the subway, I often hear women pine over lost love, why this guy did or didn't call. It gives me that bittersweet feeling since I've been that girl—I *love* that girl. She wants more from life. For me, "more" means less hassle. So when Sam doesn't call or e-mail me again, I go back to my reading, remembering that *those* books provide an entertaining escape, but, in real life, *romance doesn't exist.*

As the weeks go by, I am productive and find deep pleasure in helping with writers' careers. These stories come from talented people. I vow to work even harder and also spend more time with my mother and her academic friends. So, during my mini-depression, when Mom asks me over for one of her soirées, I accept. Being with loved ones is a good first step.

In addition, I start to think about the bigger direction of my life. I'm at that scary age when things start breaking down. Also, is there a next place for me to go, like California? Do I want to drift? Since my love life is over, I consider what I could do to fill up the empty space.

There's always the *Eat, Pray, Love* trip to shake up my world. I could go to an exotic place and accidentally get run over by a hot Hispanic importer who lives in Australia. But I have no vacation time left and don't like flying, so I can't do a world-opening voyage where I meditate, whittle toys for needy children, and live in a hut. But I could be courageous and try something different.

Waiting helps me the most. My circumstances are bound to change, so why not just chill? The answers will come, and, true to my name, I wait for them through most of September. I'm grateful for any push in a new direction—away from Sam and Tarken and toward whatever is next.

In those few weeks of wild thoughts, high highs, and medium lows, my mind keeps going back to Sam and why he contacted me. It could have been the start of an unusual friendship, but nothing happened. In a rash moment, rebelling against waiting, I reactivate all my dating profiles and sign up for nonrefundable months of romantic possibilities on Match, Chemistry, Nerve, and eHarmony. It is a half-hearted gesture, but I figure it's for my own good.

Despite this, I can't stop thinking about the phone call with Sam, how easy he was to talk to, the effect his voice had on me, how he made me feel safe. Why would this person appear on my path and then disappear? My years of romance reading tell me there's a reason, a big reason, but my brain tells me to dismiss him. *Don't even bother with Sam. You already wrote to him. He barely answered.*

Because I've ruled him out as Prince Charming, I am allowed to check his Facebook page on a daily basis. Sometimes twice. Okay, twenty times.

I notice that his Facebook status updates become increasingly morose:

It's all about money . . .
It's all frightening . . .

Why would he be blue? The man gets to see the world and speak French. He has the freedom to roam the earth however he wants. I can't read too much into it. But of course I do, and I wonder what would be so bad if I wrote to him again. It goes against all the dating rules. The more I think about it, the more frustration sets in. Maybe I'll make one last attempt at contact.

I don't have a thing to lose. If he blows me off, I will continue as before. One act won't make or break my nonrelationship with Sam. He won't leave me covered in pig's blood in a gym while I have my period.

After my big epiphany, I stay up late and think of ways to casually contact Sam. I channel my favorite Emily Giffin character and do as Darcy would do: meddle to get what I want, break the silence, have more fun. I'm an editor, so I can craft an e-mail and then rework it into effortless, cheerful correspondence.

The Moment reveals itself the next morning. During my scrolling of Facebook, I come across Sam's latest morose status update:

Again, it's really all too depressing.

This makes me chuckle. Good! I'm glad you're depressed, buddy boy. You deserve it. Especially since you blew me off. You should be depressed that you publicize your depression like that. What a lame bid for sympathy.

I make my move by pressing the "Like" button to his status update—having no idea that it will change my life forever.

Within minutes, I get a message from Sam:

You are a woman after my own heart!!!

I smile big. I'm sure this satisfaction is an everyday occurrence for Darcy, but for me, this small risk is a huge victory. Our courtship begins.

CHAPTER TEN

———◆◆◆◆———

Is This My Romance or One of Those Strange Friendships That Goes Nowhere?

September–December 2009

Modern love stories often start over a computer. Eons ago, they might have started over letters or introductions from friends. You could meet someone at a party, a worlds-colliding-in-one-night thing, and you or the other would pick up the thread, go out on real dates, which would expand into bigger dates.

These days, we're a bit lazier. If you just click your mouse, you can embark on a new journey with a new friend. There are more choices, and you don't even have to leave your desk. For a sloth-at-heart like me, this long-distance flirtation with Sam is perfect. Minimum risk for me (what else am I doing at night—*Real Housewives* with a cheeseburger and fries and a bag of knitting projects), maximum enjoyment because my level of investment is not as high as it used to be. In a logical manner, I've ticked through every possible scenario for my future with Sam, though his sudden appearance mystifies me. I'm not sure what's happening. All I know is that I feel good. Every night, I have somewhere to go. Sam is my new secret male friend, my confidant, my evening party.

This sounds like the beginning of an erotica novel, doesn't it?

It should be, except with Sam, it's pure romance. I discover early on that he's a gentleman, respectful of boundaries. He never asks me, "So what are you wearing . . . ," as a prelude to phone sex. We don't discuss *that*, though I feel chemistry from across the ocean. He says "please" and "thank you" and "I didn't mean to interrupt." He listens and doesn't vanish for no reason. We talk as strangers might over coffee. It feels like a romance novel with those butterflies, the expectation and fast-and-furious e-mails.

As my personal life—once again—becomes complicated, I know of one woman who would appreciate the glory of blossoming love: Marie Ferrarella, one of the authors I edit, who has written more than two hundred romance novels. Over the past ten years, I've spilled the beans about my boyfriends to Marie—because she asks, as would any good fairy godsister in a romance. She cajoles, lifts me up, gives me that one-liner that guides me forward. Each time I crash and burn, I write, "Oh well, it's not meant to be." She answers promptly that somewhere out there, my husband is waiting for me, most recently writing: *Somewhere in that throng of eight million people there has to be the kind of man you deserve who needs a good person in his life. If I could write you a happy life, I would in a heartbeat, but all I can do is light candles and pray. You are always in my thoughts. Love, Marie.*

See what I mean about the fairy-godsister thing? Her e-mails keep me smiling, and she signs each missive with *Love, Marie.*

Many years ago, like fifteen, when I first did research on romance, I saw Marie's name everywhere. In her photo, she was this blond bombshell with a bold stare and feathery hair. She looked right at you, could nail your character with a quick once-over. I heard she only wore high heels and short skirts. I kept picturing her as Ann-Margret and Doris Day mixed together, a woman who purred at her typewriter and loved socializing with the postal workers.

I even read a few of her books before I went to Harlequin, never thinking our paths would cross. At my first Romance Writers of America conference in Anaheim in 1998, I walked into the hotel and stood in the lobby, overwhelmed by the flood of romance writers. Imagine, two thousand women in one hotel, all pitching woo on paper, wanting to sell their books of love. As I scanned the area, I suddenly saw *her* across the way with a herd of Harlequin editors. So many people were paying homage to Marie, the essential romance writer who lived the part. She seemed happy and bewildered by all the attention. To me, it was like seeing royalty. I treasured that first glimpse of her until three years later, one of the executive editors came into my office, closed the door, and sat down.

"We'd like for you to take over working with Marie Ferrarella. We need this to happen right now," she said.

My hands started shaking, as if I would soon encounter a favorite celebrity, like Duran Duran or Julia Roberts. Are you kidding me? Of course I'd work with Marie. What was the catch?

"You have to be really organized."

"No problem."

"I mean, she writes *a lot*, but she's just lovely," the executive editor said.

"How much is a lot?"

It didn't matter to me how much. I had this covered. Organization was my thing. Hello, those French teachers didn't rap my knuckles for nothing in first and second grade.

"She writes a book a month," my colleague said.

Oh holy crapwagons, Marie was insane. "So we publish twelve books each year?"

"That's right."

I sat back in my chair, frightened yet giddy. Me, work with Marie? How lucky am I? Though I also knew that if she were writing a book a month and had done this for many years, she would stay on the treadmill at warp speed for eons. This is the drug of writing romance, and when you have the ingredients brewing in your head, you're going to get it down fast. She *needed* to write a book a month. Only one thing would stop her—the flu or death.

Then I talked with Marie on the phone for the first time. She was like that fun neighbor you want to see every day over coffee to gab about the latest goings-on, the type who brings you soup when you're sick, writes you many e-mails asking how you are, sends you gift after gift after gift for every possible holiday. She's all about chocolate on Christmas and Valentine's Day. For Easter, it's a nice chocolate egg with some kind of sugary filling. I was right; she is definitely that combination of Doris Day—chipper, saying all the right things—and Ann-Margret with her vavavavoom.

When Marie and I first started working together, I was in love with Russell Crowe and did Buddhist chanting so that I would marry him someday (Patrick said this would work). It's true. *The Insider* and *L.A. Confidential* had a visceral effect until he started seeing Meg Ryan, and then I turned away, out of respect for Meg. Marie fed my Hollywood crush, and within a couple of years, I owned most of his movies.

If Marie had a problem, she was apologetic about it. I edited her books with pleasure, though the pace of her work was dizzying. How does one ever keep up with Marie? How does Marie keep up with *herself*?

"Honey, I only need four hours of sleep. I don't have time for more. If I did, my family would starve and my husband would have no clothes."

Speaking of no clothes, her romances are the kind that readers keep devouring. Though each one is different, there are a few trends in her stories: the perky heroine, often blond, often positive about life (much like Marie). The heroes are gruff yet likeable. She makes her readers laugh out loud. She doesn't often veer from her pleasing romantic stories with babies, law enforcement, teachers, nights of passion, or doctors, but every now and then she'll insert a truly demented element—like a killer carving shapes into bodies or stealing a baby that is still in utero—that makes you wonder what lives in the mind of Marie.

In addition to being an author and fairy godsister, Marie could be a doctor. In the office, several of us consult Marie for diagnoses and treatment for our ailments. When I have a cold, flu, or injury, Marie sends me her recommendations for recovery, then a box of See's chocolate, a book, or a DVD. She counseled me on my insomnia issues, going over all the different drugs on the market. Marie was especially helpful getting me through the stomach flu of 2007, which she did from California.

It's hard to keep from considering her part of my family. She's written books using the names of my brother, me, and several editors in the office. It's kind of hilarious that I'm a heroine in a romance novel—a veterinarian—and that Marie has me hooking up with a hero named Brady. Same for my brother, Detective Patrick Cavanaugh (my real brother is gay, but obviously a hero can't be gay in a heterosexual romance), who winds up falling for Maggie, another cop.

At this very moment, as I'm conducting this strange relationship with Sam, Marie is writing a book featuring the romance-novel version of my mother, "Bonnie Gene," and "Donald Kelley" (their actual names). I've commissioned her to write a specific story and, for kicks, delivered character profiles of my family to use as secondary characters. The romance itself takes place between a sweet virginal heroine and gruff rancher. Marie is working away, then sends me this. . . .

To: Patience
From: Marie

What's new with you? Haven't heard from you in a while and it makes me nervous.

Love, Marie

I reassure her that I'm fine: *Just trying to keep up with you, Marie.* I get this kind of e-mail from Marie every few weeks. This time, I want to confide in her about this latest Sam situation, but it seems foolish. So I'm having a long-distance correspondence with someone from high school. It's a little sketchy on paper, no big deal.

Marie's stubborn insistence that I will find Mr. Right is hard to push aside. She is love's champion. If I were on a desert island, she would assure me that someone would arrive on a boat, wanting to marry me.

For now, though, I keep quiet. Maybe I need a little "Marie" adjustment in my attitude. This is the perfect opportunity to transform into a Marie heroine: cheerful, optimistic, brimming with humor. Maybe I'll wear those high heels and not act as if I'm on stilts. Instead, I'll enjoy how much fun it is to be taller. A Marie heroine lives in the moment. For now, I bask in the excitement of new e-mails from Sam.

I discover early on that Sam is vain, and about the strangest things, too, like the hair on his back or the mole on his nose, which I like. How could a daredevil such as Sam be obsessed with his appearance? He should be trying to jump over twenty barrels on a motorcycle. Of course, I have to tease him about this:

To: Sam
From: Patience

Thanks for calling! It brightened up a very dreary day.

Have a great week and a hairless back!

p.

To: Patience
From: Sam

Hi, I enjoyed our conversation too. So, you're amused by my male vanity? Last time I was here my great internal debate was whether to treat myself to more (back) hair removal or a sky diving lesson. I did the virile thing and jumped out of a plane. This time, I'm not so sure. . . .

To: Sam
From: Patience

Whatever you decide, I won't judge any more than I have already.

p.

I want to tell the whole world about how my stomach jumps every time I see an e-mail from Sam. I really do feel like a heroine, a little like Meg Ryan in *You've Got Mail*. But aren't we supposed to fall in love in a different way? We should meet on a random New York street or at a Taft alumni cocktail party. He'll remember me, come over to talk because I'm in heels and wearing an inappropriately short dress for a woman my age (I do that sometimes, just because). Romance ensues. Maybe not.

A relationship over a computer puts us in this stagnant fantasy place. I present my best self in every encounter, which is easy when you're separated by thousands of miles. He doesn't see me remove my makeup and get into my polar bear pajamas. In real life, I present that best self for an hour or two, with harsh truths slipping out—how I hate pickled beets and that's his favorite, that I'm not the most social person in the world, and is my eyeliner melting down my face? (Why, yes, it is.)

Sam knows so little about me, but over those hours of speaking on the phone, we cover a lot of ground. Even the questionable stuff leaks out eventually . . . and this creates even more cyber-intimacy. I know I'm in danger of becoming attached, more infatuated with this person on a screen. Now my romantic life is complicated again.

At least I have a challenging workload, with three books that need massive editing. This comes in addition to the sea of Marie. I'm grateful. And the end of the year offers those holiday parties, the presents to buy and relatives to see. It's good to be busy. My annual performance review will happen soon, and I have to prepare for this. Really, I can't mess around with this boy at all. And what are the chances he'll want more than a boozy, salacious week in New York with a crazy redhead? Pretty much none.

When I consider every romance novel and every movie, I understand that the romantic heroine hardly ever does the pragmatic thing. She goes back into the house where the serial killer is waiting for her. If the hero is a jerk, she doesn't walk away and ignore him. She confronts him, telling him he's a giant ass, and then he kisses her, because heroes secretly enjoy female rage. As much as I try to keep a tight rein on my love-struck heart, I run home in the hopes that he'll call at our usual time.

"So how about I move in with you and father your children?" Sam asks in one of our phone calls.

No man has ever said this to me before. I'll be all lighthearted like a Marie heroine.

"Sure, go ahead, Sam. I have room in my studio. As for kids, you might want to find someone younger." I'm half joking but want to get it out on the table in case he has wild fantasies about impregnating me. I've seen too many friends my age suffer through infertility. I'm a little ambivalent about having children.

"I'm sure we'll make it work."

While filled with humor and not entirely serious, this is how the rush of love begins from an ocean away—with long phone calls. It could be that we're easing our loneliness. What else does he have aside from this good girl willing to listen to him? The guy has left Israel to teach high schoolers in a remote part of Switzerland. How lonely must that be at night? I'm probably the closest thing he has to a girlfriend. And if he's taken, well, that would be cruel.

These kinds of what-ifs would have killed me ten years ago. I'd stew for ages, eventually sabotaging the entire thing. But now, I keep an open mind. Maybe yes, maybe no. As I walk down the halls at work, I wonder who would want to know about this latest budding love interest. We're not really a thing, but there's more going on than just casual friendship. He calls me every day and we talk for hours. That's not *nothing*. And you've gotta tell your girlfriends all the details, don't you?

Someone.

I can't tell my married, pregnant friend Rachel, whom I've known since diapers. We share a lot about our personal lives, but she has enough to think about, and this kind of nonsense is trivial. Mom and Patrick—no. I've used up my boyfriend coupons with them.

My friend Melissa is one of my best buddies in the office. She might like this story—or beginning of a story. I tend to tell her 95 percent of what I'm doing. The other 5 percent is too mundane, even for me. Melissa would describe herself as a nice Jewish girl from Brooklyn, and that's exactly what she is: friendly, fun, and single like me. She's got this gorgeous wavy brown hair, dark eyes, and that Snow White complexion many of us—mostly me—would kill for. We are both addicted to makeup and used to go out a lot more, but the older I've gotten, the lazier I've become about leaving my apartment. Melissa likes to do things. She's someone I could tell.

But I also don't know if it's important enough. Melissa has the huge job of managing many of our Christian books. I can't bother her with too much of this, the fact that I'm about to burst open . . . sort of. Maybe I won't make a big deal about it until it *is* a big deal.

Sooner than I expect, Sam and I talk seriously about visiting each other. It's only logical. When you talk to someone this much, shouldn't you follow through with a visit? On this issue, I don't budge. I won't fly to Switzerland. He has to come to me. Maybe in December when his semester is done and he has some time off. Should he get a hotel or are we grown-up enough to be in the same room for a few days—without losing (too much of) my virtue?

I go off the rails from my Marie Ferrarella romance and invite him to stay. I know this may be a terrible idea. But am I ready to meet him in person after so little time? Of course. Especially since I don't believe it's really happening, that we're slowly falling in love with each other over Skype. This will end with me crying over computer solitaire and Kim and Kourtney stuffing their faces with In-N-Out Burger while driving the Escalade to Kmart. Our special friendship could go to hell with one false move, one misunderstanding via e-mail, one lovely Swiss Miss who seduces him with her blond braids. Sam's glowing praise for me doesn't sink in, but why not follow this through to the end?

So now that we're talking visiting, maybe I should mention Sam to a few more people. With the gradual disintegration of my mental faculties (Buddha says we're always dying), I may have strayed from the sane path. People might be horrified by what I'm doing. Most of all, I don't want to bore anyone. But there's one person who wouldn't be bored by my latest romantic intrigue. I contact Nici, my BFF from Taft, the girl who turned me on to Harlequin romances in the first place. She's also responsible for my obsession with Duran Duran. She and I have kept in touch through the years, but not like we used to. She met her husband in college and married him in her twenties, and they went on to have three boys. Though we haven't seen each other in a while, she and I have one of those friendships that picks up where they leave off, though we mostly operate as if we're still in high school. I compose a careful message to her and detail this new friendship with Sam, how it's escalating into a relationship that will soon involve a visit. Within minutes, she answers:

To: Patience
From: Nici

PATIENCE!!! THIS IS SO ROMANTIC!

HOLY SHIT!

I hope you are savoring the giddiness . . . you should revel in it no matter where the story goes; joy and excitement are feelings worth dancing around in. And honey, you are so damn funny. I have the feeling he sits at his computer grinning like an idiot when he reads your messages. I have the feeling his heart pounds when he dials your number. I have the feeling he falls asleep thinking about seeing you, and thinking about how hard it is to wait.

I would gladly be a reference; he can contact me ANY time and I will sing your praises. What are the odds of this? I don't see how either of you could NOT be excited at the thought of finding each other!

As your friend who loves you a ridiculous amount, I am feeling great love for Sam right now, for being wise enough to recognize what a treasure you are, and for being brave enough to boldly speak his heart, and not let you slip away from him. I am a total sap, a hopeless romantic and wishing on every star I see that you both get a happily ever after. Never give up on that idea!

Love you to pieces. Nici

I know Nici is probably planning our wedding and I love her for it. She knew Sam as a good guy, reminded me of his putting his butt through a window and getting stitches. Plus, as I might have mentioned, she's the true romantic in my group of friends, much more than I could ever hope to be. Because I read so much romance, I don't have a clue what's truly romantic and what's nonsense. She nails it for me.

The best part about Nici's e-mail is that she remembers Sam clearly, verifies that he is, in fact, a worthy investment, even if it's just friendship. But I know deep down, this is much more than friendship. We don't define what's happening, like say, "Let's date," or "Let's be exclusive." I don't dare venture those questions again. For once, I just wait and see what will unfold. It could be nothing. It could be something great.

"Maybe we could see each other on camera, I mean over the computer," Sam suggests one night.

This sounds very porn-ish to me. It's absurd that I'm slowly turning into a prude. I just don't like to see naked people anymore. Maybe I need to up my omega-3 or go to Mama Gena's School of Womanly Arts. Webcam indeed. Just recently Peter Cook, Christie Brinkley's husband, was caught doing many dirty things over a webcam. Really, all this time alone has made me ninety years old. So what if he wants to exhibit body parts or see mine? I can end the video call if I feel uncomfortable. That's the best thing about long-distance.

The idea that he could be a perv doesn't stop me from immediately running to J & R to get my own webcam. It's late September, and I can already tell that the end of 2009 will be an interesting one. What a way to go into the holiday season, a mere six months after Superman's disappearance.

On the first night using the webcam, I go into the bathroom and fix myself up. White T-shirt, jeans, straight hair, lots of makeup. This is just like preparing for a date, though I don't feel sick to my stomach this time. It's not as if I want Sam to see what I really look like, with the blond eyelashes and my Casper the Friendly Ghost complexion. At the allotted time, I go over to the desk, test the camera, and wait for the call.

Finally, it comes, that exciting buzz and flicker of a screen. I'm going to experience a moving Sam, a body to go with the voice. I see black at first, then his room snaps into focus, technology in motion. His place is dark, though I see his familiar features exactly as I've imagined from his Facebook pictures. The nose, the expressive eyes, the short curly hair and wide smile.

"There she is!"

My insides vibrate with excitement over the connection. For several minutes, we just look at each other and laugh, like kids discovering a new toy. Can we talk and look at each other at the same time? Indeed we can. In fact, we don't stop talking for a good two hours, during which he takes his laptop into the bathroom while he pees.

Pees in front of me on our first webcam date.

I don't see body parts, but I hear the whizzing in stereo. At first I think, *He's doing it. He's peeing in front of me. I'm in a Bill Murray movie. Who does this?* Ewww. He's a little strange, but not enough for me to end the call. From my experience, guys cross into *that* territory often, and it fits with the Sam I knew in high school.

In fact, Sam's pea-size bladder doesn't stop me from taking a risk of my own. I decide to cancel all my dating profiles, even the paid ones, like Match, Chemistry, and eHarmony. I lose at least $200 because the enrollments are nonrefundable. I resign from these sites for myself. For Sam. Well, mostly for me. The relief is palpable.

I even break a girl rule and tell him what I've done. It's not pressure so much as a statement of my commitment. If he's scared off, then he's not the person for me, especially with his public urination. I don't expect him to suddenly declare his love, but this correspondence is a *thing*. It feels wrong for me to date other people. He shouldn't either, or, at least, I don't want to get my hopes up, invest all this time if he's going to date a mademoiselle on the bunny slopes of Switzerland. It seems important that I tell him as much, to let him know that I'm serious about us.

"In the interest of full disclosure, I had rejoined eHarmony, Match, and Chemistry a few weeks ago, when we weren't in touch," I confess.

I can see Sam react. He nods, the wheels turning in his mind. Will this girl be a cheater—after all this effort?

"But I canceled all of them," I add.

Sam smiles. "Did you get a refund?"

"No."

He becomes even more animated; his face gets closer to the screen. "How much did you lose?"

"About two hundred dollars. At least."

His eyes look glossy and he glances off to the side. His face changes and when he looks back, I notice his eyes are filled with tears.

"You gave up all that money for me . . ."

I start to laugh. Most guys would be horrified by this. And if Sam were a girl, he'd cry over my commitment to him. Sam is different. He is deeply moved by my financial sacrifice. Throwing away my precious dollars touched his heart.

I explain that it feels wrong for me to date other guys. I don't want to date period, but I'm willing to see what comes next. In between his peeing, we continue discussing our families, our checkered pasts, funny stuff in our daily lives. We don't delve too much into the serious issues, though I know it's only a matter of time. There's a reason why we're in our current situations.

There's a reason why this is moving fast.

Is it just loneliness or could there be something more? In a Marie Ferrarella book, there would be this special conflict, an obstacle that keeps us apart. Our big external obstacle is the distance, the lack of common ground aside from high school.

The easy resolution of internal conflict is why romance novels often don't seem real to me (probably why I love reading them). The heroine is an orphan but manages to conquer her abandonment issues to trust in the hero. All it takes is true love, and she's healed.

Perhaps the hero was beaten by his drunk father but, with the heroine's love, can accept her embrace.

From my experience, it doesn't work this way. Problems linger no matter how happy you are. Love helps, but it's a transient friend, ebbing and flowing. I can only rely on myself for those really awful moments. Plus, I have no idea anymore how to rely on someone every day. To me, everyone is in danger of leaving. Especially Sam.

While he brightens my day, I don't see happily ever after. So what is there left to lose? This is why we start telling each other everything.

He confides in me about his mother's death, how this affected his family. Sam grew up in Miami with two brothers, one who is seven years older and another who is severely disabled. Sam's father lives and breathes selling insurance. Sam's mother had been ill for years, which made the brothers fend for themselves in some ways. Though the father is a loving, warm man, raising three boys couldn't have been easy.

After high school, Sam did some college-hopping and wound up graduating from Columbia, with a focus on French literature. He met his wife at Columbia and they married in his late twenties, though he knew almost immediately that he'd done the wrong thing. I knew from the beginning that Sam was divorced and I didn't think much of it, especially since they didn't have children. In many ways, his experience sounds like a "starter" marriage, where the husband and wife get together young and learn how incompatible they are in their thirties. But I could tell Sam was a little shell-shocked by what he'd endured, getting his first teaching job in Israel with a new wife and experiencing a tumultuous downward spiral in his relationship. Toward the end of his marriage, living and teaching in Israel, Sam was waking up with thirteen cats and the knowledge that he had to extricate himself from a terrible situation.

After his divorce, he rushed into another engagement, and that went sour after a few years. He went from one volatile relationship to another, though I know deep down there's a reason why you go out with certain people. His exes must have provided some happiness, and they fit a pattern of sorts. I have my own patterns.

He pours out his heart to me, makes it seem effortless, as in he's done with his past. In some instances, I know he's still upset and confused, but he's the type who lands on his feet, survives, and maintains a sense of humor.

So what about me? What really messed me up? Why am I still single?

Uh, where do I start? It's the most moronic question, really. *I'm single because I'm a complete loser,* I want to say. It would be easy to blame my spinsterhood on my parents' divorce and their remarriages, but that was thirty years ago. People are just messy. I'm messy . . . and trying to avoid repeating my parents' mistakes. I had a lot of growing pains; so does everyone.

But since he's told me so much, I feel like it's time to relay the Big Story, the one I live with every day and in every relationship. It's no longer the most important part of my life, but it's always racing in my blood.

I begin, trying to keep it short, adult, no crying.

Sam listens attentively as I explain how everything might have been different if Jane and I hadn't ventured out for a drink one January night in 1991, a mere seven months after I graduated from college.

Jane and I had gone to school together, partied in the same circles, smoked Parliaments. People billed her as the next great theater director, and, after college, she wanted to put on a play in Cleveland, where I'd moved. Because I lived in the neighborhood, she asked for my help with her show. I hung around rehearsals, ran errands, and helped keep details on track. Most of all, I liked having her as my friend. She created fun wherever she went and this new city was lonely.

At about eleven P.M. that Monday night in January, while walking a block to a bar in the Flats—not the most populated or safe part of downtown Cleveland—a car pulled up to us. A man jumped out and pointed a gun at us, saying, "Get in the car."

For a moment, Jane and I looked at each other. Do we run? We weren't mind-readers and there was a gun on us, so we got in the car with one man driving, another with the gun pointed at us.

This is the end, I thought.

For the next ninety minutes, we made stops at ATM machines in order to drain my bank accounts. I punched in the numbers while a gun was in my back. They talked in Jamaican accents, played Prince's *Purple Rain* album—one of my favorites—and threatened to find our friends and kill them. At the end of our tour, they stopped in a remote neighborhood and raped us both. They then ordered us out of the car, and we ran, hiding behind cars in a remote parking lot. Eventually, we found a neighborhood bar and the bartender let us call 911.

The rest of 1991 was a blur before I moved to New Mexico. Jane and I spent half the year in court as witnesses, helping put the two men in jail. I won't say it was vindication, though it felt good to know they were behind bars.

There were bumps along the way. One judge rendered a shocking sentence that would release one rapist (whose charge of rape was dropped without our knowledge) early. This caused media contro-versy, to the point where he wound up staying in jail for a few more years.

Then in 2004, the district attorney's office found me and informed me that my rapist was up for parole. This resulted in crippling in-somnia that made me miss a lot of work at Harlequin. I was embar-rassed that I couldn't get out of bed. Every time I went outside, I felt this oppressive microscope bearing down on me. I wanted to crawl under the covers, so I did.

On the day of his parole hearing, a Monday in June, I couldn't stay home because I had used up my sick days. My good friend in human resources, another Sam, very kindly gave me the reality check I needed by suggesting I come to work or take some kind of "leave," which scared me into action. What would I tell my mother? That I couldn't sleep? Mothers don't sleep either. They should be the ones to get the days off, not me. So I hadn't slept in a few days, and no amount of medicine would knock me out. I had to go to work, even on this horrible day.

I dropped off to sleep at two A.M. to an episode of *Wings* but woke up at four A.M., stiff as a board. After several days of seclusion, I couldn't stay in my apartment anymore, so I showered and dressed. If I could get through the next twelve hours, I'd be home free.

At five thirty A.M., I crept to the subway and went to work, think-ing it might feel safer to be around people. The DA's office wouldn't find me. I didn't want to get that phone call at work, and I never check my cell phone. Maybe, before everyone arrived, I could sleep on the floor in my office. My legs shook all the way down to Harle-quin's office in the city hall area, though I hadn't eaten in a while either. I had turned into this fragile waif, all from a stupid phone call that might tell me *he* would be set free.

Once I reached the office, I closed the door and tried to sleep on the floor, feeling completely insane. Then again, I probably wasn't the craziest one in the room. My stress was understandable, too. How often did I have a meltdown? Not often, so this was okay.

The hours went by, dark turned to light, and my colleagues drifted in. By ten A.M., I sat in our editorial meeting, still shaking, feeling as if I might break in half. The doors closed, people started talking, and I did everything I could to pretend I was normal.

My friend and colleague Gail sat near me. She had been at Harlequin for eight years before I started. She is Rhoda, basically—funny, emotional, supportive, and a bright light. She's someone whose conversations you want to overhear because everything that comes out of her mouth is interesting and hysterical. We didn't talk all that often, but for some reason on this day, I pulled her aside after the meeting. We went to my office and I closed the door.

"Do you ever feel as if you're going completely crazy?"

She grabbed my hands—which she always does, and I love it; so does everyone—and reassured me. "Are you kidding? At least once a week. And whatever it is, it'll be fine. I promise. Don't worry, sweetie, okay?"

It's like a standard thing to say, but coming from Gail, it sounded like the wisdom of the ages and meant a lot to me. This was why I never felt too compelled to leave Harlequin. If you had periods where you were sick of romances, there were always the people who worked on those romances. I've met hordes of special people braving the romance deluge and life with me. We visit in one another's offices, congregate in the kitchen, constantly send e-mails to one another, check in through various other means. We read some of the same books, see shows, go out to restaurants, nod conspiratorially at conferences and meetings. Through any upheaval, my friends at work provide continuous friendship.

And Gail was right, as my colleagues are about most things. It *was* fine. I still have those crazy moments. I still get panic attacks and have difficulty sleeping. At night, without medication and fully under my subconscious's reign, I dream about intruders coming into my apartment, my car, pushing guns, knives, into my face, the whirring thoughts that only fear of further violation can unleash in my head. I've tried having tea with my imaginary assailants. Tried telling them I forgive them (I don't, really). Tried to understand the plight of the criminal. All I can say is, "Screw you." A few times, I've said this, but they still haunt me.

Both attackers wound up in jail for thirteen years. Getting this sentence involved many court appearances, letters to judges, parole boards, and media intervention. After the first few years, I didn't want to know anything more and stopped sending forwarding addresses to the parole board. Usually, though, someone would find me, and by 2004, I knew one or both of them would be released. They had to get out sometime. While I don't have trouble talking about this period of my life, the reality of it—like a phone call from Ohio—can cripple me for a few days.

It's no wonder I sought out the world of romance. These stories are a boost, no matter what mood I'm in, who I'm dating, and what my situation is. And over the years, some authors captured elements of my experience, what it feels like to move on after rape. Claudia Dain's *The Holding* and Justine Davis's *Clay Yeager's Redemption* made me cry buckets because their heroines learn to believe in love again after trauma.

As the words tumble out of my mouth, I feel stronger. There's that tiny part at the pit of my gut that wonders, *Will Sam find me too pathetic now?* I mean, this isn't the cheeriest topic. And it's not as if I haven't told this story a million times—in some instances to create intimacy that wasn't there in the first place—but telling it to Sam feels different. I don't need him to start crying for me. We don't have to keep talking about this either. In fact, maybe we should change the subject. But Sam does react in a way that feels right.

"Three thousand miles seems too far away right now."

He gives me a smile, the kind that doesn't quite come across a webcam, but I know he cares. It melts my heart. I feel thoroughly enveloped by his signature warmth. This is a good guy. We may not turn into a real couple, but I'm grateful to connect with another human being, no matter how far away. It's worth telling my ugly story.

We talk more about what happened and he asks questions. Eventually, Sam and I do move on from this unveiling, discuss the lighter side of things, his students, the Marie stories I'm always editing, along with managing the romantic suspense romances. He becomes part of my routine. If I don't hear from him, my day isn't the same.

But when he books an actual ticket to New York, arriving December 17, I suddenly realize: This is more serious than I thought. He's going to be here tomorrow. Maybe the next day, too. And the next.

He is planning to stay in New York—with me—for a week. Once the visit is over, he will go back to Switzerland or Miami and look for another teaching job. His crossroad fits perfectly into my schedule. And with my Harlequin hero taking all the risks, I have nothing to lose.

I bite the bullet and tell Marie about this new potential romance. I expect cheerfulness masking disapproval, since our story is a little . . . unconventional. Instead, I get vintage Marie approval: *Can I write your story?* she asks.

Sure, Marie.

Or maybe I'll write it.

PART III

Sometimes a wind comes up, blows you off course. You're not ready for it, but if you're lucky, you end up in a more interesting place than you'd planned.

—Nora Roberts, *The Calhouns: Suzanna and Megan*

CHAPTER ELEVEN

The Airport Scene

When it comes to romantic comedies, I'm firmly in the Julia Roberts camp. She's like sunshine on the screen. My brother and I see her movies together and for two hours, no natural disaster can stop us from worshipping the goddess.

But from the moment I see Sandra Bullock in *Speed*, in 1994, I think, *Oh God, that's actually me.* Only I'm red-haired and far less vocal.

I am melodramatic during a crisis (though I can drive through Manhattan with a panic attack). I spend a lot of time in my pajamas crying over failed relationships just as Sandra does in *Hope Floats* and *Practical Magic*. I'm so mortified by some of the situations I've been in—dating jerks, traveling through four states to visit jerks, spending thousands of dollars and oodles of time on jerks—that I resort to my jammies and bags of knitting. And as I age, this hermitage gets worse. In addition to being alone (which I like and hate), my body is breaking down. I complain about my joints, for goodness sakes. Does Julia do that? No. Sandra, yes. She may not say it, but she does a fabulous sulk.

I'm also the girl who, when wearing high heels, looks like a bear who's been kicked hard in the ass. And then I'll fall as Sandra does in *Miss Congeniality*. My heart gets broken easily, too, and I cry a lot over stupid things when I'm alone, like when the cupcake frosting is mushed when I take it out of the bag.

Julia cries at beautiful things, like opera with Richard Gere, when talking about Susan Sarandon's precious children in *Stepmom,* the stress of fighting injustice in *Erin Brockovich,* the paparazzi publishing naked pictures of her in *Notting Hill*. Sandra just bawls all day long over stupid men and the crappy hand fate has dealt her.

Julia is the woman you want to be. Sandra is the madcap woman you already are, which is why, I think, so many people love her.

As I converse with Sam over Skype, I try to exude as much Julia as I can, playing up the red hair, the glamorous makeup, optimum black turtlenecks and flattering T-shirts. Behind the scenes, I'm all over the place: Happy and calm because I just feel good. Grateful that this friendship is even happening. Scared of what might not happen. I think of where Sam will go after his one-week visit with me.

It's only natural that I'd turn to both Julia and Sandra during this time of questioning. I rerent *The Proposal,* that story where Sandra is a workaholic, has no social life, then makes her assistant fake-marry her so that she can stay in the country. Sandra plays a Canadian. I work for Canadians. We have so much in common.

The only difference between me and her is—well, a whole lot of things. But as it happens, I'm living in a romantic comedy. There's this interesting new friendship developing quickly. I feel those butterflies, as if a special event is taking place. With the butterflies come the obstacles, like distance and how unlikely it is that I'll trust another boyfriend. Like Sandra, I bury myself in work because it's solid ground. If everything goes to hell, I will at least go to the office and read these luscious romances. I've read love stories even through—especially through—the most devastating breakups. Separation of work and real-life love is easy for me. I have no delusion that my life will be a romance novel. How could it?

But maybe all that love stuff has sunk in too deep. I should be completely neurotic about the whole situation. Why am I not more freaked out? I just feel good every time I talk to Sam. I always have this sense that he will call again tomorrow, so I don't wait by the phone.

He's out in the middle of Switzerland by himself. When he leaves and the semester is done, he wants to start over, find a new school, get a teaching job. What will that look like? If anything, he needs me more than I need him. I've started over a few times. I know I can count on myself. He might disappear from my life, but I will retreat to movies, books, work, and family. No problem.

Maybe I have turned into Julia, after all.

Sam and I remain fast and furious on Skype, talking to each other every day. His ticket is booked, and I've mentioned to a few people what's going on—like Melissa at work, my mother, my brother, my friend Nici, Rachel, and Marie—but I am trying to keep the day-to-day excitement to myself. This whole idea is insane. What could possibly happen with this Skype relationship?

We know what Julia would do. She'd continue to sparkle and understand that the guy will appear.

But because I've been Sandra for so many years, I keep the lessons of her movies in mind. He may show up and it'll be great for a week before he goes for the Pamela Anderson lookalike on the sixth floor of my building. In an Ambien moment, I'll smear cat shit on the door and then hang out in my bathrobe with no recollection of what I did. Of course, Keanu Reeves will be the cop who comes to investigate me for vandalism and harassment.

As the days pass, I see new layers of Sam. He posts photos of himself skiing on Facebook. Because of his daredevil ways, I worry he may die on the slopes. Wouldn't that be perfect? The guy I'm falling in love with hits a tree, mere weeks before he's about to see me for the first time in twenty-six years. He assures me that for once in his life, he's opting to wear protective helmets. If there's anyone who needs one, it's Sam.

Since communication over Skype is far more satisfying, our e-mails are sparse.

To: Sam
From: Patience

I got a Snickers bar to celebrate the Full Moon, yeah, that's right. I'll only eat half and bury the other half in a plant. I guess that's a little Wicca-ish.

Happy hiking!

xoxoxop.

The part about burying the Snickers is not really true; I wouldn't do that unless I was feeling very into nature. Julia would give her chocolate to nature. I eat the entire Snickers and tell myself I'm going to hell, which is so Sandra.

To: Patience
From: Sam

Subject: Sending from my yahoo to your hotmail
Doldrums after hike. Was thinking of you on the way back down the mountain. The thought of Patience lifted my spirits. (Won't comment about the Snickers.)

This is a red flag—that Sam is a health junkie. I throw out hints about my rabid chocolate eating and he doesn't seem to share in the obsession. I worry that he's into eating seeds and might be a vegetarian. This is not a deal-breaker, but what a bummer for me since I love cheeseburgers. I've tried vegetarianism many, many times, but because I've been a runner since childhood, when my father took me to the track, I get weak when it's just tofu and vegetables.

To: Sam
From: Patience

It's my pleasure to lift you out of the doldrums. Serious about the Snickers.

As the weeks go by, there are feelings I don't dare express. *I want to date you in a normal way. I wish we lived in the same city. I'm falling in love with you over Skype.*

These feelings strike me as normal but ludicrous. I've been

through this before. *Not really.* I say nothing, though I remain cheerful. It's easy with Sam. He has no problem being effusive with his affection. He even teeters on the edge of "I love you" a few times, but I know it's too soon. I mean, we haven't even met yet. As scared as I am, or rather reserved, I do relay often how much his friendship means to me, no matter what it turns out to be.

During this fall courtship, I have one obstacle in addition to the three books I have to edit: a writers' conference in New Mexico. I accepted the invitation long before Sam appeared on the scene. I wanted to go because I adore Albuquerque and plan on spending my golden years there. Also in New Mexico is my dear friend and mentor Lou, whom I don't get to see much.

But I'm terrified, because what if I die in a plane crash? It would be the ideal ending in a story of unrequited love. Those winds flying into Albuquerque are a nightmare and, I'm sure, could bring down a jet. In the days before I have to fly, I am miserable, very Sandra, crying, cursing, wishing I could cancel due to some unforeseen illness, maybe a blood clot in my leg (not funny, I know). It's shameful because I'm forty-one and still fragile when I have to get on a plane. There has to be a way out.

There isn't. I have to do my job, go to the conference. If anything, the job reminds me to keep my sanity, not give up everything for a guy who may not pan out.

The night before my flight, I buy a card just for Sam and write a heartfelt message: *If I die, please know how much this correspondence has meant to me.*

I leave the card on my desk so that my mother will see it once I die and send it to Sam. I even triple the amount of postage so that it would get to Switzerland. A "good-bye and I love you" message for him, even though I haven't yet said *that* to him.

Funny thing: Once I get on the plane I am okay (with a tranquilizer and deep breathing), ready to give my best editor performance. After five hours of air travel, I arrive, put on my faux-leather skirt and aquamarine sweater, and do my conference thing. I give the occasional "weird" talk, as in think too deeply about what I want to say, as if suddenly conference-goers want to hear a more philosophical speech (they don't—they just want to know what you do and how to get published). My talk topic this time is how Facebook might be impeding the writing process. What the hell do I know about it? The more I say, the more I hear the crickets in the room. Big mistake. Huge.

Facebook is important for authors, as is Twitter. In fact, social media is vital for promoting books. Oh, hey, and am I not the one who wouldn't even have this relationship with Sam if it weren't for Facebook? I love Facebook. So why the brain freeze? Oh right, Albuquerque is five thousand feet above sea level. It's the altitude. Live and learn.

The flight home is uneventful, even with my usual impulse purchases in the airport, prayers to the Cosmic Goddess, and sudden yet quiet freak-outs 37,000 feet in the air. When I step on solid ground this time, I feel double the euphoria. I am home safe. I am going to meet Sam. Only fifty-two days left.

Then thirty.

Twenty-five.

With all the expectation, the building of momentum, the deepening of our relationship, this is turning into a real-life romance novel—minus Jake Hunter's millions and Protestant upbringing, and plus the eight years Sam spent in Israel shackled to his first wife. Romance-hero Jake wouldn't be caught dead in Israel. Maybe Afghanistan, and he'd single-handedly bring down the Taliban for all the crimes they commit against women (Cassie gets kidnapped by the Taliban, but nothing bad really happens to her). Sam and I are turning into a romance novel because we are leading up to a happy ending of some kind (though it could go terribly wrong, too). We're taking so much time to get to know each other, time I could have been soaking up the Kardashians and Housewives. If that's not love, I don't know what is.

As the big day draws closer, I blithely forget all my cynicism about romance—that it would never happen to me, that I wouldn't experience that swoon-inducing fairy tale. This whole experience couldn't be more real. With my last few boyfriends, I had the thought, *Well, this is wrong, but I can live with it.* With Sam, I feel no reservations, just free-floating excitement. I *want* to live with what I've seen so far. Of course, we could crash and burn. We both are riddled with problems, but at heart, we are solid people who care about each other.

Sam and I plan for every kind of disaster, too. I joke that he'll kill me in my sleep; he jokes that I'm secretly crazy. Even though we flirt like mad over Skype and talk half-seriously about our life together, we don't kid ourselves. This might blow up in our faces, and we reason that he can always return to Florida, Switzerland, or Israel to teach. I will continue to edit romance novels, and one more failed love story won't destroy me.

With sixteen days left, even with our guards up, Sam goes onto Facebook and posts a picture of himself holding what looks like an IV bottle with the caption: *Swiss saline solution sold in IV bottles saves me money on my contact lens care. The bottles make great canteens afterwards. I love Patience Smith.*

By this time, the "I love you" has been said a few times, though with the knowledge that we might hate each other on arrival. Sam said it first in mid-October, first by repeating the word *love* over and over in a sentence and finally just saying, "Sam loves Patience," in the third person, just like Julius Caesar. For me it took a couple more days, because I don't like to just throw it around, and there's still some afterburn from previous botched "I love you"s. But finally, without reservation, I just said it to him over the webcam, and now Sam has said it to everyone via Facebook. But it's an "I love you" with an asterisk. In the flesh, there could be boredom, ambivalence, revulsion, and "What was I thinking?" The worst for me would be an empty apartment, which is a speck on the timeline of life events. For Sam, it would mean figuring out where to go. He has no plans beyond getting another teaching gig or staying with his father in Miami at some point.

Family. Now, there's another issue.

For a couple of months, I've mentioned "my friend Sam from high school" to my mother and Patrick, not expecting them to hop on board this potential train wreck. I would slip him into conversation in the usual way, as one might bring up an acquaintance. Certainly there's no mentionitis, as in I have to bring up Sam or pine over him with my relatives. I've cried wolf far too often. But when Sam books his flight and our relationship escalates, I have to be frank with my family. There may be a new man in my life. This whole romance may sound strange, but here it is. My brother's reaction is his usual diplomatic one: He shows support without giving an opinion. The poor guy has endured my many breakups, endless phone calls with me whining. What are the chances that this could work out? Very slim.

Carlos, my brother's boyfriend, is another story. He hasn't heard my tales before, the desperate phone calls. This darling man loves a good romance. He's sassy and has strong opinions. His eyes light up when he hears the details of me and Sam, the progression of our relationship from e-mail to phone to Skype to visit. But he's ready with advice like, "If he takes advantage of you, you kick him to the curb," spoken in his thick Peruvian accent.

So Carlos has regularly asked me how things are going with Sam. Am I excited? Is he as cute now as he was in high school? He's even hotter, I answer. At least from what I see on the webcam.

My other gay best friend, Jose, who used to teach with me in Albuquerque, is also supportive and sends me uplifting e-mails, asking for details. In addition to the opportunity for salacious exhibitions via webcam, he's fascinated by my potentially becoming Jewish, like Charlotte from *Sex and the City*. I wish it worked this way since I've always loved the idea of having a religion. Jose continuously e-mails me positive messages. Did I show at least my breasts? Did we celebrate Yom Kippur via webcam?

I'll never tell.

As my mom and I get our manicure/pedicures, I drop in little details about Sam—that he's an academic, a Francophile, a bon vivant—but she doesn't really seem to be paying attention. She's listening though not that interested. He could be another Barry the Teacher, Superman the Finance Guy, Nathan the Spanker.

"I've invested too much. I can't go through it again," she says. Losing a potential son-in-law has got to be painful, especially since she bought Barry the Teacher a very expensive tie from Barneys a few months before he broke up with me. Investing in Sam is not an option right now.

But then she calls me one Friday night in November, breathless.

"I was talking with Nancy . . . from the College Board . . . and [wheeze] *she knows Sam*! I told her my daughter has this friend who's coming to visit. He teaches French. 'Do you know him?' I asked her."

It turns out Nancy does know Sam from their days at Columbia and reassured my mother that he is a "great guy."

How random is that?

Mom is now invested in an academic potential future son-in-law. In my book, Nancy is another one of those angels. She appeared at the right time and gave my mother the assurance I couldn't have provided.

After this, my mother Googles Dr. Sam like crazy, analyzes his scholarship, sees that Sam's got potential in his field as a Proust scholar, had a rough time in his marriage, dropped out of the circuit for a while to hide and start over, and now he's ready to re-enter life.

In addition to Nici, my work BFF Melissa and childhood friend Rachel show interest in my budding romance. Suddenly, there is a whole army behind me. They want to know what happens next. How long did we talk last night? Boxers or briefs? Is he still a daredevil? After so much time on Skype, will we have the same chemistry in person? What if Sam moves in and does nothing? What if he takes advantage of me? What if it's just a fling that goes nowhere? What if he's a big lush and wants to rappel down buildings just for fun?

What if, indeed.

These are all questions I've thought myself—often. I'm not a moron. If Sam wants to steal my fortune, he's foolish since there's not much to take. If there are evil ulterior motives, so be it. I have nothing to lose. I'm not looking for marriage or babies. Bad things have already made their mark on me. He couldn't do much damage, and if he did, I'd pick myself up.

I'm not expecting miracles, but it's more fun if you can share these exciting moments. My friends are mostly with me. Except for Patrick. Though not unsupportive, he's cautious, and I don't blame him. We have a complicated relationship—95 percent loving siblings, 5 percent childhood ick. We've risen above the ick, to the point where as my father exited from his paternal role, Patrick took over.

He's the one who advises me on the big issues, the proud parent when I do something great. I want his approval more and more over the years. All this time, Patrick has been the most important man in my life. It should have been my father taking some of the slack, giving me those pep talks through my twenties and thirties—like *you're doing fine, maybe I'll come see you in the city, what are your friends like?* Patrick always took that time with me. Now I just hope he'll give his blessing on this last journey because, surely, I can't go through this emotional ordeal with anyone else ever again.

It's true love with Sam or single girl forever.

It's Wednesday, the day before I go to meet Sam at the airport. He arrives on Thursday night at eleven P.M. and I'm taking the A train to meet him at JFK. My boss approved my taking Friday and Monday off. Normally, I'd take this kind of exciting day off to have a nervous breakdown, but this time I don't. It doesn't seem fair to stay home again since I work from home on Wednesdays. What am I going to do all day on Thursday—watch romantic comedies, practice talking in the mirror, and get my nails done? No, I'm an adult. I can talk into the mirror after-hours. For now, I need a distraction, the romances on the page that pay my bills.

On Wednesday, I do my usual waking up late. There must be

some homing device planted on me since I get a phone call from Lesley, one of my regular Resurfacers. It's a rule that the minute you're "taken," you'll get a rash of signs asking, "Are you sure about this?"

Something is up with him, otherwise why would he call me? He knows all about Sam, that in a day I'll be cohabitating with this person for at least a week (or maybe permanently). Soon, Lesley won't be invited into the apartment anymore. We haven't fooled around in years so that isn't an issue. But is it improper for me to be friends with him?

From our talks, I get the feeling Sam doesn't like my friendships with men. Some seem to threaten him—like Lesley and Superman, both of whom keep in touch with me. But I'm so far beyond my exes, and, damn it, Lesley and I have been friends for eight years. Can't I even talk to him if I want to? Sam and I aren't married. We haven't even seen each other in person! No guilt.

Lesley and I go to the nearest coffee shop, where he tells me about the latest book that he's writing. Ah, there's the rub. He's almost done with it, this seven-hundred-page masterpiece. I'm a single girl with nothing better to do than grant him a massive favor. I usually don't mind when people give me stuff to read. It's my job, my passion. But when I notice the bizarre timing, I get apprehensive. I can smell a request, and I steer the conversation toward Sam and my monogamy. It gets steered back to making his book into a movie, and wouldn't it be cool if we could write a screenplay together?

It might be a cerebral hemorrhage that prompts me to invite Lesley to my apartment on Wednesday, to hang out, not do anything improper, but to look at photos, talk more about Sam. I have this feeling that inviting him over might be the wrong thing to do the day before Sam is due to arrive.

So, when Sam calls the night before he's about to leave, I'm both excited to see him and burdened with my faux pas. Our big moment is twenty-four hours away. He asks me about my day, and I'm terrible at keeping secrets.

"Lesley came over to talk about his new book. And then I did some editing, and then I went to the gym. . . ." Cover up the big event with minutiae. This shows how inconsequential Lesley's visit was. But I notice Sam is upset.

"You had your ex-boyfriend over the day before I come see you . . . ?"

"He's not an ex-*boyfriend*. Nothing's going on. He just came over. It's been platonic for years."

"Don't you think that's crazy?"

Oh God, of course it is. I can see Sam wilting on the other side of the webcam. Did I just screw this up majorly? He has to know that his visit is the only thing I've looked forward to in years. Years. Not since I got to see all five original members of Duran Duran onstage at Madison Square Garden in 2005—a miraculous event. Meeting Sam is a miraculous event.

"I'm sorry." I don't know what else to say. "It was the wrong thing to do. Please, I hope you'll still come tomorrow."

The conversation is awkward and by the end, I wonder if he'll even show. I don't see how he wouldn't. We've said "I love you" so many times. He's not exactly perfect, and neither am I. Relationships are complicated, aren't they? All this and I'm not even into Lesley. We have a long history, but we both acknowledge that the spark is long gone. I want Sam.

After this conversation, I get angry. If Sam doesn't show, then he's a jerk and not worth my time. I made a stupid decision—I will make many in the future—but the lesson is that I'm, occasionally, dumb as rocks and too eager to please. When friends call me asking for things, even less-than-altruistic friends, I tend to get sucked in over and over. That's probably the worst Sam will encounter, those dumbass choices that don't move me forward. If he's threatened by a guy I barely had relations with, then it's not really about me.

I try to calm myself down, rationalize my fears, and sleep. But the truth is, I'm kind of a mess.

"Are you excited?" my friend Melissa asks in the office the next day. She's all smiles, hugging me. By now, she's firmly on Team Sam. Sure, she's seen the Facebook pictures of him, knows every piece of our correspondence.

Overnight, Sam seems to have forgiven me about Lesley. Maybe when he arrives, he'll be convinced I want him and no one else.

"Yeah." It's hard to articulate how I feel. It's like this happy glow inside. This is what the romance novels show at the end of the book. These books leave readers with that glow. I feel the glow.

It's the kind of glow that doesn't feel strange or weird or misguided or red-flaggy. Just a glow. Yes, I'm still nervous as hell, but I know I'm moving in the right direction, no matter what happens. There should be a movie camera on me. Seriously, my poise is commendable. You should always go to work before a big event. The distraction alone is worth it.

I'm not sure how, but I go about my day in a normal manner even though this is not a normal day. I edit part of a book, give my assistant odds and ends, choke down yogurt for lunch (I can barely eat), and go to my editorial meeting.

During the meeting, we discuss books we've bought, and publishing and company news. At the end, we go around the room and mention something good that's happened. I usually try to be funny because otherwise I feel awkward. But this time when it's my turn, I say, "I'm about to see an old friend after twenty-six years and we're going to cohabitate."

I know, crazy to spew like this to my colleagues. Everyone kind of knows the story, and I don't share that much about my personal life except in bursts at staff lunches or holiday parties or in moments of sheer paranoia. Melissa and my HR friend Sam know just about everything, though. Overall, my colleagues are happy for me, rooting for this to work, even though deep down, they may think I'm insane. It's like having an office of mama bears secretly pulling for your happiness.

After work, I dash home for my five hours of primping. I'm taking a few days off, and it's close to the holidays, so no one is around anyway. It's time for me to meet Sam.

My phone rings. Mom.

"We need a mani/pedi before your big meeting, don't you think?" Mom says.

She's the best. Suddenly, she's so excited for his arrival. We sit in the salon downstairs from my apartment building. I can tell she wants to be a fly on the wall. In some ways she is.

"So, maybe you and Sam would like to come over for a cappuccino tomorrow morning. Would you like that? Think about it," she says, with the eyebrow raise.

Sure, Mom. Sam and I are going to spend our first night together, then come see you for a cappuccino in the morning. Oddly enough, Sam would enjoy this twisted offer. He's the type who can walk into a roomful of strangers and convince someone to wrestle him in a pool of mud.

With my nails red as sin, I'm alone for a while. My clothes are laid out: dark jeans, white sweater. I washed and straightened my hair and now have about two hours to kill.

The only thing that could calm me down is a movie. Something appropriate—not *Citizen Kane*—but something not completely awful, either. I can't watch a Julia movie because in my quest to be Julia, I've memorized every line of her movies.

This time, I need Sandra. I will honor those years I've spent in my bathrobe, whimpering about lost love. Also the girl who's started over a million times with a new person. I'm a bit repressed on the outside, but in my sweet little cave, I'm all emotion. I want to be accessible, that girl who doesn't need to be perfect. Sam will see the real me since I can only pull off perfection for an hour or two.

I go through my collection of DVDs and pull out *The Lake House*, a gift from Marie. I remember that I paid actual money to see it in a theater. What did I expect, the fireworks of *Speed*? No, but Keanu and Sandra are golden together on-screen. So much gorgeous brunette in one frame; they just fit.

I pop in the DVD and the waterworks begin immediately, and thank goodness I have ample mascara and Pond's cold cream to help apply and reapply my makeup. Sandy (I can call her that, can't I, since we're imaginary best friends?) doesn't smile through most of the movie. For some reason, she and Keanu connect over the bridge of time and write these highly literate letters to each other. They present their best selves on paper while toiling through their mundane real lives. Sandy is a doctor who feels too much. Keanu works construction but is an architect, too. His father, Christopher Plummer, is a block of ice and eventually dies, which makes Keanu sad. Sandy comforts him. They discover, too, that they did meet earlier, though this seems like a contrivance. How would you ever forget kissing Keanu or trying to save his life? If you see Keanu, you remember him for always.

But the Paul McCartney song "This Never Happened Before" and that last kiss have me blubbering like never before. The movie mirrors a lot of what Sam and I have gone through over the past four months, and it captures my mood. By the last scene, I'm a howling mess because Sandy is finally happy. She's not wearing a bathrobe anymore—just an awesome red coat that stands out in the tall, dry grass. Keanu practically mauls her because he's waited for her for so long.

This is the big last scene of *my* movie. I can't believe it. The moment I've waited for my entire life. Not my wedding. Not having babies or owning property but the deep sense that *this is it*. My heart belongs to Sam. Finally, I get to see my Prince Charming.

I'm on my way, my brother texts me half an hour later once I've cleaned myself up. I'd planned on taking a train to JFK, but Patrick, surprisingly, offered to drive me.

Usually when I have a huge event, I am nervous, like sick nervous, want-to-stay-home nervous, sometimes cancel-at-the-last-minute nervous, or I just suffer while trying to remain present. Unlike those other times, I feel great, ready to meet my destiny. It's easy for me to leave my apartment and rush outside.

Patrick swings by somewhere around nine thirty P.M. He's smiling, that hesitation in him gone. This feels right, like the father driving his kid to a date, giving me away.

He doesn't give me fatherly advice. We don't cry over the fatefulness of this whole experience. He just drives, plays music, and distracts me. Again, the future isn't here yet. He could be driving me to meet a friend with whom I'll connect and then go back to my old life.

"Have fun! Let me know what happens!"

"I will! Wish me luck!"

"It'll be great. And if he hurts you, I'll cut him," he says before dropping me off at the terminal and air-kissing me on the cheeks.

My brother is not the type to drive people to the airport in New York City. Public transportation is just too efficient. He's super busy and doesn't have time for this. It's a big deal to me that he would go out of his way for me on this potentially strange night. Patrick has been there through many important moments, especially the bad relationships. He's listened patiently to repetitive tirades with me asking, "Do you think he likes me?" He's met a parade of fools, even sort of liked a few of them. He's taken me out when I've felt poorly. He's let me off the hook when he shouldn't have since he has a life, too. He's told me point-blank when he's been worried about me. Also, like a parent, he's trusted me to figure out my own problems and met me at the other end of hell.

My beloved brother—that quiet yet expressive boy who put on plays for the entire neighborhood—grew into a strong man. At the end of my life, I can see us hanging out in our walkers at the same nursing home. I'm lucky in so many ways.

And now it's my turn to chase a dream.

JFK is a funny place past eleven P.M. There isn't as much frenetic activity, but people are still traveling, navigating jet lag and the jarring nature of country-hopping. I wait by the walkway, gasping as groups of people exit, searching for loved ones or the bathrooms. Sam could be anywhere. He has to go through customs first, which takes a long time. I brought a book with me, *Eat, Pray, Love*, but can't read a single word. Instead, I text my brother over and over again: *Not here yet.*

I have "This Never Happened Before," that Paul McCartney song, in my head. This kind of romance hasn't happened to me before, for sure. I have gone on many, many dates, but rushing to the airport to meet someone who feels this right—never.

Eleven thirty passes. Even eleven forty-five.

The crowd thins even more. Not so many travelers coming through the terminal anymore. He might have missed his connection in London. I'm sure his flight has already arrived. In fact, I know it has. Maybe something happened on the way. He got stopped at customs—one more obstacle for us.

After twenty-six years, it may not happen. I've long since forgotten the fact that Sam and I never knew each other in high school. There was one dance and that picture we took together. We discussed those memories, though they feel distant, like amusing artifacts we have in common. What's happening now is more colorful. The stakes feel high. I should be more nervous since I might be going home alone in my Skyline car.

Suddenly, I see one lone guy in the distance, apart from the other travelers. He's wearing a striped sweater that I recognize. The short curly hair from the webcam sessions. The olive skin, thin physique. He's coming closer and I know it's him.

He sees me, smiles.

There is no rush into my arms. No songs playing in my head or quickening of my heart.

In fact, it's very strange.

"Hey," I say.

"Hey," he says before we hug. And not that crushing hug one might expect between a couple separated by an ocean for four long, excruciating months. This isn't the Keanu-Sandra moment at the end of *The Lake House*. There's no kiss. Maybe it doesn't feel natural since, well, we don't know each other in the flesh.

"Wow," he says. "You're three-dimensional."

I smile appropriately, noticing how dazed he looks. On the web-cam, he came alive, smiled, spoke animatedly, and provoked me. JFK-Sam-in-the-flesh is reserved, maybe tired. He just traveled for the past fourteen hours. Perfectly normal.

"Do you need to use the restroom before we go to the car?" I ask. So romantic.

"Yeah." He goes to the men's room and I wait on one of the seats. Talk about anticlimactic. But God, I feel so much. I'm a WASP, which means I have forty years of buried feelings. My ulcer will reopen. Or a stroke, right here in JFK.

Sam is so handsome in person. It's possible that I was just a dis-traction to get him through those last few months in Switzerland. Or that he just needs a place to stay before he goes to Florida. If I think about it too much, I'll start crying. Four months of contact, and I'm a basket case. The truth is that he may not feel the same way. The whole Lesley thing messed us up. He's probably overwhelmed by it all and just wants to go home. This is the problem with believing in romance. Reality is so disappointing. At least I only wasted four months. Now to figure out how to get through the next week with Sam.

I should play it cool, act like a good hostess who just wants to have fun in her old age. It should be high on my radar that he could spill the beans to people at Taft—not that I'm in close touch with anyone, but I don't want to have a reputation. I'm paranoid. Note to self: Be like Mom, who always makes the best out of uncomfortable situa-tions.

As he emerges from the bathroom, we continue to stare at each other as if we're both from outer space. He really is better-looking in person. Like I could hug him again. All those hours of talking and talking into the night. Now he's here. This will be a painful week because he is just that cute.

"Let's go to the car," I say. Since he's barely touched me and definitely didn't kiss me, it's obvious he's not attracted to me. Not everyone is. This was a giant miscalculation but not fatal.

We get into the big car and our driver commands our ship speedily across the streets. It's wintry and damp, though no snow yet. The weekend is supposed to get a downpour and I already warned Sam to bring a winter coat, as if he wasn't coming from Switzerland.

The car takes us over the highway on the smoothest ride ever through late-night New York. I wonder what the hell is happening. Who is this stranger with me in the car? I know so much about him, but he seems almost bashful. It's obvious that he doesn't like me *that* way, I just know he doesn't.

But one gesture can change everything. Sam moves in closer to me, puts his hand on my leg, his head on my shoulder. Now I *know* he likes me. It's a slice of webcam Sam. The leg touch is a dead give-away, and those butterflies are stirring inside me again, along with relief. He likes me. The conversation may be slow to start, but I imagine he's exhausted so I stay quiet and don't force it. He's coming home with me. Hand still on my leg.

The car sets us in front of the building in Chelsea. I help him with his giant suitcases and backpack. We go to the elevator and take it to the sixth floor. We smile at each other, discuss his long trip quietly. It's close to one in the morning.

He's not so talkative, very different from Webcam Sam, even Taft Sam.

I take out the key and open the door to the apartment. It's pitch-black and I'm tempted not to turn on the light, just like in a sexy thriller. But I'm a reasonable person. The cat must be hiding behind the couch now that he hears this strange noise, this new presence.

"You said you had a one-bedroom," Sam comments, smiling and joking just like he did on the webcam, as he wheels in his luggage. "You lied to me."

"I did not."

He's smiling, fidgeting with himself; he doesn't know quite what to do. This is my Keanu-Sandra moment, so after four long months of talking to him, never touching him, I go over and kiss him.

A romantic heroine usually doesn't initiate the kiss, but again, I have nothing to lose. And in personal encounters, I have this sense that my boy is shy. In romance, that first kiss causes fireworks and waves of ecstasy that make the heroine's womb contract. I don't experience those exact sensations, but the second I kiss (maul) Sam, I know I want more, to the point where I practically lock him in my apartment from the outside so he can't leave. What about those dating rules I'm supposed to obey? I'll admit to a little amnesia. If I have to ruin a relationship, I'll have as much fun as possible first.

CHAPTER TWELVE

———— ◆ ◆ ◆ ————

Eat, Pray, Move in on the First Date

Romance novels contain juicy conflict on every page. The hero and heroine take a break from the angst to have sex or eat a meal (usually a "garden salad," protein, "crusty bread," and lots of iced tea—who knew? No veganism because that's too fussy. Sadly, the heroine will go for the apple instead of cake—and sometimes we have to hate her). After these happy commercials, the characters grapple with their mommy or daddy issues, lost love, feelings of inferiority, family trauma—basically, all those humanizing things.

Most of the conflict Sam and I have is the usual stuff, like are we too screwed up, and will this end? I don't want it to, it doesn't feel temporary, but, of course, I worry. And because I can't lose such a divine catch, I vow to look gorgeous at all times—put on my face, wear flattering clothes, and—gasp—straighten my hair, a process that takes hours. This goes out the window fast thanks to my studio apartment. He sees the raccoon eyes when I emerge from the shower. I see a snoring corpse when he sleeps with his mouth wide-open. We can't hide.

I take a break from reading so much romance and delve into two happy-making books: *Eat, Pray, Love* by Elizabeth Gilbert and *The*

Happiness Project by Gretchen Rubin. I started Gilbert's book earlier but never got around to finishing. Now I'm devouring every word and feeling inspired. The same with the Rubin. For the most part, they both urge readers to chill out and follow the bliss.

Speaking of bliss, I normally wouldn't recommend moving in on the first date. My circumstances with Sam are unique, so I let many rules slide. After several days, I'm fairly sure that he's staying with me indefinitely. Though he has numerous couches where he can crash, I want him on *my* couch.

Our exit strategy is such that he can disappear at the first sign of trouble. He's a popular guy, can find friends even in remote areas of the globe. I have no doubt he's the type who loves being with others. Will he adore living with me, snuggling while watching TV, cooking dinner, doing laundry together, and taking walks around the neighborhood? Sam isn't a hermit like me and enjoys the company of others. I seem to have the opposite problem of so many—I'm used to being by myself. The adjustment is huge, for both of us.

I love living alone and have avoided the roommate situation. No one is snoring or having sex in the next room, there's no coordination of bills, no one fights over whose food is in the fridge or the messy toilet issues. At my age, I'm petrified to live with a man. My father and brother were neat, took care of their hygiene, but plenty of people are slobs behind closed doors (like me). I've lived alone for so long that the odds aren't good that this will work.

Our first night and day have gone swimmingly. We're happy to see each other, and, like most nauseating couples, we have to show how fabulous we are together. Should we go have a cappuccino at Mom's? Of course, Sam insists. Meeting the parents on day number two would have given my past boyfriends hives. Not Sam.

We trudge over five whole blocks to Horatio Street in the West Village. Here we go—this could end everything. I've introduced Sam to my entire family via pictures and anecdotes, so he knows what's coming. We walk down the hall and open the apartment door to an airy, light room.

"Why, hello, Sam. Nice to meet you," Mom says in her unique way. She's incredibly charming from the first second and makes him a frothy cappuccino.

I keep hoping Sam will fall under her spell, because he hasn't had a mother for a good thirty years, and my mother is game to expand her brood.

Then Sam and my stepfather lock eyes. Yes, *that* stepfather, the curmudgeon who barks at dogs and people, loves his mysteries, and is stubborn. Time stands still as my new roommate goes to shake the hand of this befuddling intellectual historian. My stepfather doesn't smile often, but this time he does. Maybe it's the love he sees in Sam's eyes or that Sam actually engages him in conversation. In fact, Sam hangs on Don's every word and the connection builds from there.

It's a little twisted, this man-love. I almost start laughing outright at the strange hetero mating dance between men. Sam keeps watching my stepfather as if he's a *Sports Illustrated* model, a beguiling creature you don't quite get but want to keep looking at. Sure, the man is a genius, but he's also a giant grumpus. What's the appeal?

"You don't understand. He just draws you in," Sam says as we walk home.

"You're in love with him."

"I've finally met the right person," Sam says.

I'm fairly sure at this point that Sam is a little deranged, but I can handle this. We return to our domesticity.

———

The most mystifying habit I notice right away is that Sam doesn't eat. The first few days, we hang out on the couch. I swallow my penchant for bad television and read alongside him. This will be good for me. No more crappy reality TV. But then I pull out my bag of M&M's and offer him some.

"No, I don't have much of a sweet tooth," he says.

Uh, yeah, me too. I feel deep shame over my sugar addiction. How in the hell am I going to order pancakes every Sunday? Scarf that ice cream at eleven P.M. right before I go to bed? Perhaps I could restrict my junk-food habit to the afternoons—like secretly, when he's not around. What would Elizabeth Gilbert say to this? I can't be on a starvation diet. I'm a girl. I've tried this before and it never works.

The hours go by on that first weekend. Mealtimes pass. Sam sits all skinny on the couch, reading smart books. No *People* magazine for him, so I hide mine behind the bookshelf. He can't even tell the difference between Julia Roberts and Sandra Bullock, for God's sake. The man wasn't in this country for the *Sex and the City* craze either, which leaves us with little in common. Well, I can fix that. I put on the first episode of the first season. But the minute he hears that music, sees Sarah Jessica Parker in a tutu, his face is awash with disdain. He can't bear the cackling, the chatter, the shopping, the stuff most of us girls adore. So, the potential love of my life doesn't do anything that I like to do: eat, watch bad television. He might be more like Liz in *Eat, Pray, Love*, after all—a lover of travel, an observer of culture, a flaneur through marvelous sites.

"Maybe we should get some fresh air," he suggests on the second day of our new lovers' weekend.

This is the part I've dreaded—the outing, the walking around for hours—and if I keep up with his not-eating, I'll die. Low blood sugar makes me insane. Let's face it, M&M's are not lunch. (They should be.) While I feel better when I eat well, I can't stomach the idea of a carrot nibblet.

This worry creates a snowball effect of panic, but I keep a bland smile on my face. "Sure. Let's go!"

I'm still sporting my perfect makeup and hair, though I have dialed back wearing contact lenses. Even over our long-distance courtship, he did see that I am incredibly nearsighted and don't wear contacts all the time.

Overnight, the snow must have come down, blanketing the city as we were sleeping. It's almost as if Christmas arrived just for Sam (who is Jewish). We go outside and the snow is deep, to the point where there are snowbanks all over Manhattan. Surely Sam and I won't walk far. Maybe a few blocks, then turn around. We're old, after all. Of course, I conveniently forget that Sam spent the semester climbing mountains and therefore has excellent endurance. That and not eating make him an enigma.

Bundled up in our snow gear, we trudge through the snow, and for several blocks, I'm fine. We won't be long out here in the white winter wonderland. It's freezing out, my tootsies are already numb, and in my head, my diva complaining has begun. But then I remember my BFF Rachel, who is pregnant for the first time. We grew up together and now she's embarking on this new journey (without an epidural). That must be hard. Secretary of State Hillary Clinton spends half her life on airplanes and meeting people, being out and about, eating bad food, and trying to live on fumes. She wouldn't be a wimp about walking a few blocks. Really, I'm so spoiled.

We wind up walking two miles to Central Park. Low blood sugar has hit, thanks to Sam's manorexia and my trying to keep up with his no-eating regimen. He goes over to get some cider, which I'm not into. Summoning my inner Julia, I remain stoic and sparkling, not complaining once (maybe a couple of times). I just want for him to think I'm a cheerful girl, up for anything—which I'm not, let's face it.

I do enjoy the moment, though, relish that happiness that will build if I keep up with Gretchen Rubin's maxim to carve out time to do what makes me happy (I even make lists, as she suggests). I like being outside. This snowy weather is heaven to me. I like and love Sam. The bottom line is that I'm with the man of my dreams. We're soaking up the sun and lovely snowy weather. It's a gorgeous day even if he just threw a snowball at me. I'm such a lucky girl. A year ago, I was in such a different place.

Sam and I take pictures. In each one, I have a big smile on my face and I feel it clear through. We frolic in the snow, laugh a lot, and take the subway home. By the time we arrive back in Chelsea, I'm ravenous. There's no time to waste with this not-eating thing. Sam also gives up his manorexia and we order greasy burgers and fries.

The next hurdle is unveiling my shelf of DVDs (I'll leave the Duran Duran stuff for another time, when he's locked in). Though I hide the more embarrassing ones, he's bound to discover my obsession with Steven Seagal movies, romantic comedies, Queer as Folk, The L Word, and 95 percent of Julia Roberts's repertoire.

I start out slow, convince him to watch a benign romantic comedy. Being on his best behavior, he is amenable to watching Maid in Manhattan. I love my Jennifer Lopez in movies, so he has to adore her, too. No reason why he shouldn't since she's infectious and her smile lights up those somber halls in the hotel where she works as a maid (the romance tropes and stereotypes are cringe-worthy, but it's J.Lo and I have to watch).

Although Sam seems interested in the movie, he asks after twenty minutes, "Wasn't this nominated for an Oscar?"

Ha ha, so funny.

But he succumbs to J.Lo's magic. I look over and see tears running down his cheeks just as Jennifer gets fired from her job cleaning Ralph Fiennes's hotel room and defiantly tells her mother she's not going to clean houses.

Total wuss. I might be able to do this. Finally, we find a show we both love, *The Closer*, which oddly enough stars my brother's friend (my former embarrassing crush from *Equal Justice*) Jon Tenney as Kyra Sedgwick's long-suffering boyfriend. Each time JT comes on the screen, Sam screams out, "Jon Tenney! He's so hunkalicious!"

Lesson learned: Never tell someone everything about your life. . . .

By the end of our first week together, it's clear that Sam will stay longer. We get along great but disagree enough to keep things interesting. The original plan was for Sam to leave on Christmas Eve, but now he will experience my family during the holidays.

Christmastime is special to the Smith/Kelleys because it's Patrick's birthday and there is a present exchange that can only be described as wrapping-paper carnage. We're gathering on Christmas Eve, with another family dinner the next day. I'm not sure how Patrick does it, but he manages to keep his birthday going for weeks, with a minimum of two parties to celebrate his arrival into the world.

I should be worried about Sam and Patrick meeting for the first time. I want them to like each other, but I'm too used to Patrick's guardedness. He doesn't want anyone to hurt me, which I understand. I haven't had great judgment in the past. In contrast, Carlos already loves Sam, so I rely on his gentle coaxing to win over my brother.

On the day itself, Sam and I accidentally both wear blue and we don't notice until we get to my mom's apartment. As we walk in the door, Don looks up from his latest mystery. He puts his book aside to stand, smiles, and gets up to shake Sam's hand. That's what people in love do. It's clear that Don and Sam have a special connection that I'll never understand.

I know that as we walk home, Sam will talk about Don for the rest of the evening: "Did you notice how Don lovingly put the salt around his margarita?" or "I like how he tells Bonnie no and then does what she says. Did you see that?" He's terribly infatuated. Not a day goes by without his asking about Don, his health, his interests.

Patrick and Carlos are usually late, but once they come in, I can feel electricity—not tension as with other times when I've brought people home, but a sense that this is the best person I could possibly introduce to my family.

As Patrick and Sam shake hands, I soak up the moment. Their smiles, the playful jibing. When Patrick punches Sam in the arm—as one would a little brother—I know my brother is sold.

Sam loves being around family—his own, mine, and any other related people he can find. He and his brother, Warren, talk every day at least twice, to the point that I can predict when the phone will ring—when Warren is on his way to work or home, when Sam comes home from the gym, or at seven forty-five A.M. The Blooms also visit one another often, planning last-minute trips to New York or

Orlando, where his brother and his family live. Sam's family is eager to meet my family, or at least to see what Sam is getting himself into.

Within a couple weeks of Sam's descent into New York, his brother, sister-in-law, and two nieces arrive from Florida to meet most of the Smith/Kelley clan. My mother and I nervously make arrangements to dine at a West Village restaurant. Patrick and Carlos can't make it.

As usual, I need to pop a tranquilizer, because you never know how these things will go. Will everyone get along? Will my stepfather behave? How bored will the nieces be? Does everyone hate me? Will my mother bully me into ordering an appetizer? (If she doesn't, something's wrong.)

The older niece, Kyra, feels under the weather and stays at the hotel, leaving Gaby, a blue-eyed, light-brown-haired teenage cherub, to deal with the adults. Gaby is poised throughout the entire meal, even when my stepfather uses the F-word. It doesn't faze her one bit, and she goes back to texting her friends. My mother is a dynamite conversationalist and keeps it all going, talking with Elise, Warren's wife, who resembles Gaby. I don't think I eat anything during the entire meal, but I feel a deep satisfaction that everyone is getting along. Later that night, we meet up with Kyra, a beautiful brunette with a love of theater. We've all met now, and it doesn't seem to be killing the relationship so far.

There are those moments in a relationship when you truly clash, even if it's in a nice way. In the books I edit, couples mesh beautifully during times of forced proximity. If Jake Hunter has to use Cassie's house in order to spy on the evil neighbor (whose landscaping business is a front for selling busloads of heroin), they live together harmoniously—maybe bicker a little, which masks their burning attraction. In small ways, they surprise each other. He knows how to make an omelet (all heroes do, oddly enough) and she is easy to love.

For our first few weeks, we settle into our blissful cohabitation and acknowledge that our relationship has no time limit. Sam miraculously finds a teaching job for the spring semester and has a few days to prepare for class. I have my own work, thus making us an employed couple. We're the easy-to-love Cassie and Jake, until reality sets in. Sam snores his face off at night. I have to tap him and tell him to turn over. Sometimes he yells at me that he won't do it. Sometimes he's complacent.

With his no-eating regime abandoned, Sam eats my yogurt, my leftovers, and my packed lunch. I buy groceries; they disappear fast. He eats my food without apology. So I learn to buy two of everything. Still, it disrupts my harmonious landscape.

It's soon obvious to him that I have trouble sleeping, that my habit is to stay awake forever, and to get myself to sleep, I often resort to clubbing myself in the head with a horse tranquilizer. This doesn't always work. Sam is dead to the world within five minutes of hitting his pillow. He wakes up at two A.M. to read, then falls back to sleep. He says he can function with five hours of sleep, but let's be serious: He gets eight a night, plus an afternoon nap. This is not fair. Cassie and Jake never experience such discord in their sleeping patterns.

I take a shower every day, sometimes two. Sam will take more than that. He loves showers, cleanliness, sweet-smelling hair, and an empty sink. He's obsessive about his towels, soaps, and face-scrubbing lotions. I don't wash my hair for three days in a row because it's so damn thick. Sam wrinkles his nose at me after the second day. My candlelit bubble baths are now done in secret since Sam witnessed one and said, "You're basically bathing in your own filth." Nice. Jake would never say that. It's obvious that Sam knows nothing about girly indulgence.

After eating, I let the dishes sit until, you know . . . a few days go by. Sam has to pick them up before he does anything else. I barely cook, preferring to have food brought to me, which often means no dishes. Sam cooks pad Thai from scratch and really should be a chef. He's so talented that my mother gets uncomfortable when he comes into her kitchen. But she loves eating what he cooks.

Before Sam arrived, I cleaned my apartment from top to bottom once a week. Now, with the endless cups set down, food eaten, dust accumulated, bed unmade, laundry piled high, I let it all go. I can't clean and work and be in a relationship. I mean, I can, but I don't. We do the best that we can with this, but it's difficult. We don't invite people over because we're slobs. To add to this, we have no interest in interior decorating, which means we live in a pit with shabby furniture from twenty years ago.

Each day, I live more spontaneously, loosely, but it feels good. We don't have to be as perfect as Jake and Cassie. Sam and I take our preferences in stride. I try to be tolerant, and he's the most easygoing person ever. We get along great, until the night he goes out with his friend Reid from Taft.

I grew up with noises waking me up in the middle of the night. City sounds, people fighting or talking loudly, parties, usually my own nightmares rousing me, a weird phone call at three A.M. My bad dreams make me lie awake shaking for a good hour afterward. Now that I'm in my forties, I hate for my sleep to be disturbed.

Because I'm in this new relationship, still acting as Cheerful Girl, I am so happy that Sam wants to hang with a friend. Why not? He needs to have a fun boys' night out and blow off steam. Maybe since I have to go in to work the next day, he could be in by midnight? Sure, darling, no problem. We embark happily on our separate evenings.

Toward the end of the night, I wait and wait. No word from Sam. Finally, I put myself into a coma, hoping that he won't wake me up, but if he does, I'll be fine with it because I'm more relaxed now about everything.

At about two A.M. the door opens and in walks Sam, very quietly. He barely speaks, immediately takes off his pants and coat, and gets into bed, lying unmoving for the next few hours. I can tell he's beyond smashed out of his brains, mostly because he's so quiet and careful. I almost laugh, except I hate this kind of thing.

On the one hand, he should party if he wants. On the other, is this a habit?

I don't talk to him for about a day because of how neurotic I feel, waiting for him to come home, wondering if he's a crazy drunk, and why can't I loosen up and let him have a fun night out with a friend? All my worrying ruins my day. Also, there's the fact that he was inconsiderate, never thinking that such a late arrival would upset me. If we had a separate bedroom, it wouldn't have been a big deal. Do I want to get involved with someone who goes out until two A.M.? I'm really a square and only a brain transplant will change that. He knows I hate this middle-of-the-night coming home. Why did he do this?

Luckily, this happens only once and my revenge occurs as I watch him go to teach his French class at nine the next morning. He is miserably hungover.

I knew Sam was truly the One early on—maybe with the Facebook declaration with the Swiss saline solution. During the first few weeks and months of our living together, he prods me ever so gently out of my shell—getting me to be more social and less of a tight-ass, laugh more. But then . . . something happens that might be the deal-breaker.

"Let's go to Miami," Sam says, a bright gleam in those irresistible green eyes.

My resistance flares. What the hell, traveling? That, for me, is the downside of a relationship, which a normal person would see as the good side—you have to go places when you're with someone. Oh dear God. I have to be on a plane with this man. Dibs on the window seat or he dies. For some reason, if I can look out the window of the plane and see where I'm going, this means I'm psychically managing this aluminum tube. I'm so not Elizabeth Gilbert and I *want* to be.

There is no way out this time because I have to fly to Florida anyway for a romance writers' conference. I just thought I'd be going alone, freaking out by myself on the plane, as usual. Why me? Of course we'll go to Miami together.

"Oh yeah, I have to meet your dad," I say. If I have to fly with Sam, I will buckle down and do it. Meeting his father is a necessity. Not only are Sam and his brother obsessed with their father, talking about him incessantly, but I just want to meet the man responsible for Sam.

"He wants to meet you."

I've always wanted to spend serious time in Florida, and this is the only way I'll do it. "I'd love to go." And I vow to be a calm adult in my serene forties. What are the chances it will rain on the actual day? I hate flying in the rain.

Of course, the day we leave, it's pouring buckets. My spirit guides are laughing their asses off at the misery they've caused. The sky mists over, kind of like the haze that plunged JFK Jr., his wife, and her sister into the Atlantic in 1999.

These kinds of thoughts plague me as we sit in traffic on the way to LaGuardia. We have about two hours to spare and we watch the skies carefully, me hoping for a blessed cancellation and ultimately a delay to our travels.

No such luck.

We have plenty of time in the airport. Sam grabs a beer and I buy four celebrity magazines, my frantic, quick reading material for the two-and-a-half-hour flight. I keep repeating my mantra: *I will behave like an adult.* Even with a whirlpool of pain brewing, I won't let him see it. If I have to barf, I will gracefully excuse myself and go to the bathroom—though I have the feeling that Sam would gladly hold back my ponytail as I yak into a bag. If I were going to let him do that, I would wear my hair pinned back and contact lenses, since glasses could fly off during heavy spewing. Or so I've seen in horror movies.

All aboard. I glance outside the window and see a sky littered with angry clouds. I've flown my entire life, all over the world. I once flew through three storm systems (thank you, Toronto, circa October 26, 2005) and did just fine. How could one little trip to Miami kill me?

I suck on about half a tin of Altoids, my saving grace in any crisis, and, yes, I take half of a large animal tranquilizer. My nerves are there but not unmanageable. Sam reads the paper and begins to look sleepy. He leans his head back as we start takeoff, when my terror begins.

The first ten minutes are full of bumps. I curse inwardly and pray to the white cloudy sky to show some mercy. Though drifting to sleep, Sam reaches over and takes my hand. Not overt support but just enough so that I relax instantly.

I know in my heart that I love him. I'll love him forever. He is the one for me. No doubt about it. He doesn't mind the crazy girl in me. This man is smart enough to leave me be during a panic attack.

After riding out the storm, I settle in to watch a beautiful view outside the window. This is the post-traumatic relief, the good side of adventure. I breathe. We veer out over the Atlantic Ocean, something I haven't done in decades, and for a moment, I want to rush back to France, a country I once called home. We land in beautiful Miami at night, and the lights of the city captivate me. I can't stop smiling. We survived!

Sam whisks me off to his father's large condo in the Coconut Grove section of Miami. Sam's father, Bill, well into his eighties, emerges from the back room and greets us warmly.

He is a classic charmer, the kind you'd call "a swell guy." Within minutes I can see where Sam gets his sparkle. This is what Sam will be when he's eighty. His father has the family's bright green eyes; clear, tan complexion; and wide smile.

"Nice to meet you, dear," he says.

When an older man calls me "dear," I'm pretty much a goner. He grasps my hand and we tear around his condo together.

That first night in Miami, I sink into the bed and instantly fall asleep. I don't think of the future with Sam, if we will ever get married, buy a house, spend all our days together. With him, I feel no pressure to do anything except relax. I'm sure that this is the right path, no matter where it takes me.

For three days, we frolic around Miami. Walk around Grove Isle every morning, work out in the building's gym, swim in the sparkling pool, go out to fancy restaurants in South Beach. The beautiful palm trees seduce me since I've only known the Northeast foliage and the New Mexico desert. The weather hovers in the eighties and we peaceably stroll in shorts and T-shirts. Sam makes like Miami is same old, same old, but I'm sure he finds some joy in his home away from Big Bad New York.

If traveling is this fun, I will go anywhere with him.

At some point Sam goes through his closet. Because he's traveled so much over the years, his possessions are scattered—in a storage facility, with his brother, at his father's, and now with me. But he does know where he kept the picture of us from the Taft formal oh so many years ago.

Sam pulls out a shoebox and sets it on the bed. He goes through picture after picture and pulls out the one of us.

I am speechless. He kept this picture all these years. I don't even remember the moment, but the fact that it stuck in his mind touches me deeply. This guy thought of me as more than just a passing thing. I stayed with him.

The photo itself is hilarious. There I am with my cool mullet, that blue dress, and Sam in his tux. We have disparate expressions—me with slack-jawed surprise, Sam with an almost stoic smile. Over the past few months, we've shared our memories of each other. Mine are hazier than his. I remember the dance, him as a legend, but not that we took a picture together. He remembers the picture, me in the halls, calling out to me from across the pond, catching me smoking with another boy. If you add this up, Sam had a little crush on me way back when. And if someone had told me that the popular boy was accessible to me, I would have sprinted after him.

Who knew that so many years later we'd be meeting again, living together, and perhaps even contemplating a future?

◆┤◆├◆

CHAPTER THIRTEEN

Where There's a Ring

I will follow *Sex and the City* wherever it goes, even if it shoots out lackluster sequels, even if there are a million copycats. I love stories where women hang out together and wear great clothes and hash out their relationships. Now that it's out in theaters, I have to see *Sex and the City 2*. Given that my office is focused on the business of romance, we have a group field trip to see this latest movie.

I have to admit, there is a certain plushness to working in the romance field. We're committed to trend-chasing, like seeing which shows and movies and books rise to the top. How can this help our business?

Once a month, as a group, we'll watch a movie at work and discuss the story, how it relates to our field—sort of like a mini English class. We do the same with books that we read, either from the company or outside. With such a rare event as a *Sex and the City* movie, it's to be expected that we'll all see it. We trek en masse over to the Regal theater near the West Side Highway and settle into our seats.

Many of us were at Harlequin during the height of *Sex and the City*'s fame, and we cackle the loudest. My heart stops over Liza

Minnelli singing "Single Ladies," though I never thought that Stanford and Anthony would ever work as a couple. After this, Big and Carrie have some marital woes in that she likes to go out and Big wants to stay in and lie on the couch (as if that's a bad thing). When the boredom hits an all-time high, the girls go to Abu Dhabi. They just pick up and go because they can. Out in the desert, they wear flowing dresses and artfully arranged scarves, and they ride camels. They get to stay in this palatial hotel and each is served by a personal butler. The eternal question for me remains: Which one of the girls am I?

It's with great eagerness that I watch the film and reidentify with the central female characters. There are some of the usual fashion shows of earlier episodes, women squealing, and somewhat lame problems: If you're married to Mr. Big (alpha, but turns into beta with an edge), do you really want to screw up your life with Aidan? I mean, really? I don't buy it, but I watch anyway, liking that at least Aidan comes back since I thought he was the great guy Carrie should have married. And at least Samantha gets to bang that hot businessman on the jeep on the Fourth of July.

The only misgiving I leave with is the mundane life Carrie has after marrying Mr. Right. Why wouldn't she be happy with that? I am so ready to lead a boring life since I've had enough excitement—moving to Ohio, New Mexico, New York, not to mention all the relationships. Sam and I definitely have our mundane moments, but it's more common that he makes me laugh hysterically every day. I wonder if we're just weird. Maybe marriage does get mundane and I would go looking elsewhere. I shudder to think of it.

I leave the movie theater with my colleagues. My friends Gail and Ann Leslie ask me how everything is going with Sam. Both women are wearing beautiful sundresses in this hot weather. I'm in a khaki skirt that I keep meaning to throw out but haven't because it's convenient. They seem interested in how my love life is progressing. Because I'm living with Sam and we're happy, I feel as if I've joined a special club.

Do I love cohabitation? Do I think it'll get more serious? Wouldn't it be nice if I got married? They could help me plan the wedding. J.Crew has some nice dresses. And then they tell me about how they got married, how long ago it was, and wouldn't it be spectacular to have another wedding in the office? A baby, perhaps? At Harlequin, there is at least one marriage, one engagement, and/or one baby per year.

This is one of the many benefits of working with women, because you talk about these fun things all the time. You have an instant support network, especially during periods of your life when you need all the encouragement that you can get.

"Sam and I are just having fun," I say to Ann Leslie and Gail. And it's true. I feel no pressure to do anything except enjoy Sam.

The stories I read don't quite cover this part of a relationship. The romance should turn to a marriage proposal fairly soon. In a novel, there's not a whole lot devoted to making dinner or doing laundry together. In earlier relationships, I felt that sense of urgency—*I have to know what the future holds now. Does the guy feel the same way I do?*

I have none of those questions about my relationship with Sam, no need to know. We are a dream come true. I love folding the laundry after he brings it upstairs. I love going into the kitchen while he's cooking and having him tell me to leave his territory. I love how obsessed he is with getting silk long johns to wear in winter. I love when he laughs really hard. Going to a restaurant is a pleasure with him because we talk as if we're strangers again, getting to know each other. I love how when I'm mad at him, he finds a way to make me smile and defuse my anger. There is so much that I love about Sam that anything else—like marriage—would be a bonus I don't exactly need.

When I get home from the movie, I see Sam put a little box in his pocket.

He does it semi-covertly, without emotion, until I notice his fingers twitch. When nervous, he tends to fidget and avoid eye contact. Sweat beads on his shirt. I don't want to admit that I suspect what's in the box or that I've picked up on hints. I'm just going to enjoy this fully.

"It's happy hour at Mary Ann's. Wanna get some margaritas?" he asks.

Even though the early June weather is already warm, he slips on a sports jacket over his white shirt and dark pants. Formal wear for a casual night out to a Mexican restaurant? His hair is combed back, interesting considering he didn't have to work today. His class at Barnard is done for the summer, and he's scheduled to teach three classes in the fall.

"Sure. Let's get margaritas."

I can't stop smiling. My life has changed so much in the past nine months. The Universe is laughing its ass off at my determination to stay single after Superman's sudden disappearance, my many starts and stops in love. How did this joy happen? Was love supposed to feel this good? For six months now, we've had our ups and downs, but now I can't imagine not having him in my space.

For the long walk of three blocks, I watch him and memorize every second. People will be asking for our story. The hazy sun, my too-big khaki skirt and black shirt. Neighbors walk by, recognize us. We usually hold hands since we're a new couple, but this time we don't. Something is different. He keeps his hands close to his sides, as if guarding his pants.

I check myself for nervousness. None. How weird is that? Everything makes me a little nervous: the walk to the subway, going to the gym, running on the treadmill, being at work, leaving work, going to bed, meeting anyone for coffee. And here I am about to get engaged, and not a single eye-twitch. Instead, I feel like a mother helping a boy off to his first day of school. Sam is going to propose, and I want to make it as easy as possible.

"How was your day?" I ask, then look down at my sandals. My face feels hot. Sam is so handsome, I am struck when I take note of it. I look at him and think, *Wow*. He has those rugged good looks, along with that class-clown thing. He can go from *GQ* gorgeous to Jimmy Fallon in seconds.

I feel his gaze and glance up. His smile charms away my shyness. This is the grin that gets me through the day. His smile is a lethal weapon and will keep us safe. And then there are the eyes . . . For an instant I am lost again, wanting to stop him and kiss him on the sidewalk—we do that—but this time we just keep walking.

"I had a *great* day," he says, imitating how my mother says "great."

In a way, I feel like I was married to him the moment he came into my life, that first time we talked on the phone or when he said, even though it was a bit of a joke at the time, that he wanted to move in with me and father my children. I am so sure of how I feel that no nerves are needed.

We reach the red structure that is Mary Ann's, which serves Mexican food. It's part of a chain throughout Manhattan. It's always bustling; customers seem to return over and over again. The décor is fairly minimal but it has a "Mexican" feel. Sam and I often eat here. Plus, they serve large frozen margaritas that he can slurp down, easing the stress of a long day.

As we sit, I pretend not to know about the ring box. Once again, we say things like: How was your day? So glad it's almost summer. Love how festive everything gets with people on the streets. Should we go back to Miami? Your father is a sweetheart.

There, I do my best with chatting. The silence is inevitable after our smirking waiter brings drinks, as if he knows. I sip my drink and pretend to be absorbed in the table surface.

Plunk. Sam sets the box in the middle of the table, stopping me midsip.

"I wonder what this is," I say coyly. In fact, Sam is terrible at keeping secrets and I decoded several phone conversations Sam had with his brother. We live in a studio. There are no secrets.

Without hesitating, I pick up the box and open it, knowing I'll love whatever is inside. Forty-one years. My moment. My prince. Open sesame.

That's what one looks like. And it's mine.

The round diamond winks at me, beckoning me to pick it up. I've seen dozens of diamond rings, worn a few, all belonging to friends and relatives. This one is for me.

My first and only one.

I instantly fall in love with a gem, a gold setting, an achingly beautiful piece of jewelry. It is a ring of protection and love. Smiling, overjoyed, I slip it on my ring finger. Though I rarely search for it, I like tradition when it presents itself. This is my future. I didn't need a ring, but I'll take it.

"Wow!" I almost forget to look back at him; I am that transfixed.

"And I have a question . . . ," he says softly, slurping his drink, his hands shaking. You'd think someone so handsome and smart would ease into this with flair and ceremony. Not *this* groom. He is about to soil himself.

"Will you marry me?" he asks, his eyes darting around the room.

The proposal is matter-of-fact, almost laughable—should we order Chinese or Thai? Sam displays more exuberance, but I know he must be nervous. As someone who easily slips into panic mode, I find this is the perfect way to propose to me—casually, without fanfare, with my having some knowledge ahead of time.

"Yes." Two seconds later, I feel that rush of giddiness brides-to-be are supposed to experience. OhmyGodIhavetotelleverybody . . . *and change my Facebook status to "Engaged"*!

This isn't how I—or anyone—thought my life would turn out. My family expected me to be alone forever, and I wanted to be alone. Who else could stand a crazy girl who preferred to stay indoors?

Sam has changed this. He brings me out of my head. I forget to be scared and go with whatever love wave we happen to be riding.

Slurp slurp.

"How do you feel?" I ask.

"Good. No dread like the first time I did this, or the second," Sam remarks, referring to his ex-wife and rebound fiancée.

I still can't stop smiling or staring at the ring on my finger. The food arrives—I don't remember what I ordered—and instead of eating, I stare at the ring, at Sam, then ponder the shock my family will exhibit upon hearing the news. I can't wait to tell everyone. Can we leave now? Oh, I'm going to be one of those women with a dress, walking down the aisle, with family maybe. Or we could elope to Vegas or city hall. We're not exactly rich enough to throw a big wedding.

This prompts a discussion of *when.*

"As soon as it's convenient," the groom says. "Maybe in a year, like May."

I'm thinking more like February, but whatever. A year seems too long to wait. Oh God, I thought I was one of those casual girls who doesn't care, who waits for everything. Now the diva bride thing is happening.

"Maybe we could get married even earlier, like over a long weekend. Presidents' weekend," I suggest.

"Sure."

We smile at each other, and a warm sensation creeps into my heart. He prepared for this moment, thought about it for a while. A friend said that an engagement isn't real unless there's a ring. I have a ring.

I'm not sure if I eat. Maybe I take a few bites of rice, then look at my ring. Again, where are the nerves? I love this calm and feel that the ring plays a big part. Sam enjoys his second margarita, and I'm about to bust out of my chair. Must. Call. Mom. She's going to have a cow. I cannot wait to shock everyone. This is engagement narcissism, and what fun it is.

The minute I arrive home, I call my mother and give her the news. This woman is used to calls of woe, me crying into the phone about all kinds of awful traumas. I want to tell her about this good fortune immediately. Usually, she is overflowing with things to say.

This time, she's keeps saying the same three words. "Oh my God. . . ."

"And then he gave me the ring. . . ."

"Oh my God. . . ." Mom is never this inarticulate.

"So, I need to get regular manicures now and not the crappy ones I do myself."

"Oh my God. . . ."

She does regain consciousness enough to ask me when we want to have the wedding.

"Maybe February or May," I say.

"What about September this year?" she says. "We old folks need it fast. I'm going to have a heart attack. Oh my God. . . ."

The rest of the conversation is full of more "Oh my God"s and little bursts of praise for Sam. This boy will be her son-in-law. She'll have him full-time, her very own academic to play with. I can't even begin to think about the future lovefest between Sam and Don. They will be related.

As soon as I get off the phone, I call my brother. Instead of "Oh my God," he keeps saying, "Wow." I can hear Carlos yelling in the background. Our family keeps getting bigger and bigger.

"Should I tell Dad?" I ask. I really don't want to, but I guess it would be rude not to say anything to my father, to let all his relatives find out over Facebook before he does. Though a malicious part of me wants to do it that way.

"You need to call him."

Yeah, so how would that go? The sooner I call him, the sooner I can change my Facebook status to "Engaged." Engagement narcissism is second only to Facebook narcissism. The likes will boost me into the happiness stratosphere even though I'm already happy because I am engaged, in case that's not clear. Engaged. Engaged. Engaged.

I completely forget that Sam is in the room.

With the phone in my hand, I go into the bathroom. Sam is in the rest of the studio calling his father and brother, telling them the news. I can already hear Sam describing the ring to his father and explaining why he didn't want to save money by choosing jewelry from the family's safe-deposit box in Miami. It makes me laugh.

I dial my father's number, hoping my stepmother doesn't answer because then I'll have to speak to her.

"Hello?" Thank goodness, it's just my father.

"Hi, Dad. It's me."

I already know I have a good two minutes to get my message through before he wants to get off the phone. I'm sure he'll be polite, just not gushing. I'm paying him a courtesy before I shout my news from the rooftops.

"I'm engaged to that guy I e-mailed you about."

"Oh . . . well, congratulations." He sounds surprised, and not upset in any way. I like to think he might be happy for me and the fact that despite everything, I found a decent person. "So, tell me about him."

"He's teaching French at Barnard. He lived in Israel for eight years."

"So, I guess he must be on Israel's side."

"Well, he has more knowledge of the Middle East than most of us who've never been there. He loves Israel, but he thinks each side has the enemy it deserves."

My father chuckles. I can hear him judging my fiancé, though perhaps it's envy. My dad never got to fight in a war or go anywhere truly dangerous. The worst nail-biting moments he's had came from mountain climbing (though he's had some life-and-death moments). I doubt he's ever had to stay in a shelter or live in fear of a suicide bomb going off in a restaurant. My father, at heart, is an adventurer, but one who's been homebound for most of the past thirty years.

"Congratulations," he says.

"Yep, I'm actually getting married, probably early next year." No talk of the ceremony or his participation.

The few minutes are up and we discuss the upcoming Smith reunion, where I will bring Sam to meet him. It might be a good idea for them to meet before we get married. Plus, I can't resist the Smith starchy foods, and they are nice people. I don't worry a bit about introducing him to my mother's side of the family either. The Sullivans will love Sam because he'll eat great piles of their food. He will love them for yelling at him to eat more.

Finally, it's done. My dad knows. Mom and Patrick know. And now I go to Facebook and change my status to "Engaged," close my eyes, and wait for the flood of "likes" and congratulations. I am going to marry Sam Bloom.

A ring on your finger makes a difference. I always thought it wouldn't, but it does. Dare I admit that I like that feeling of ownership? It's so unfeminist of me. Out of defiance, I tried out different rings on that finger: a hematite ring, an amethyst ring, then a fake wedding band for when I wanted to be left alone. This new engagement ring feels right. I used to be bothered by these traditions, but now I'm swimming in them, willingly.

Going to work engaged feels fantastic. On the subway, I keep peering down at my ring. I have one now. With new energy, I get my engaged breakfast and engaged coffee, take out my building pass with my left hand, flashing my ring as much as possible.

The newly engaged usually enter the Harlequin office to squeals and demands to see the ring, hear the proposal story and wedding details. Very little gets done by the affianced lady, because who can stop looking at her ring? Not me, and I am no different. Though I stay in my office—since I don't want to be too obvious and showy—I quickly whip out my hand and give details to anyone who asks.

My friend Sarah, the editor for our nonfiction line, examines the ring and says, "It's a good setting. That way the diamond can breathe." If it weren't for Sarah, I wouldn't have a clue what I wanted in a ring. She gave me some websites to scour at a point when I overheard Sam talking to Warren about "waterslides" and should he get one "waterslide" or "three waterslides." I figured out that *waterslide* meant "diamond."

The ongoing pleasure of the engagement is indescribable. It's like a bubble bath, cake, and champagne rolled into one—all day long. Sam and I are a little nicer to each other, not that we weren't before. We smile more, hold hands more, and I'm sure we're nauseating the general population.

For months now, he's had plans to go to Israel to visit a sleep clinic. I know, why would he need a sleep clinic? Between you and me, I'm not sure either, though he does have a problem with snoring and waking up in the middle of the night. At least he's proactive about getting help, almost comically so. I just witness and support him as much as I can. Health care is cheaper over in Israel (if you ignore those thousands of dollars for a plane ticket), and Sam has convinced himself he has serious sleep issues. I've learned to just nod my head over his latest health fixation.

After a couple of weeks of engagement bliss, Sam leaves and I'm alone for ten days. It seems strange to have the place to myself again for such an extended period. I keep thinking how wonderful it will be—watching movies all day, reading until three A.M., eating as much crap as I want. My solitude is back, though not enough for me to miss being single. I just have some time to adjust to this new phase, sort of like when Carrie and the girls go on a trip together—returning to the source before they all get into more permanent relationships. I'm returning to me.

For the first forty-eight hours, I'm deliriously happy in this decadent living. When I go to play computer solitaire, I don't start crying. The television watching is epic, with various takeout delivery people stopping by with my meals. Sam and I communicate the way we used to, via Skype.

By the third day, I hate the silence. Where is my Sam making me laugh, stomping over to the fridge to eat all the leftovers? Sure, my apartment is cleaner. The bed gets made and stays made. I barely have dishes in the sink, and the bathroom doesn't carry that "boy" film of hair and who-knows-what. But I miss Sam, his voice, his playfulness, the company, and even his snoring.

And there's another thing. If I think about it too much, my legs start to shake, and I get that sick feeling. But I have to do something about it. Finally, it's time for me go across the street to Duane Reade and buy my very first pregnancy test.

I choose my favorite cutoffs, an oversize bleached-out pair that are so big that I feel skinny; my favorite tight shirt; and flip flops. I throw my hair up in a bun. No makeup. This is my comfort wardrobe for when I feel and look like hell, which is fine since I'm on vacation and having a mini panic attack. Even though it might be bad for the baby, I pop an Ativan, because the idea that I need to take a pregnancy test makes me unable to breathe properly. I can barely move. Five days late.

We've already established that "if it happens, it happens." But so fast? I guess it's a good thing, but I'm petrified. Might as well find out if I am pregnant or not, so I walk over to the Duane Reade, legs shaking, and find a test, along with some Altoids, a candy bar, and some Doritos. It's absurd that I'd be so nervous. If I got pregnant, I'd have the baby. Now that I have an actual significant other, it wouldn't be reckless. We have the money, the support network.

To be honest, I'm not one of those girls who's dreamed about being pregnant. That's not a crime, I know, but I feel guilty for it. Isn't that supposed to be ingrained in me? When I'm around children, I love playing with them. The idea of raising Sam's child makes me happy, but does that kid have to come from me?

All of a sudden, I'm dealing with it. I could be pregnant, earlier than we planned. We might have this little red-haired kid with a big nose running around eating and breaking things. I love the idea, but it's terrifying. After drinking thousands of gallons of water, I go and deal with taking the test.

In the past three days, I've accepted that we might add to our family. So much has changed, and rather quickly.

"So, I'm really late," I say to Sam.

"Oh . . . ," he answers. "You may be carrying my child."

He sounds happy, so I start to feel a bit more upbeat. The idea of children starts to excite me, though not enough to overpower my anxiety. We'll just say the balance between the two is leveling off.

"And it didn't even take that long. Wow." He sounds shocked.

"I don't know yet. It could be a false alarm," I say.

When we hang up, I do feel some pressure. If I'm not pregnant, he'll feel let down. If I am, I'll be scared out of my mind, but less so with him there. I guess I need to face reality, take the test.

I follow the directions and wait it out. And another test, watching closely as they both turn negative.

I feel that mixture of disappointment and relief. I wanted to be pregnant, sort of, especially since I could live out the fantasy of calling myself "knocked up," creating the suspicion of a shotgun wedding. How fun would that be? So I'm not pregnant. When I tell Sam, he's supportive. We already discussed the possibility that we might not be able to have children given my advanced age. We decided that we should try and see what options are open. More than anything, I don't want to go through years of IVF and fertility clinics, the heartbreak that goes with them. Having a child isn't my main objective in life (though I'd adopt in a second).

My panic stops, the adrenaline ebbs, and I regain my appetite enough to devour the bag of Doritos. I am calm again, returning to the woman I was before all of this happened. But the whole experience makes me think about the baby issue. Sam returns in a few days, and I take the time to think about the months to come.

I have a wedding to plan. The baby can wait a bit longer. In addition to my author Marie sending me not one but three wedding-planning books, I consult that beacon in any bridal storm: I join the Knot. And this is when the real fun begins.

Because I've never cracked open a bridal anything, I need a whole lot of help. Fast.

CHAPTER FOURTEEN

Wedding Planning and Taking the High Road

In a romance novel, there is no long engagement period after our rugged hero Jake Hunter proposes to Cassie McBride. He gives her a ring, then the author fast-forwards to their blissful wedding. The cause of the bride's puffy glow is anyone's guess—too many falafels? Or a belly full of baby?

Their families go ape with happiness, fussing over who's going to make what wedding dish (there's a lot of potluck in romance). Aunt Cora provides the Something Old—like a hanky blown into by a bride in 1874—and the bratty sister coughs up Something Blue, her favorite skanky garter she wears to the Rocking G-Spot Saloon every night. Cassie and Jake have these amazing nuptials—the whole town attends—and look forward to the honeymoon (wink wink), though every day is a honeymoon, if you know what I mean.

For me and Sam, the engagement begins with his trip to Israel and a pregnancy scare. With every twinge of fear about my life changing, I look at my ring and remember:

I love Sam. Sam loves me.

I also remember that my family doesn't resemble those in most romance novels. My mother is a larger-than-life powerhouse. She's the one who has to be intimately involved in my wedding. In my corner, I also have many "Aunt Cora"s, all of whom provide spunk, fun, and wisdom. I love my uncles and cousins, too. No surprises there.

My father is another story.

Often, romance heroines are orphans with little extended family. But if Cassie McBride did have a father, he would be one of the following:

1. Dead
2. Drunk and dysfunctional
3. Adorable and loving from the beginning, married to the same woman for fifty years
4. A cold jerk from the beginning
5. A cold jerk from the beginning and dying

Poor Jake Hunter is in the same situation. Usually, Jake has a hard time dealing with his father because they are so similar. Jake Hunter Sr. has worked the ranch for decades and wants his son to take over. Jake has his own dreams, but often they get sidelined due to tragedy and he has to raise his five brothers and sister on his own. Maybe Aunt Cora helps, but she's getting old. Well, not old enough to stop baking those fluffy blueberry muffins.

My dad doesn't fit into any category. He was a loving father until I reached adulthood and could feasibly live on my own. At that point, he and my stepmother had been married for more than a decade, so why the sudden chill? I hadn't lived at home since before prep school, and before that, I was the girl who stayed in her room or lingered at friends' houses for as long as possible. I didn't want to be a burden on them, so I worked through my chores, tried to be good, and used my allowance on things I needed, things parents would normally buy for adolescent female offspring. I must have made too many mistakes as an adult, ignored my father and stepmother, or gone into the wrong profession. After many years, I realize that his pathology has little to do with me. No one can truly diagnose why I fell out of favor with my father, and so I move on from it. At heart, I will always love my father, but it's best for us to go our separate ways.

Getting married stirs up that primal family stuff you'd rather keep buried. Now I have to deal with old crap, which means digging into my daddy issues, once again. For the past few years, it's been a relief to be estranged rather than to lose myself in trying to please my father and stepmother when I visit. The father I knew is long gone.

But I can't help but think, *You have to take the high road. That way, you can say you did everything you could.*

As I work out my guest list, Sam says this a few times before it sinks in. I know he's right. I *have* to invite my father to my wedding. He has to meet Sam, too, and I know the perfect time: the Smith reunion in August. There are layers upon piles of reasons why I should dis my father altogether. It would be thoroughly satisfying to withhold my invite. I picture my wedding, all his siblings in attendance, and his realizing he's been left out.

Okay, this makes me sad.

The one last glimmer of father-daughter hope we had was at my cousin's wedding, maybe seven years ago. She's a little younger than I am and had finally found her Mr. Right. I blubbered all the way through the ceremony. This girl, who'd been quiet, wildly intelligent, and sweet—multifaceted, really—she could get married, too. In her early thirties, my cousin did her work, went to church, loved her friends and family. One day, she met her husband and her whole life changed.

If I weren't so happy for her, witnessing her palpable joy, I would have scowled my way through the affair and been envious. Instead, I noshed and hung out with her brother, and Patrick, of course. At one point, with some prodding from his wife—who does the right thing occasionally—my dad came over and asked me to dance. He was one of those fun dancers, too, loved making an ass of himself . . . or was sappier than sap, the way a real dad should be.

My father and I slow-danced, with me more rigid than usual because I felt so much emotion. I wanted to have fun, but the moment was far too painful for me. We barely hugged or acknowledged each other unless my brother was in the room, and then all eyes went to Patrick. Now my dad was paying attention to me, even though it was someone else's idea.

I put my head on my dad's shoulder, the way I used to when we'd hug. All of a sudden, I thought I'd start weeping. My father was holding me, really dancing with me, as if he might have wanted to be there.

"Maybe someday we can dance at my wedding," I whispered in his ear, not knowing how he'd react to such a bold statement.

"I'd like that," he whispered back.

Seven years later, that memory is still vivid. I keep remembering it through the wedding planning, like when I go to put his address on the save-the-date card.

Maybe he'll remember that moment when he sees the announcement, that the little girl he once carried around, took hiking, ran the track with, grocery shopped with, cried with in post-divorce hell, sat in an audience to watch in every bad play—she found someone, that "pure gold" he told me to seek in a husband when I reached the age of having serious boyfriends.

Today, I have to deal with the father I have. The one who cancels at the last minute after making plans to see me in New York. The one who barely acknowledged my getting a master's degree or moving to New York. The one who doesn't answer e-mails or letters and stipulates that shared DNA doesn't mean we need to do anything more than send the occasional card once a year. And this is the father who defends his wife after she sends nasty and abusive letters to me.

If I follow that "high road" I'm supposed to take, I have to facilitate a meeting between Sam and my father. Smith family reunion. August. Only a month away. I think about *A Little Princess*, the girl who makes the best of a bad situation, and I know I can do this.

You'd think bridal planning would create euphoria in a relationship. For me and Sam, not so much. In fact, he becomes weirdly distant soon after putting the ring on my finger. Maybe it's the pregnancy scare or the fact that he's been married before. Or he could be having second thoughts. Sam isn't the type to get engaged without careful consideration.

I keep asking if anything's wrong, and he says no. I take this at face value. Normally, I would freak at the first whiff of boy-weirdness, but then I remember several things:

1. He'd make a huge fool of himself if he bailed on me.
2. He has nowhere to go except maybe to his dad's.

3. Everyone would pity me, which I'm okay with.
4. This whole love thing has been pure gravy and if he left,
   I'd survive (though it would still suck).
5. I do feel that he loves me.

With these five points, I keep planning our wedding. He shows little interest in this either, except to veto ideas.

"Maybe we could just go to city hall," I suggest to Sam one night. Seriously, that's such a "me" thing to do. It would alleviate stress. No Ativan needed. No huge expenses, because weddings, as I'm discovering, are a huge racket. Everything costs way more than it should. Plus, at city hall, no people would see me hyperventilating as I take my vows.

Sam looks up from his book, searches my face, and smiles. "I think you might want a more memorable wedding."

Because he says this, I'm reassured that he'll go through with the wedding. Sam is money-conscious. Why would he want an expensive wedding just to jilt me?

"Okay," I say. "You're right." Imagine, me agreeing to a real wedding because it's insurance against his bailing. It's sort of true, too, what he says. I do want a party. This is a huge event for me. As difficult as it might be, a bigger wedding would be unforgettable. I deserve this. Seriously, I will never go through this again.

I decide to take Sam's aloofness in stride . . . no matter how bad it gets.

I've watched hundreds of movies about weddings. Many of my married friends stressed about "location" when they got hitched, like saying you have to "book the cathedral a year in advance." I find this hysterical. I mean, how can all the places be booked so far in advance? Can't you find a nice patch of grass and get married there? No, because it's booked until infinity.

So the first bit of wedding stress I experience is over the location, since it's clear I won't be marrying Sam anywhere good. I do a little research on the Web, trying to find a few places with the following criteria:

◊ I can walk there.
◊ It's not that expensive.
◊ It doesn't look like a fast-food wedding chapel.

The first two do not exist. No matter what, if you're the bride, you'll be hauling shit, which means you need a car. And to avoid the fast-food venue, you need to max out a couple of credit cards, which is reality. Sam and I visit one place near where we live, and the guy can spend only a few minutes with us. The view is lovely, of the uptown area and its environs, but the banquet hall has a few strange corners and a vibe of faded glory. Pass.

I don't want to consider leaving Manhattan for my wedding. Anywhere outside of Manhattan is cheaper, but I am one of those annoying New Yorkers who rarely ventures away from her borough. I'm running out of options. It's summer; I'm a sweating bride-to-be and desperate for answers. Where do I even begin my search?

This is where my mother secretly intervenes. And she meddles the old-fashioned way, by mentioning my search to friends, relatives, anyone who will listen. "My daughter is having a wedding. Where should I put on this big party?" And that's how she pitches it, as a big party. Bonnie Gene Smith, hostess with the mostest, wants a big shebang. She doesn't exactly ask for help, but she's the kind of person people want to please.

Enter Uncle Bob, the husband of my mother's sister, graduate of Yale, passionate about politics and family, and another powerhouse in my family. Though he suffers from muscular dystrophy, there is no stopping him from planning massive family events from his scooter. He congregates and facilitates, can get anywhere, can argue you into considering wild conspiracy theories, talks to managers about turning down the "damn music" in restaurants, and can converse into the wee hours, telling harrowing tales of his coming-of-age and the pit of scum that is DC politics. I love watching him in action. He gets riled up about a variety of causes and breaks his back to create an occasion.

Uncle Bob makes a few phone calls and charms the event planner at the Yale Club. We have no affiliation with the club, which is why it's appalling that we have an appointment with their event planner. I chalk it up to Uncle Bob's skills of persuasion.

My mother and I go to meet Dari, a lovely smiling brunette, who ushers us into her office.

She hands us a packet of information and we review it. I do my initial gulping over the price, but it's more reasonable than many places in Manhattan. We could do this. I'm inviting no one, though.

I look over at Mom.

She nods. "We can do this."

"Are there any special requests you have, like themes for your wedding?" Dari asks.

I'm not sure what pills I'm on. Maybe it's just stress or the heat. I lean forward and declare, "I want a Duran Duran–themed wedding."

"Of course. All Rhodes lead to Nick," Dari responds without missing a beat.

My venue search is over.

The Smith reunion in August, a mere five months before my wedding, is sort of like the one I attended when I first moved to New York City. This time, there's the additional tension between me and my father and the big engagement bomb I just dropped.

Swimsuits on hand, Sam and I enter the Connecticut lake house and see the Smiths sitting at a long table, eating hot dogs and hamburgers. We're a little late to the event, which I blame on poor map-reading skills. Late is better than never, though I feel all eyes on us. Wearing his signature tan hat—one that covers the head and has a significant brim—to protect him from the sun, my father is eating Greek yogurt.

No one gets up for a minute as we exchange greetings. I can feel the unease, as in, who is this strange person I've brought with me? And what's the deal with Patience and her father? Or . . . they were just talking about us and our entrance stopped them in their tracks. Or I'm just paranoid and overly sensitive.

Sam and I go around and I make the introductions. My cousin Mike is the first to offer to grill us some burgers, which breaks the ice. We settle in and chat amiably with my relatives. I know at some point, my father will approach Sam to engage him in conversation properly. He does this on the short boat ride around the lake, an outing I avoid because I hate being trapped on a boat unless I'm the one manning it. Six of my relatives board the vessel, and from the dock, I watch everyone and toy with the idea of jumping in the lake.

Just by the way they start talking to each other, I can tell my father likes him. As he leans in, my father's expression is light, almost content. He hasn't looked at me that way in a long time. This is okay. At least, in this small way, I can see he feels I made a good choice. The boat leaves and around the lake it goes.

To burn off some stress, I whip off my shorts and shirt (I'm wearing a bathing suit) and jump into the lake. Once the boat returns, Sam does the same. Other cousins and their children follow. For a while, I feel like a kid, frolicking in the water, scared of encountering mud and eels. I swim and swim, noticing members of my family hanging out on the bank. They are fun, nice people to spend time with. I vow to make the trip to see them more often.

I see my father is angling to leave after a couple of hours. He has to get home before dark since his eyesight isn't what it used to be. Because he's leaving quickly, I'm not sure how to play saying good-bye. It seems weird for me to come out of the water, sopping wet in my bathing suit, so I stay in to see how he'll handle that. He'll either lean down from the dock to give me a kiss on the cheek or just nod a good-bye and leave. I'm ready for anything.

He makes his approach, awkward and rickety, the picture of discomfort. I know he'd rather just run and put this whole moment behind him.

He says his good-byes to family on the dock, then leans down and shakes my hand, like I'm an acquaintance and not the girl he ran up and down mountains with. This is so not like the ending of *A Little Princess*, where the daughter and father finally reunite. A few years ago, this handshake might have made me cry and spend many hours in the therapist's office. This time, I just chuckle.

I have this eerie feeling this is the last time I'll see him.

Once he drives away, the cloud lifts. Sam and I relax and play with the cousins, their children, and various pets.

"Sam's sexy," my cousin Leigh whispers to me, smiling.

Her husband, Jason, comes up thirty seconds later. "He's hot, isn't he? If you don't marry him, I will."

They are so awesome. I will invite all these Smiths to my wedding. Especially when my uncle Will, my father's brother, asks me in that laid-back Smith voice, "So what kind of date do you have for this wedding?" He pulls out his iPhone.

"January sixteenth."

He smiles as he notes it in his calendar. "Great. You're locked in." I get that rush of paternal warmth from Uncle Will that I've been missing all day.

We say good-bye after eight hours of reunioning. Even though seeing my father wasn't a heartfelt affair, my relatives are genuinely caring and welcoming. I want them with me at my wedding, family strife be damned.

"What about this one?" I ask Mom, knowing deep down I can't wear this short, sequined, tired-hooker dress to my own wedding. But we're in Bergdorf's. If it comes from here, it must be proper (and crazy expensive).

Mom winces. She likes the drapey Eileen Fisher dresses. I like gaudy showgirl dresses that I should never wear in public. It's my wedding, right?

I put back the tired-hooker dress, and we saunter around all the departments in the store. Nothing. All high-end fashion or too bridal. This choice is going to be terrible. For me, there's a short window of time since I hate shopping for clothes. What would a forty-two-year-old bride wear? A big white pantsuit. Oh God. Not me!

"Okay. I have a proposition: Macy's and then maybe some Soho boutique. There has to be a dress," I say. It's already September now. The save-the-date cards have been sent—even one to my father and that woman.

I hear that dresses are the next urgent item after the venue since they take forever to make. Why is that, unless you need beading? My grandmother whipped up a dress in minutes. I don't need the marsh-mallow puff. Just a fun, simple bridal gown for a middle-aged bride. Doesn't have to be white or complicated.

My mother, the queen of fashion in our family, seems at a loss. For once, she's stumped. If it's not a black pantsuit, she's in the wrong galaxy. She is tall and lean—with *great* showgirl legs. I'm shorter and curvaceous. Shopping for me is hell.

We race down to Macy's and I know I could easily have a panic attack. There are swarms and swarms of people in Macy's at any given moment. Luckily, the bridal boutique is practically empty.

And out comes Tanya, the sassy historical romance writer from the local Romance Writers of America chapter who taught me all the romance rules more than ten years ago. This must be the work of divinity. I remember her so well out of everyone I've met since then. Now she's going to help me with my wedding dress? She's exactly the same, with her nicely kept shoulder-length ash-blond hair, mischie-vous eyes, and quick wit.

I know she doesn't recognize me, so I reintroduce myself. Her eyes light up.

"You're right! I remember you. Well, congratulations!" she says, then goes into her bridal-dress spiel.

Even though I'm sure she still has no idea who I am, I listen and hang on her every word. There's no doubt in my mind that I'm going to get my marshmallow bridal dress from *this* woman and no one else. It's fate.

Mom follows, stunning me with her reticence. Usually, she has an opinion, and it's humbling that she's letting me make the decisions. Or maybe she hasn't the foggiest idea what to do. We're navigating virgin territory, but we dive in, loading up on bridal gowns, ones I think might not be too Casper-ish on me and other, less hideous garments. I take one huge taffeta meringue just for fun.

Mom sits on a couch, a difficult thing for her to do. She crosses her legs, as if tamping down her own energy, which would otherwise compel her to scurry around the store. She waits and watches as I go from rack to rack.

The first, second, and third "ivory" meringues make me look like one of those old-fashioned ghosts in *Poltergeist*, like a dead lady looking to find her way back to this century. I can already hear the guests remarking, "Why is she so pale? She must be nervous."

That does it. No white. Not even freaking "ivory," which everyone recommends. But I turn to see Mom's reaction. She nods her agreement: White and ivory suck.

"Maybe I need to wear a real color," I say to Mom and Tanya.

"Let's look at the bridesmaid dresses," Tanya answers.

We go through dress after dress, all perfectly fine but not bridal enough for me. It seems hopeless, that shapeless ivory pantsuit a whisper away, when I see it.

The dress.

A long, sleeveless, strapless, nearly backless black gown with a fitted bodice and less fitted skirt. It calls out to me. I love the shape, especially with how it would fit to my curves and hide a few fat deposits.

The attendant finds my size and sets me up in the dressing room. My senses are heightened, sort of like what happens to humans when they become vampires. I notice the soft light in the boutique, the cool air conditioner relieving the intense heat from outside. Magic begins.

With the errant thought that now Tanya has seen me in my underpants, I slip off my clothes and just as quickly put myself in the gown. Then I see myself in the large mirror and gasp.

This is the dress.

It rests against my body like a beloved blanket, snug and comforting. The black complements my skin, bringing out my paleness in a better way, highlighting the red hair. Though I know I can't wear a black wedding dress.

"It comes in dark blue," Tanya says.

"Perfect!" Just like the blue dress I wore to the winter formal where I first danced with Sam. In this gown, I am astonishingly beautiful, the gorgeous goddess I'm meant to be, always intended to be.

With some trepidation, I step out into the waiting area. If my mother doesn't like it, well, what can I do? It's my day, right?

But the moment my mother sees me, she doesn't wince. She eyes me with curiosity, as if thinking, *Huh, I can work with this.*

There's no crying. No big hugs over this milestone. But I'm filled with pleasure when the saleswoman puts a veil over my head . . . and my mother gasps.

Later on Facebook, I post: *I said Yes to the Dress!*

Having the dress doesn't alleviate the tension at home. Sam and I are still close, but there's a distance between us. I try to let the tension slide because I overreact anyway. Weeks pass with my trying to adopt a bright, sunny, wifely attitude. We continue our separate agendas (agendae?). Our marriage is only a few months away, and we might be disintegrating as a couple. Sam wouldn't dare leave me, would he? I would recover, but he's changed my life so drastically in a few short months. I want to keep up this fun time he's shown me.

As I peer around my studio, a small space that has housed me for seven years, the place I swore to die in, I try to imagine what it would be like without him, my romantic hero. This feat is near impossible now. That's the problem with meeting Prince Charming. If he vanishes, there's no going back to what you once were.

With Sam, I'm always in the moment (unless I'm distracted by work or TV). I want to go for walks along the river and even travel with him. He *did* that. Now we're on shaky terms. At night, we touch base but rarely speak about this upcoming milestone. Several weeks pass in a blur and my nerves remain close to the surface. This is what couples mean when they talk about a widening gap in marriage. Any minute now, I expect a phone call releasing me from this relationship.

But for some reason, I feel as if this will work out. My love for Sam makes me happy, not so afraid. It makes me want more for myself and for us. Life is easy with his smile and constant jokes. His absence would create a giant hole, and this is hard for me to admit. In the past, I would pride myself on the walk away, the excising and blubbering over a bad person. It would be mind-numbingly painful if Sam left. Sam is the right person, and I wish he would just come over and say how hard it's been for him. We could be close like we were at the beginning.

I escape through television until, one night, when I can't stand it anymore, I ask him again: "What's wrong?"

"Well, you might remember that I've done this before," Sam answers.

Oh right, *that*. The ex-wife is always a problem. My mother is an ex-wife and she's been a ghost in my father's second marriage. In romance novels, the ex is usually pernicious or dead. Every now and then Jake Hunter is friends with his ex and they amicably share custody of their child. Of course, Jake Hunter's ex left him because she was a cheating whore, but she's nice.

Sam's case is one I don't quite understand beyond masochism and a need to be honorable. His first marriage started out okay but deteriorated over time. The relationship ended with an ugly string of events, after which, Sam fled.

For several years after his divorce, Sam left no forwarding address and no phone number, and lived under the radar. No one could find him. He was vague with people about his whereabouts, though he remained self-sufficient and productive in his field. Any inquiries about Sam went directly to his father or older brother. Sam tried to be invisible. Anytime his ex wrote to him, he ignored it.

It dawns on me powerfully that by marrying me, his life as a nomad will have to change. He'll have to be Mr. Bloom, resident of Manhattan. Which means his nightmare could find him again. Luckily, I look over my shoulder, too. Two people looking out for each other are better than one, right?

For once, I really listen to Sam and add up the evidence of a tattered soul, a guy who flinches sometimes when touched, who has nightmares several nights a week. I doubt he was a model husband (who is?), but he did what he could over a long period of time. I know it's a painful subject. Sam's not the type to talk extensively about his feelings, though he's aware of why he is the way he is.

I give him as much support as he'll accept, then try to work on my own neuroses. If I bug the crap out of him these last couple of months, he is sure to bail.

So, I distract myself by doing one of the most frightening things ever: I sign up for National Novel Writing Month (www.nanowrimo .org), which is where you write a book in a month, during November. As with my initial romance with Sam, I don't broadcast my new project, except to one person.

Dear Beloved Editor, you're crazy, Marie Ferrarella writes to me. *You don't want to put added pressure on yourself. You're about to get married.*

I know, Marie. It's totally insane, but if you only knew how scrambled my brains are. I need this outlet to wipe out my mania. I have one hell of a book to write, where I say good-bye to ghosts and invite this handsome, caring new stranger into my life.

"He won't come to the wedding," Sam said after that Smith reunion. "It would cost him."

I know he's right, which is why I write to Dad after he expresses some distress over my save-the-date card: *I will understand whatever you decide to do.*

He answers formally that neither he nor his wife will attend my wedding. *Love, Dad.*

It might have been an "appropriate" e-mail if not for the *Love, Dad.* The clarifying missive shocks me. Yes, clarifying, like those lotions that clear the blemishes on your face. My father doesn't love me, not really. After forty-two years, I have my truth.

I take a breath. And another. Not so bad. Within minutes, a lightness fills my chest. Isn't that a good thing? Dad just wrote me a terrible, terrible message. Why am I not crying? Why don't I have a big knife in my chest?

Because I never, ever have to talk to him again. I don't have to try anymore. I feel like I've been through this before. The release from bondage of a sort.

My father isn't coming. No fake-happy walking the daughter down the aisle. No pretending that I'm glad he's there looking uncomfortable and embarrassed. He made the choice. Just for good measure, I reread the e-mail and let it sink in further. The anger will come, probably tomorrow. But now I finally have good reason to dislike my father. He doesn't care.

"Your father is an asshole," Sam says after reading the e-mail.

Right. Some people turn into jerks over time. And now, this item is off the list. I have other elements to make me nervous. Like the fact that November is flying by. We're getting married in January, right after the holidays. Two months left, really only one.

The walls are caving in.

Two hundred people on my guest list, some of whom I've never met. My simple dress is at that moment being altered somewhere in Italy. The invitations are in the mail. I will go on a starvation diet immediately. Thoughts are swirling. Are we having a honeymoon? Oh God, another plane ride somewhere weird.

I order myself to have more fun with this wedding planning, first by ordering a sequined "The Bride" T-shirt. I have the dress, the guests, the invites, et cetera. Our officiant is my dear friend Lou, from New Mexico. Next I have to incorporate Duran Duran into our wedding somehow.

I've got it: I will walk down the aisle to a Duran Duran song.

Immediately, I write to Duran Duran Mission Control, or at least the one person who might respond, Katy Krassner, an entertainment executive for this band, along with many other artists. Not only does she provide online content for their website, answer fans' questions, write volumes, but she also knows everything about Duran Duran and is accessible. I listen to her and Nick Rhodes do their Oscar podcast every year. In my almost daily Duran Duran scouring (for twenty-eight years now) and worshipping from afar, her name has been there the longest, so I muster up the courage to write to her, outlining my plea. *What is the perfect DD song for a wedding ceremony?*

She responds quickly, saying nicely she couldn't possibly comment on such an important decision. It's embarrassing how much I'm shaking like a teenager in the front row. I've never been this close to Duran Duran before (if you don't count the thirty seconds John Taylor knew my name).

No problem, I write back, exhilarated to get a response. I'll figure it out. Duran Duran or bust. I take a page from my mother's playbook and ask around, just casually mention how I need Duran Duran somewhere in my wedding. As it turns out, my brother has a friend who plays guitar. Sam has a cousin who plays the flute. Together, they develop a long-distance collaboration of "Rio."

This brings me into December—the homestretch.

I grab my coat and purse, and we go to our scheduled tasting at the Yale Club. An hour later, Sam and I stare down at a table full of crab cakes, three kinds of salads, a spinach puff pastry, and herb-encrusted salmon. The filet mignon comes out just as I wonder if I'll ever fit into my wedding dress.

For the first time in months, I notice that Sam is his happy, boisterous self again. Maybe it has to do with the food, or that it's closer to the wedding, or that he finally believes that nothing will stop this wedding—not even a ghost from the past.

"This is the best part so far," Sam cracks in my ear. "And it's free!"

"Oh yeah, this is free, Sam." I roll my eyes and take a leisurely sip of my wine. I'm a little bombed from half a glass. Light brightens the airy restaurant on the twenty-second floor. About three other tables are filled with club members.

Our wedding coordinator, Dari, comes from the kitchen and sits back down with us.

"Have you decided on your two appetizers?"

"Crab cakes and this eggplant thing," Sam says.

I nod since I don't care so much about the food. We move on to the entrées, the filet mignon and salmon for sure, even though Dari seems to push the Chilean sea bass. Sam does his best to finish everything on all of the plates. He is beyond wasted and happy.

"I guess the dessert is the most important part for me . . . ," is my contribution.

"Of course. Let me get them."

Within five minutes, Dari returns with a tray of mousse, fancier mousse cake, shortbread s'mores with hot fudge and caramel. The groom sticks with the wine while I dive into each dessert—feeling both buzzed and sugary. I want all of them—and wedding cake.

By the late afternoon, having made all our choices, we stumble out of the Yale Club and weave our way home, slurring and laughing.

"This wedding is going to be *great*!" Sam yells, slinging an arm around me.

"The best!"

We kiss in the middle of the street, in the crosswalk with horns honking at us, just like we used to at the beginning. I start to feel like a real bride who is adored by her groom.

"Taxis cause so many deaths in the city. In the crosswalk," Sam says too loudly. "I don't want to die like that."

"Me neither."

We hug dramatically and then get the hell out of the way. Our arms link as we saunter down toward Penn Station. Maybe I'm premature about premarital problems. We're a fun-loving couple, mostly happy together.

"I've got a couple of hours left of grading and then I'll come home. Maybe we can eat again," Sam says before kissing me good-bye.

I sigh as he walks away. I can't wait to be Mrs. Bloom. This little princess is shedding her dad's last name in favor of a new one. Plus, doesn't "Patience Bloom" sound like a hippie heroine in a novel?

CHAPTER FIFTEEN

Happily Wedded Ever After
(but Someone Will Puke)

One of my fears is fainting as I stand to take my wedding vows. There are examples of this on YouTube, and they are frightening. Normal people fall over on the big day. I will easily succumb. As a semi-agoraphobe, I am uncomfortable standing in a crowd for too long. The ground swims, I lose my footing, and I begin to sway in wide circles. My breathing grows shallow and I look for the exit. At publishing cocktail parties, I sometimes position myself next to a chair or wall that I can grab so I don't fall over.

Tragic events, happy events, casual events, I usually have this reaction, but not every time. So at this happiest event of all, how the hell will I stand unsupported, holding a bouquet and staring at Sam? It's a recipe for disaster.

To offset this rush of negativity, I think of my favorite "wedding" in a romance novel: *The Sheik's Arranged Marriage* by *New York Times* bestselling author Susan Mallery. From the first page, I became a Mallery-aholic. It was another instance of losing an entire weekend to reading.

In this story, Heidi McKinley returns to the fictitious Middle Eastern kingdom of El Bahar, where she is an adoptive daughter to the king—adoptive because of her parents' deaths in a freakish accident. All she wants to do is translate ancient texts of El Bahar (she's studied to do this, followed by a stint in charm school)—certainly not marry an icky man. Sixteen months ago, I was so like Heidi. The king of El Bahar guilts Heidi into marrying his son, the ever-gorgeous, unfathomable Prince Jamal. Though traumatized by his first marriage to an ice queen who didn't like having sex with him (imagine), Jamal couldn't give two doughnuts whom he marries. He has no problem marrying Heidi. He finds her awkwardness amusing, and she wears glasses and her hair in a bun (just like me). To get her libido going, Heidi masquerades as "Honey," the prince's hot mistress, and they have passionate sex. Of course, as any sighted person would, Jamal knows that Honey is his gawky wife, Heidi. A wig and contacts can only do so much to hide your identity. Heidi gets pissed that Jamal didn't fess up that he knew who she was, and she's just repressed anyway. Like me, she needs constant assurance that he's in love with her, that theirs isn't just a marriage of convenience. Finally—and this is where I start bawling—to prove his love, Prince Jamal arranges a traditional El Baharian ceremony where he declares Heidi his "true" wife, which means she's the only woman he will ever marry or love again. Prince Jamal wears kohl around his eyes, and it's completely hot to me when a man wears makeup like that.

I feel exactly how Jamal does. Even if Sam were to drop from the face of the earth, he is the only one I'll ever marry. I can't go through this again. I'm lucky things turned out the way they did. But first, I need a village to get through the ceremony.

I call my mentor on all matters, Lou from New Mexico, also the one conducting the ceremony. I tell her my anxieties, the fact that I'm a nervous Nelly, which she's known about me for the past almost-twenty years.

"It'll be okay," she says in her slight Southern drawl. "The ceremony is short. And I'll make sure you don't fall over. Sam can pick you up when you start to drop. You're okay, Patience."

Her voice alone reassures me. She is like earth and rock, unflagging in her support. Everyone needs a "Lou" in her life, and this bride needs extra help. I relay my worries about staying upright to Sam and others. They nod and I can tell they think I'm nuts, being a nervous bride. What about rushing me to a doctor for some balance-enhancing horse pills?

Standing strong is serious business for me, so I embark on a holistic plan without telling anyone. For the six weeks before the ceremony, I do a yoga-esque exercise by standing on my tippy-toes with arms outstretched for ten minutes. I alternate standing on one leg and seeing how long it takes for me to fall (about two minutes). This works well, along with the knowledge that my mother has taught class with a 104-degree fever and pneumonia. If she can do this, I can stand for ten minutes without fainting.

I'm sure that Heidi McKinley from the Susan Mallery romance is just as neurotic as I am, maybe even more so since she does a dance of the seven veils to seduce her husband. I don't go nearly so far.

The next obsession is whether I should eat before the wedding. If I do, I'm sure to feel sick beforehand, and then I'll vomit on the groom and it'll go on YouTube. If I don't eat, won't I faint? Oh God, which hell will I choose? At the Harlequin holiday party in December, one month before my big day, I'm supposed to relax, but no, I chase after my colleagues for help in solving my persistent conundrums.

Our party is in this large, sunlit restaurant on the southern tip of Manhattan, right at South Ferry. It's practically on the water, and the company puts on a big shindig to celebrate the end of the year. The CEO (also a redhead) and several other Toronto staff fly down for the event, to give out awards and mingle with us. But do I focus on any of this? No, because I can't relax one bit. Wearing my semi-Christmassy olive-green jacket and black skirt, I rush around the room asking my married colleagues what they did before their weddings. Did they eat? What did they eat? How did they feel after they ate?

Who is this strange bride-to-be on the loose?

I pray that my boss, her boss, and the CEO don't notice this red-haired headless chicken darting from table to table, asking insane questions. But still, I must know what to do: *How do brides handle pre-wedding eating?*

One colleague says of course I need to eat a meal before the wedding. That way I'll have energy for the big day. Like pancakes and eggs, some orange juice. My insides churn with anxiety over this response. She's saying I'll pass out if I don't eat. My rational brain remembers for a second the many times when I ate little for days during times of stress and still managed to act like a normal person. So I find another married person to pester, Glenda.

"Did you eat before your wedding?"

Glenda, who runs Kimani Press, our fabulous African American romance imprint, smiles and answers reassuringly, "Maybe you should eat a little something, just a little."

It's a viable answer, but she's obviously more mentally balanced than I am. She's not telling me I *have* to eat something but that I *should*. I'll take that. But still I'm not satisfied, so I go to yet another bride, the no-nonsense, tell-it-like-it-is managing editorial coordinator, Kristin. She'll give it to me uncensored.

"Did you eat before your wedding?" I ask.

She gives me the best possible response. "You try, but you don't."

I sigh with great relief. And this woman got married at night, so she waited an entire day. I'll try to eat something, like my go-to panic food: a yogurt honey peanut Balance Bar, which I associate with panic, but it's still comforting. I'll do that.

There are lots of things for me to do. Oh wait, no, that's not true. The details of the wedding are done. Now I have to focus on myself, which I do. Sam appears to be serene and ready for marriage. I'm doing my best to enjoy every bit of this pre-wedding time, despite my anxiety.

I'll redirect any insanity, rechannel my thoughts toward what gives me joy, aside from reading: watching movies and TV. This could be a fun way to prepare me for the event. I pick a wedding-themed movie or show each day, skipping *Father of the Bride* for obvious reasons. So here is my list:

1. **Mr. Wrong** (I'm sure Ellen DeGeneres, the star, would agree that it's one of the worst movies ever)
2. **Mamma Mia!**
3. **How to Marry a Millionaire**
4. **Sex and the City** (the peacock feather is still ridiculous)
5. **Baywatch: Hawaiian Wedding**
6. **Notting Hill** (there is a wedding at the end)
7. **Mickey Blue Eyes**
8. **Sex and the City 2**
9. **Best Friends**

10. **Here Comes the Groom**
11. **Only You**
12. **Say Yes to the Dress**, season 1
13. **In & Out**
14. **Sense and Sensibility** (again)
15. **Wedding Slashers** (a horror movie)
16. **Conversations with Other Women**
17. **The Proposal**
18. **The Mirror Has Two Faces**
19. **Driven to Kill** (Steven Seagal goes to his daughter's wedding)
20. **The In-Laws** (the one with Michael Douglas and Albert Brooks)
21. **Love Actually**
22. **The Wedding Planner**
23. **Bride Wars**
24. **The Groomsmen**
25. **A Wedding** (directed by Robert Altman)
26. **Monsoon Wedding**
27. **My Big Fat Greek Wedding**
28. Every wedding episode of **Will & Grace**
29. **Pride and Prejudice** (the Donald Sutherland version—where I can pretend he's my real father)
30. **My Best Friend's Wedding** (Julia, of course!)

Not a bad list, eh? With every movie, my wedding becomes a real event, once in a lifetime, a celebration of dreams coming true, dreams that are beyond what I imagined for myself. I never thought I'd ever come this close to marriage. Even the ring was a stretch. Now it's happening to me. People come out of the woodwork, conveying their happiness for us. Sam is my dream groom and the idea that I will spend my life with him makes me excited because *he* is exciting every single day.

One night, right before New Year's, I wake up in the middle of the night to go to the bathroom. As I stand, I feel as if I'm falling. So much so that I have to sit down on the edge of the bed. Sam is asleep. This is like that scene in Mario Puzo's *Fools Die* where the woman suddenly dies of an aneurysm. I'm dizzy as hell. Of course, I'll die right before my wedding and then this will be a beautiful tragedy. Sam will go on talk shows to tell his sad story. There will be a documentary on us, maybe even *Love Story* 2.

I go to the bathroom and then lie upright in bed. This happens to me sometimes, the vertigo when the weather gets cold. I wonder if this has anything to do with nerves. I'm sure it'll be better in the morning.

Except it isn't. I'm still dizzy when I move. Somehow, I go to work and try to read, but moving my eyes makes me dizzy. If I stay in one place, it's not so bad. But when I stand, turn my head, or walk, the world starts to spin. I don't want to alarm anyone, but it's damned uncomfortable. How can the bride walk down the aisle like this?

Four days of dizziness. I tell Sam about it, but he chalks it up to another one of my weird psychosomatic fits. I must be overreacting. Like I'm the hypochondriac who spends three thousand dollars to fly to Israel to a sleep clinic (he did wind up having mild sleep apnea, but he did nothing with this information).

I finally realize I need to see a doctor. If I have a brain tumor, I'm going to enjoy life as much as I can over the next two weeks, then wither away in a comfortable chair with my knitting. Poor Sam will be okay.

A day later I'm in the doctor's office. This nice physician's assistant comes over to me with one of those nose prods. She looks like Natalie Wood, though I don't say this. We all know what happened to her. I rattle off my symptoms, thinking I may be sent to the ER to have a brain scan.

"Let me look up your nose," she says, impaling my nostrils with the prod.

I wait. You'd think I'd be allowed to have a peaceful wedding, but no. I'm not meant to be that romantic heroine. Cassie McBride would make it down the aisle without falling over because she thinks she's going down steps on a flat floor. Cassie would eat breakfast beforehand, too.

"You have a sinus infection."

"So it's not a brain tumor?"

"Probably not," Dr. Natalie says.

My eyes fill. I know it's silly of me to react like this. Ooh, maybe I shouldn't cry. The dizziness makes me sway on the stool. "I'm getting married in two weeks and you just saved my wedding."

It's difficult, but I try to keep myself from hugging her. She probably has no idea how high the stakes are here. After twenty-five years of dating and so many romance casualties, I've met the man of my dreams and I could have missed my one moment to be his bride.

She saved the wedding.

"Here you go." She hands me my prescription. And within a few days, I'm sure-footed again.

Everyone expects me to have a nervous breakdown, but I'm doing *great* right before the wedding. My mother is the one who loses her marbles about a week before. Every few minutes, a new phone call.

"What about the guest list?" she asks, practically screaming.

"Taken care of."

"Does Bill Bloom have a place to stay? Oh my God, what are we going to do for them?"

I'm not sure what she means. What *can* we do for them? Breast-feed? "He's staying at the Lotos Club."

"Did you get Lou a cab from the airport?"

"Done, Mom."

"What about the dress, oh God, there are so many things to remember!"

"There's nothing to do."

Hahaha! Is it bad I'm giggling over her nerves? She has to buy a new jacket, a new suit for Don, and how will her siblings get to the Yale Club, and is there a reservation for whozeewhatsit at the hotel? And maybe we should organize another big brunch!

All taken care of, because I love organization. Someone should hire me to organize them. This bridal planning is a snap. Now we just have to sit back and enjoy.

Except . . .

The week of the wedding, we get word that we're going to be in the *New York Times*, and they would like to do a feature video on us. Okay, sure, no problem. Sam and I glitz ourselves up and walk around Chelsea with an impressive camerawoman, answering her questions and praying we don't seem like idiots. I already know my

Marge Simpson voice is out there for everyone to hear. Despite this, the excitement of this celebration builds and builds. I cannot wait for it all to start.

And then Wedding Eve arrives.

I am packed with all of my to-do's crossed off. I'm going to be spending my last single night at the Yale Club, while Sam stays home. We do follow tradition by not being together the night before the wedding.

My matron of honor, Nici, arrives, bubbling with enthusiasm, telling me about her dress, and have I got everything packed? Nici and my actor/comic/nurse friend Langdon from California bond like macaroni and cheese in my studio apartment. It's fun to see them together because they are so similar. Nici I've known since high school. I met Langdon after seeing him in a terrible play in New York. He was terrific and I've stalked him ever since. Now these two dynamic people are in the same room.

On the other side of the apartment, on the couch, Sam is wearing his baseball cap that says "Groom." We're all laughing, talking, and having a good time. The rehearsal dinner starts in a few hours. I've attended so many weddings in real life and in romance novels. Now it's my turn. I'm feeling that bliss from the books that I read—and it's real.

Finally, I got my wish. My groom is here.

I stand in the foyer of my studio apartment, watching the mayhem of my friends interacting, wildly gesturing over something awesome. As the voices fade away, I suddenly feel *it*. That wave of fear, that the world is spinning too fast, that my head might split in half.

Sam looks over at me, his eyes register my panic, and he smiles.

"What's up, Red?" he asks playfully, rising from the couch and coming over to me. I step into his embrace, knowing that he will always make things better. Marriage might be an adjustment, but I still want him in my life every day.

"Maybe you should get out of here," Sam whispers in my ear.

I nod and bury my head in his neck. "I'll go to the hotel." As I stand in his arms, I remember the first time I saw him (again), that striped sweater, that dazed look coming down the walkway at JFK. That now-familiar glance. He is my one "true" husband.

I felt that need to be closer to him in every way. I still feel that. He walks into a room and I go to him. When he's in the kitchen, I go to the kitchen, too. (Not the bathroom, at least not every time.) We work in the same space, too. And he's the perfect date for a party. Everyone wants to talk to him, and I like to watch. This is the biggest gamble of my life, though I gambled several times with some good outcomes—the moves to New Mexico and New York City being the two biggest. This time, I am letting a strange man change the course of my life.

I can't believe he's finally here.

Sam is not Devlin or Jake Hunter or a British duke with a sprawling estate he'll inherit if he marries the plain commoner from the next county over. Even with all the romances I've read, with the loveable heroes who captured my imagination, Sam is even better than all of them. It's hard to believe that he could be, but he is. I had a picture of my perfect romantic hero—a little James Bond, a little Darcy, and a little Shane MacKade. But Sam surpasses them, too.

My friends continue to talk madly about every single wedding detail, how fabulous the dresses will be and then flowers and what a cool mom I have and oh God Patrick is so awesome, wait till you meet his hot boyfriend.

What in the hell would I be doing if I wasn't getting married tomorrow?

Lying on the couch and watching movies I've seen before. Contemplating my exes. Again. Knitting endless baby blankets for pregnant friends. Playing computer solitaire and crying. Maybe happy to some extent, but not this kind of happiness.

"Aw, you guys are so cute!" Nici cries, and Langdon joins her in cooing over us.

The two of them watch us hugging, the soon-to-be-married couple, their beaming smiles almost convincing me that this whole wedding will be a piece of cake. My next move will be getting from here to the club without losing my mind once again.

This happy abundance bubbles in my chest. I love Sam and want to make a life with him. Gone is single life. No problem saying goodbye to the past. But right there, in the studio apartment, bags packed for my last night as a single woman, Ambien and Ativan stowed, makeup, pins, shoes, lingerie, thank-you gifts, lists, license, candles, jewelry, cameras, and all the somethings (old, new, borrowed, blue), I think I might have the nervous breakdown to end all nervous breakdowns, just the panic attack I was due to have.

My legs shake, my hair trembles, and I need to get to the hotel to be by myself. Before anyone knows that something might be terribly wrong with me.

I'm going to do things differently, I think over and over again. I won't have a panic attack, won't shy away from the spotlight, won't avoid the big moment or give in to the fear. I'm going to love this—all the rituals involved with marrying Sam. This propels me through my long walk to the Yale Club, with my two suitcases near to bulging with wedding regalia. I am strong as an ox—though sometimes mentally fragile.

My friend Langdon, with his spiky blond hair and brash personality, escorts me. The great thing about him is that he can talk endlessly or be quiet, as needed. All I want is someone to walk with me while I daintily lose my mind. His presence soothes me, the perfect wedding gift.

Once I get inside the bridal suite, I breathe a sigh of relief. No people. A few precious hours before the craziness truly begins. People assume I'm running around and leave me alone. My cell phone is silent. I have a big bed, many magazines, and a television.

Tonight, I have to pull myself together for the tradition entitled the rehearsal dinner. Automatic pilot, right? I eat a yogurt honey peanut Balance Bar for energy and just let myself stare at the walls.

Four hours later, having regaled and smiled and cried away my makeup—tears of joy—I settle into bed, this time for the night. I see the bottle of Ambien on my bedside table and know some ghosts will never leave me. The only advantage to nightmares is that they test your strength, put the little things into perspective.

I can't forget how I got here.

The truth about love is that the right spouse is obvious. I know for sure that Sam is my Prince Charming. He will come through for me. As a teenager, he took the time to charm the wallflower at the other end of the gym. I spend my last few hours sifting through memories of Sam, how we met, how he bewitched me even then.

I am soon thinking about all the good in my life; even some of the bad stuff was good. There is a long, rutted road from there to here and I count my blessings.

———

There is a knock on my door at nine A.M. My hair person. I'm already showered and ready to go. I open the door and prepare for the profanity.

John, a dashingly handsome, loudmouthed hairstylist, bounds into the room with his cases of curlers. "You are a cunt for having your wedding at noon. That means I have to wake up at the fucking crack of dawn."

You know it's going to be a good day when someone calls you the C-word.

He sits me down and gets to work on my hair. It's an unruly mane and I know it'll take a couple of hours to tame it and make it into wedding hair. As he works, other people sift in: my lovely cousin Claire; my matron of honor, Nici; Patrick and Carlos; and my wedding photographers, Natasha from New Mexico and her boyfriend. How could I not stay in touch with such a vibrant person as Natasha? She stayed a close girlfriend, leaving me screeching, obscene messages over the years. Plus, I need her enthusiasm and mad photography skills.

I think of the other side of town, Sam waking up and getting ready, meeting my mother and Don, since they're going to come together in the same car.

Sam sends me his last text as a single man: *Mark Harmon is the comeback kid!*

Yes, ladies and gentlemen, this will be my husband, who, it seems, just discovered *NCIS* the night before. This is just another part of this wave of celebration building up to the big moment.

Quietly, my brother does my makeup, just as he did growing up when we put on plays for the neighborhood. I can feel his joyful energy, the history between us, his taking care of me and now acting as the one who's passing me to my husband. He zips up my dress, arranges my bridal wrap, fastens it into place with an elephant pin (I collect elephant anything). Carlos is with him, critiquing, praising, and finally cheerleading.

Three hours later, I'm ready.

Dari enters the room. "It's time."

The people in the room disperse and we take our places. As we walk through the halls of the Yale Club, I feel an intense quiet. Guests are in the library, waiting for me, the bride. This is it, that hush.

I walk down the hall, and we fall into place, with Nici in front of me, Patrick and I linking arms.

The music starts: Duran Duran, just as I wanted. With the first few strains of "Rio," played on flute and guitar, I start cracking up. Not many people would know what song it is. My mother is mortified, no doubt. I am such a diva, walking down the aisle to my favorite band—brides can do this!

Patrick and I giggle and start our walk. The guests rise and watch. Here comes the bride, whose name is Rio and she dances between the stacks of books at the library in the Yale Club.

As Lou promised, the ceremony is very short. I remember very little about it, just how happy Sam looks, how steady I feel (no swimming floor or wavering walls), how pagan our ceremony winds up being, how I can feel my mother's gaze, how I screwed up who got which ring, the applause at the end, Sam and I walking down the aisle as husband and wife.

It is the happiest day of my life. I remember so many parts of the reception:

How great I feel the entire day.

The handkerchief that brides in my family have carried in their bouquets for almost a century.

The flowers and food, which are perfect.

Hearing the Taft table cheer as Sam and I dance for the first time to "My Eyes Adored You" by Frankie Valli and the Four Seasons—a song Sam had randomly started singing to me one day, not knowing what a fan I am of this group.

Friends from work dominating the dance floor. Harlequin employees dancing till they drop.

Giving my bouquet to Melissa, my BFF from work.

My mom socializing like crazy, carrying children, hugging strangers, schmoozing like the dickens.

How I have a new name, and a new father in Bill Bloom.

My stepfather being his merry self but overdoing it (I won't say what happens).

How I keep holding food but never get the chance to eat until after everyone leaves.

The DJ playing a lot of Duran Duran.

How moving it is to see my father's family and how my mother weeps with joy to see them after thirty years. Even without my father's presence, this wedding reunited several families.

At the beginning of the planning, I wondered how I'd get through the six-hour event. And by the time six o'clock rolls around, I'm stunned that it's over. Sam and I say our good-byes and sneak up to our bridal suite . . . and watch the Golden Globes.

All through the night and on most occasions (except when he pisses me off), I look into Sam's eyes and remember how certain I was—and still am—that this is the one who's meant for me. I realize that as a bookish girl who narrowly escaped death in her early twenties, dated like crazy, and then chose to live quietly, this is truly my own romance novel come to life.

I have the amazing hero and that romantic pull toward him 95 percent of the time (5 percent of the time, he drives me insane), the juicy conflict (which makes life interesting and never gets totally resolved because we're human), the wedding experience, and someone who wants to share the ride with me. My happily-ever-after is more than I ever imagined for myself.

And you know, those books were right—about everything.

Acknowledgments

Many wonderful people supported me through this unforgettable experience:

Thanks to my mother, who pushed me to write when I first expressed an interest in storytelling. I hope this book gives me a pass on ordering an appetizer at dinner—forever. But I'll continue to enjoy your recitation of the menu. You're the best, Mom!

Thank you, Patrick, my amazing brother, who encouraged me over and over to dream big and never give up. After a while, it sunk in.

Big thanks to my agent, Jeff Kleinman, who discovered my story by accident and believed in it. His encouragement and insight made me work harder (and nearly throw up, but in a good way). Everyone needs someone who can push you to do better and support you at the same time.

I am deeply grateful for the spectacular Dutton team, who made this process a pleasure. A special thank-you to my editor, Jill Schwartzman, for giving me brilliant editorial guidance and unflagging support. During my diva moments of self-doubt, Jill lent me her confidence in the project and helped me keep my eye on the prize. Thank you to Stephanie Hitchcock, who made such valuable suggestions, which helped shape this story. Thank you, Ben Sevier, for being such a champion for this book. From the beginning, he helped me feel welcome at Dutton. Thank you, Brian Tart, for taking a chance on an unknown. Thank you, Christine Ball and Emily Brock, publicists extraordinaires, for guiding me in this foreign field, which turned out to be an exciting one. Marketing director Carrie Swetonic provided a vision of the places this story could go. I'm thankful for art director Monica Benalcazar's artistic translation of the story into such a fetching cover. Thank you, LeeAnn Pemberton, for all that you did to shepherd this book in the production process.

Thank you to Brandy Rivers, of the Gersh Agency, who saw the potential for *Romance Is My Day Job* on-screen.

A special thank-you to Sam Warren for being my super-secret first reader (and such a good friend).

I'm lucky to have my fantastic family and friends, some of whom may not have been mentioned specifically in the book but who are always part of the bigger story. Thank you to the Mercurios, Nesters, Sullivans, Smiths, Gallants, Blooms, Kelleys, Carlos Cano, Lou Liberty, Rachel Astarte Piccione, Nici Derosier, Natasha Chornesky, Langdon Bosarge, Joseph Weyers, Leslie Aaron, John Haracopos, Diane Echlin, Jenny Bent, Louise Fury, Joseph Mauricio, and my Facebook, Oberlin, Sandia Prep, and Taft families (*hic haec hoc*, Mr. Cobb).

If it weren't for Harlequin, there would be fewer pages. I'm especially indebted to Melissa Endlich, Gail Chasan, Ann Leslie Tuttle, Sarah Pelz, Allison Carroll, Dana Hamilton, Rachel Burkot, Mary-Theresa Hussey, Allison Lyons, Natashya Wilson, Glenda Howard, Shana Smith, Susan Litman, Margaret Marbury, Theresa Linton, Margo Lipschultz, Reka Rubin, Kristin Errico, MRF, my amazing authors, Dianne Moggy, Loriana Sacilotto, Donna Hayes, Craig Swinwood, and Tracy Farrell, who hired a Latin/French major so many years ago.

My thanks to all the romance writers out there. You inspire me.

And, of course, the biggest thanks to Sam W. Bloom, who makes me happy every single day.